# Faith and Action Rooted in Christ

*Reflections on Spirituality, Justice, and Ethical Living*

# Faith and Action Rooted in Christ

*Reflections on Spirituality, Justice,*
*and Ethical Living*

Obiora Ike

*in Collaboration with* Chidi Ilechukwu

Globethics.net Co-Publications & Other

Globethics.net Co-Publications & Other

Director: Prof. Dr Obiora Ike, Executive Director of Globethics.net in Geneva and Professor of Ethics at the Godfrey Okoye University Enugu/Nigeria.
Series editor: Dr Ignace Haaz, Globethics.net Managing Editor

*Globethics.net Series Co-Publications & Other*
Obiora Ike, *Faith and Action Rooted in Christ Reflections on Spirituality, Justice, and Ethical Living*

Geneva: Globethics.net, 2021
ISBN 978-2-88931-415-7 (online version)
ISBN 978-2-88931-416-4 (print version)
© 2021 Globethics.net

Managing Editor: Ignace Haaz
Assistant Editor: Nefti Bempong-Ahun

Globethics.net International Secretariat
150 route de Ferney
1211 Geneva 2, Switzerland
Website: *www.globethics.net/publications*
Email: *publications@globethics.net*

All web links in this text have been verified as of June 2021.

# TABLE OF CONTENTS

This Book is dedicated on the 40th Priestly anniversary of Obiora Ike and 25 years - silver jubilee anniversary of Chidi Leonard Ilechukwu in humble gratitude for the opportunity and vocation given to us to serve Christ and humanity through witnessing to the Good News of salvation, to spirituality, reconciliation and love.

# ACKNOWLEDGEMENTS

"You are the light of the world; allow Christ to burn in you, whatever the cost. Do not be afraid." (Pope Benedict XV1, evening Prayer Vigil with enthusiastic young Germans, Freiburg/Breisgau, 2011)

The Christian life must continually measure itself on Christ: *"Have this mind among yourselves, which is yours in Christ Jesus"* (Phil 2:5), as Saint Paul says in the introduction to his Christological hymn. With this mission, the pastoral witnessing of the team of pastors at St. Leo the Great Parish, Federal Housing, Enugu, led by Msgr. Obiora Ike under-took to share with our parishioners, and Catholics in other parishes, Christians of other denominations and indeed all people, the spiritual riches embedded in the Word of God. On our own, we have been challenged by the word of the scripture as we let it illuminate our thoughts, meditations, actions, deeds and sharing. This agrees with the theme of our parish weekly, the *Peaceland Weekly: Pray With, Think With and Work With*. In more than one way, we have put ourselves continually into reviewing our relationship with God in prayer, in participation at Masses, parish, social and cultural activities, in exploring our faith through meditation on sacred scripture and study of the Catechism of the Catholic Church.

The spiritual wealth reflected in this volume has been made possible through the support and sharing of the Church Fathers' meditations and reflections in the Patristics, brilliant teachers, theologians, social ethicists, philosophers, wise sages, simple saints and renowned preachers. We acknowledge rich resources and instructional materials from Father Charles Irvin, Joseph Lobo, Ernest Munachi Ezeogu, and Salt and Light TV. In many cases, we found the sermon of these inspired teachers so honest, touching, prophetic, salvific, challenging and demanding that in some part, we have adapted or outrightly adopted them for the spiritual reflection of the people of God and our personal growth.

We have chosen to offer spiritual reflections to the faithful at the parish and larger public as a spiritual guide and a life programme. We are called to witness the divine milieu and share Justice, Love, Peace and Development in our life and in the world's context and circumstances. As the Holy Father, Pope Benedict XV1 in his homily at the Freiburg Airport in Germany, said,

> "God desires the salvation of His people. He desires our salvation. He is always close to us, especially in times of danger and radical change. His heart aches for us, and He reaches out to us. We need to open ourselves to Him so that the power of His mercy can touch our hearts. We have to be ready to abandon evil, to raise ourselves from indifference and make room for His word. God respects our freedom. He does not constrain us."

We hope that the spiritual reflections contained in this volume shall continually awaken in us the spirit and mind that is in Christ Jesus, who in His own time makes all things new and beautiful. He can do in us infinitely more than we can ever think or imagine. We re-affirm these words as true: *"Paul plants, Apollos waters, but God gives the increase."* To Him be the glory and praise forevermore.

*Obiora Ike/ Chidi Ilechukwu*
Geneva, June.2021

# FOREWORD

On the cold plains of a rough Galilean countryside many moons ago, eternity entered time. The Word became flesh. God became man. Christ became Immanuel. Time and history embraced Timelessness, wrapped in swaddling bands and lay in a manger. All these happened, while the shepherds watched their flocks by night.

As Christ entered our history on that holy night, the humble and pure of heart, who spent the night watching their flock in simplicity of heart and station, were awake to hear the thrones, hosts and dominions of heaven, as they intoned the "Gloria in Excelsis Deo"! They were also profoundly fortunate to witness that outpouring of peace, which heralds the opening of heaven's gates.

St. Augustine and many other Church fathers spent a lot of ink on treatises and disquisitions, to make clear to the faithful, that one of the first attributes of the Kingdom of God is peace. Whenever heaven meets the earth, peace flows in the hearts of all men of goodwill. That was the whole essence of that Lukan account of Christ's nativity. Christ, apart from being the wonderful counsellor, as Isaiah prophesied, is ultimately the Prince of Peace. That he is the first son of God means that peace is the first attribute of heaven. This is why anyone, who desires to become a son of God, must be a peace maker. For blessed are the peacemakers, for they shall be called the sons of God. (Mt. 5:9)

Peace is the promise of heaven. It requires an essential platform for its existence. St. Augustine makes this clear, when he reminded us, that 'He who created us without our help without our help will not save us without our consent'. Peace, being a gift of heaven, can never flow into our hearts and homes, if we do not provide a basis for it. That platform is justice. Without justice, there will be no peace.

To that end, since justice is the cornerstone of peace, one can surmise then that justice is the bricks for the construction of God's Kingdom on earth. In that light, whoever works for justice is creating the kingdom of peace. Little wonder the venerable Pope Paul VI etched it for all times, on the stones of our hearts, that if you want peace, which you must work for justice.

Those who work for justice, over and above building an abstract City of God, in the Augustinian sense, are making God forever Immanuel (God dwelling among men). They are bringing about the reign of God's kingdom, just as Christ prayed and taught us to pray- Adveniat Regnum Tum.

Peace is what happens, when God makes an entrance into our space and history. For God to make that entrance, we must heed the prophecies of Isaiah. We must prepare the way for the Lord and make his path straight. We must fill every valley and make every mountain and hill low. We must make the crooked path straight and make the rough ways smooth. The summary of all this, is that we must do Justice. When we do that, we are then rooted in Christ. And that is when all nations would then see God's salvation. This means that the incarnation never ended. God will continue to take flesh in all those who work for justice, and dwell among us. These ones bring us a heaven of peace on God's earth.

Msgr. Prof. Dr. Obiora Francis Ike made it his life's mission to work for justice. His life and work  have brought about a heaven of peace in Enugu, his home; Nigeria his country, Africa his continent, and to our world as a global citizen. Rev. Dr. Leonard Ilechukwu has essayed in his life to follow those footsteps as well.

At stages in their life, both men; Obiora Ike-40 years ago, and Leo Ilechukwu-25 years ago-prostrated themselves in humility before the people of God, to receive their sacrament of Holy Orders, as catholic priests. On rising, they individually decided to dedicate themselves to the gospel of justice, as a way of making God accessible to men and women of their age.

These reflections you hold in your hand, testifies to this vision. They were the products of the vision shared with their brothers and sisters in their home parish, and by extension to all God's people. This compendium of reflections comprising 89 themes is not only their gift to God's church. This book, together with their life's work, has been their song to their maker, in the tradition of the psalmist of old. With these, they have continued to make the psalmist's words their own in practical terms. This book, together with their lives, have been their prayerful song before God's throne of mercy, saying - "Your justice, I have proclaimed before the great assembly. My lips I have not sealed. You know it, Oh Lord"-as they both continue in their journey to seek and do God's will.

You can make this compendium and prayerful meditations yours as well. Each chapter is a treasure trove of insights, rich in inspiration. May this book inspire you the reader, with those gifts freely given to all those, who avail themselves, to become instruments and channels of God's Peace, just like St. Francis of Assisi prayed.

*Onyemaechi Emmanuel Franklyne Ogbunwezeh, PhD*
Senior Research Fellow & Director for Genocide Prevention in
Africa, Christian Solidarity International
Zurich, Switzerland.

# IN MEMORIAM

*Archbishop Oscar Romero - "A Future Not Our Own"*

"It helps now and then to step back and take the long view." The kingdom is not only beyond our effort; it is even beyond our vision.

We accomplish in our lifetime, only a tiny fraction of the magnificent enterprise of God's work. Nothing we do is complete, which is another way of saying that the kingdom always lies beyond us. No statement says all that could be said. No prayer fully expresses our faith. No confession brings perfection. No pastoral visit brings wholeness. No programme accomplishes the Church's mission. No set of goals and objectives includes everything.

This is what we are about. We plant seeds that one day will grow. We water seeds already planted, knowing that they hold future promise. We lay foundations that will need further development. We provide yeast that produces effects far beyond our capabilities.

We cannot do everything, and there is a sense of liberation realising that. This enables us to do something and do it very well. It may be incomplete, but it is a process, a step along the way, an opportunity for God's grace to enter and do the rest. We may never see the results, but that is the difference between the master builder and the worker.

We are workers, not master builders; ministers, not Messiahs. We are prophets of a future, not our own.

*Archbishop Oscar Romero was murdered during the celebration of Holy Mass in his cathedral in El Salvador, South America, 1984*

# THEME 1
# THE POWER OF TRUTH

*Jeremiah 1:4-5, 17-19; 1 Corinthians 13:4-13, Luke 4:21-30*

Many persons do not wish to be duped or lied to. We want the truth, even the unpleasant and painful truth. You want your doctor to tell you what you are suffering from, that you have cancer, for example. How would you feel if you had cancer and your doctor did not tell you? People agree that it is far better to be told the truth than to be consoled with a pleasant lie. If your child's teacher calls you and tells you that your child is failing in school, you would, of course, be upset. If your child fails, how would you feel if the teacher lets you feel good without telling you the truth? Still, we know that many people also feel bitter when they are told the simple truth they often do not want to hear. While we agree that there may be things we do not want to hear, let alone discuss and would rather have that they were buried, truth is different from a lie, and to be told the truth is far better than to be lied to. This brings to mind the phrase we may have often heard, *"My mind is made up. Please don't confuse me with the facts."*

Today's gospel account presents us with Jesus in His hometown having just given His *Inaugural Address* in His home synagogue, among His family and friends. He was the toast of the town, well-received, holding their rapt attention. The gospel account tells us *"All who were present spoke favourably of Him. They marvelled at the appealing discourse that came from His lips" (Luke 4: 22)*. However, very soon, it all turned to hatred. Moments later, they took Him to the brow of a cliff and attempted to throw Him over the cliff's edge to his death. They suddenly changed and turned on Jesus when He told them a truth they did not want to hear. What had He said to them? Well, He reminded them of two events in Jewish history. One was during the life of Elijah, the prophet. The Hebrew in Elijah's time were suffering from a horrible drought; people were dying of starvation. A prophet of God came to a widow in the pagan village of Zarephath, and because of her faith, God saved her. The problem was that she was not a Jew; she was a Gentile. The same is true in the story of Elisha.

Leprosy was spreading throughout Israel, but God used a prophet to save only one leper, and he too was a Gentile from Syria. This was painful for the Jews because they had come to believe that they were God's Chosen race; that non-Jews were damned, and that God's love and favour were manifested only in and among the Jews. The people of Nazareth and those in other Jewish settlements, especially in Jerusalem thought they had a monopoly of God. It was axiomatic in their thinking. In times of conflict, God would come to their aid. When all else failed, God could be counted on, and non-Jews would suffer and die outside of God's favour and love. Jesus' words deeply offended them because He suggested that what they believed about God's favour might not be true.

Centuries later, in Italy, it was commonly believed that the earth was the centre of the universe. Everyone believed that the sun revolved around the earth and that the earth was the centre of the solar system. A Polish scientist named Copernicus argued otherwise a century earlier, but nobody took him seriously. Then an Italian scientist named Galileo came along and showed them through a telescope that they were wrong. Italians, including distinguished Cardinals in Rome, were shocked and horrified. Galileo was arrested and silenced because he upset their ways of seeing reality and their self-inflated attitudes about humans being the centre of God's universe. Their minds were made up, and they did not want to be confused by the facts that came to them through a telescope.

The problems come, you see, when we are confronted with a truth that requires us to change our attitudes towards people of other races, to change the way we behave, to change our patterns of living. This is what Jesus was about; He was not interested in merely having friendly intellectual discussions about provocative ideas. He was not merely talking about tidbits of history. He was calling for a thorough-going change in the way they understood themselves, God and what they should be about in their ways of living and relating to other people. The people of Nazareth realised what they were facing, namely, a prophet of God who was confronting them not with a mere debating subject but with a radical change in living. You see, if it was true that God cared for non-Jews, for Gentiles, then it was likewise true that they had to do the same. Well, they had no intention of doing that, they probably told their racial jokes about "those Gentile people"; they certainly put Samaritans in their proper place. They were not about to change their prejudgments. How do we react in the face of such confrontations when challenged, much like the hometown folks of Nazareth were challenged? We kill the messenger "If you don't like the message, well then, get rid of the messenger." If you are in a court trial, make the prosecuting attorneys and the police look like bullies or fools. Destroy the witnesses by discrediting them or by ruining their reputations. If the message you hear upsets you, destroy either the content or destroy the messenger.

We like to pride ourselves in thinking that we want to hear the truth. We even tell our wives, husbands, and children that we want to hear the truth from them. However, if they present us with a truth that requires radical change, then watch out! We tell God we want Him to reveal His will to us. In our piety and our prayers, we tell God we will do anything for Him. We had better be prepared, however, for what He will tell us. Be careful about what you pray for; you may get it. Thus, if the truth hurts, well, perhaps it should! Too many of us want to shape God to be just like us. We fancy Him as seeing things just as we see them. All such ideas about God need to be challenged, and then we (not God!) need to change. What hope do we have to grow and be saved if we only worship a God who is as small, as mean, and just as petty as we are? The people of Nazareth are a lot like us and we, too often, are too much like them. Thus, when the truth hurts, when it confronts and challenges us, we ought to ask ourselves "Why are we so upset? We ought to take a second look and see if God is causing us growing pains. We will never be saved if we worship only a God who suits us because we have made Him over into our own image and likeness. When we pray, we should expect change, for prayer changes us, not God.

# THEME 2
# FISHERS OF MEN

*Isaiah 6:1-2, 3-8; 1 Corinthians 15:1-11; Luke 5:1-11*

Simon Peter was a fisherman. It was his livelihood. He was not a sport fisherman, fishing simply because he liked to fish. His life depended upon his skill and talents in catching fish, so did his family's security and happiness of his family. Not only was that, the livelihood of the men who worked for him as well as the security and happiness of their family members, dependent upon him. Peter was aware of his personality and the responsibility that went with his person. We find him in today's gospel account in a moment of failure. We shouldn't think it was his only failure. He probably encountered many such other moments in the years he had been in business. Was this failure the last straw? Was this the final failure for him? Was he about to abandon his fishing

business and start all over again in a new business? We don't know.

But many of us do know the feeling; many of us have had moments of such profound doubt that we were ready to give up. We've had times, haven't we, when we've been beset by certain nostalgia and sentimental memories of earlier days, days when we began our careers and marriage with high hopes, with dreams and expectations of our futures? Such moments can be pleasant reveries, or they can be memories of times of terrible doubts. In them, we can severely and harshly judge ourselves to be failures. Have we made a difference in the lives of those around us? Can we yet make a difference in the lives of those around us? We had high hopes back in those early days. When we began our careers, we entered into our marriage and started our families. There were such seemingly happy days, days of happy anticipation over all that we were going to accomplish all that we were going to do. All of that was before life dealt us its cruel blows, causing us to enter into moments of depression, a sense of loss, and days of living in failure.

In writing his letter to the Ephesians, St. Paul wrote: "For our struggle is not with flesh and blood but with the principalities, with the powers, with the world rulers of this present darkness, with the evil spirits in the heavens…" He was reminding them that we are dealing with immense forces in our world, forces that seemingly seek to beset us and destroy us, destroying our spirits, corrupting our souls, and reducing us to regarding ourselves as little more than failures. In today's first reading, we find the prophet Isaiah in such a state of mind. His soul was heavy; he was in near defeat. His nation was divided between the north and south. The Assyrians had conquered Israel's northern kingdom and then carried away the Israelites into captivity in Babylon. The southern kingdom of Judah was languishing in one civil war following after another. Religion had fallen into little more than observing a series of formalities. Real belief in God had all but vanished. King Uzziah, once wise and trusted, had fallen into disgrace and had recently died in dishonour.

On top of all that, Isaiah, whom history would later regard as one of the greatest of all Old Testament prophets, found himself held in contempt by those to whom God had sent him. No one was listening to him; some wanted to get rid of him by killing him. Isaiah was, to say the least, very conscious of his failures and limitations. Once again, you and I are presented with the problem of failure. Moreover, failure raises questions, questions about us and questions about God. If God is so good, we are asked, why is there such terrible suffering in our world? Why did God allow the Holocaust? Why does God allow babies to die? And then we are told: "I can't imagine a God that would allow evil and pain to afflict innocent people." But isn't that the problem? Why do we need to ask, should God be limited by our puny little human imaginations? The problem, you see, is with us not with God. Do our limitations limit God? Do we allow ourselves only to worship a God who is so small that He fits into our little intellectual categories?

Peter was offered a window of opportunity when he least expected it, after a night of failure. He took the chance, gave God what he did have, namely hope and trust, and suddenly defeat was transformed into victory. Peter, admitting he was a sinner, became the Rock upon which Jesus would build His Church. Jesus was saying to Peter: "Look, I know you are brusque, impulsive, strong-willed, and even a racist bigot but you've given me your best, and now I'm going to give you my best." Isn't it true that people who have been wounded become great healers? Recovering alcoholics become the best rescuers of drinking alcoholics. Slow learners become great teachers. Aren't some of our greatest athletes' people who have been told they have no talent? Remember that Ludwig van Beethoven wrote his greatest symphony when he was stone deaf. Winners never quit, and quitters never win. If we try to limit God by our own limitations, we will only succeed in limiting ourselves. The great Jewish prophet Isaiah was like Simon Peter, given a window of opportunity amid failure. He took the opportunity and said: "Here I am Lord, send me." Having confessed that he was a sinner, Peter heard Jesus respond: "Do not be afraid; from now on, you will be a fisher of men." Peter responded to the challenge and became the chief of the apostles.

How, then, do we respond to failure? Do we see it as a challenge and then at a deeper level, see that every challenge is but an opportunity? Do we respond as did Isaiah and Simon Peter? To do so, we cannot limit God by our own myopic imaginations. We are not responsible for everything that happens in our lives. We are responsible only for our responses. No one else is, only we are … not God, not others, not life.

Such, then, are the challenges of faith, for faith is not simply our adherence to a creed or a set of doctrines. Faith is how we act in life, the arena in which God comes to us. You may think that everything depends upon you, but you would be very wrong-headed in thinking that way. You may think that you are a failure and will never make a difference in the world. You would be equally wrong-headed in thinking that way. The only way to face life is with the belief that "with God, everything is possible" and then live our lives while depending on Him.

# THEME 3
# REJOICE FOR YOUR REWARD
# IS IN HEAVEN

*Jeremiah 17:5-8; 2 Corinthians 15:12, 16-20; Luke 6:17, 20-26*

"Happy are you when people hate you, drive you out, abuse you, denounce your name as a criminal, on account of the Son of Man. REJOICE, for then your reward will be great in heaven." Lk. 6:22.

Dear brothers and sisters, the message of today stands resounding in the ears of all. In the gospel, Christ proclaims blessings to His people; Happy you who are poor, happy you who are hungry, happy you who weep now. And to all these, a blessing is attached. The teachings of Jesus called the Beatitudes, recorded in the Gospel of Luke (6:20-23), are an invitation to a way of living that brings true happiness and both inward and outward peace. The beatitudes call us to a radically new way of being when we centre our lives on God, and we become transformed. The beatitudes call us to true happiness and the deepest of joy as we find our true identity in our relationship with God and true peace both inwardly and outwardly. Beatitude is Latin for "abundant happiness". In His lesson on the Beatitudes, Jesus calls us to abundant happiness that makes us complete and whole, in which we find our true selves, the person that God intends us to be. God leads us to a transformation of ourselves and gives us the ability to see what needs to be transformed and find God's help in that transformation. They lead us to a feeling of peace and joy here and now: in knowing Christ's Living Presence. Just as He did over 2000 years ago in Galilee, the Living Christ brings joy as He seeks us through and accompanies us in our pain. He brings a joy which sorrow and loss and pain and grief are powerless to touch, happiness that shines through our tears. This is a joy that nothing in life or death can take away, because nothing in life or death can separate us from the love of Christ (Romans 8:38-39). As Jesus said, "No one will take your joy from you" (John 16:22).

Each Beatitude begins with the word "blessed." The Greek word translated as "blessed" means "extremely fortunate, well off, and truly happy" because one is favoured by God. To live the Beatitudes is to be centred on God and God's desires for our life. They invite us to live with a true inward peace that leads to a desire to be outward peacemakers, bring reconciliation, seek out opportunities for mercy and compassion and pursue justice and righteousness as a pang of hunger and thirst. We live the Beatitudes where we are right now, one day at a time, one leading at a time, and one action at a time. We live them realising that we are imperfect, that we make mistakes, and need forgiveness. We live them with confidence in Jesus' promise of joy and peace that only God can give.

However, it seems that Jesus calls the poor and suffering blessed because they are likely to recognise their need for God. They are more motivated to turn to God for God's help and strength, just as the crowds in the gospel came to Jesus with such eagerness, hoping just to touch Him. Jesus addresses warnings to wealthy and popular people because they may well fail to recognise their need for God. Throughout His gospel, Luke recounts stories in which the well-heeled do not use their wealth to help the needy. They tend to be trapped by their possessions and to fall short in their trust in God. It is too easy for them to place their trust in other things, in themselves alone, or just in the present experience of satisfaction. In this Sunday's first reading, the prophet Jeremiah proclaims a similar message. He compares those who place their trust in human beings or earthly powers to a barren bush that is lifeless. He likens those who entrust themselves to God to the tree planted beside the water that receives bountiful nourishment and refreshment.

You and I know very well that we are called to place our ultimate trust in God and not in other things or other people. Nor are we to place our ultimate trust in our own personal or professional accomplishments. That is not news to any of us. Each of us has probably experienced times in our lives when we have recognized our absolute dependence on God and God's grace, particularly in an intense way. It might be a time of struggle with school, deep disappointment in a friendship or other relationship, an experience of illness, or merely the recognition that even our best and most sought after accomplishments do not fulfil us completely. At times like that, we may feel like the people in the gospel who reach out to Christ to touch Him and experience His presence and power.

This simple message, though, is one that we need to hear over and over again. It is a word that we need to meditate on with attention. It is just so easy for any of us to lose sight of where we are putting our ultimate trust. Amidst the pressures and temptations of life, it is so easy for us to transfer our trust to something (or someone) other than God. But when we do make a conscious effort to orient our lives and our decisions toward God, we discover a deep joy and satisfaction that nothing else can replace. When we try to live each day with trust in Christ, asking for the strength and the grace we need for that day, other things in our lives tend to fall into their proper place. We find ourselves deeply rooted, like the tree planted next to the life-giving waters. When we live in communion with Christ, we experience a resonance with the heart of reality that can sustain us through difficult times.

As people who come to the Eucharist to be nourished at the table of the Lord, we celebrate and reaffirm the fact that we belong to Christ. We are His. Deep down, I suspect that all of us realise that we are truly happy and we experience real contentment when we place our deepest hopes in God and make our decisions in the light of our relationship with God. This God, whom Jesus reveals, is not a heavenly tyrant who wants to keep us in our place. He is a gracious God who offers us true freedom and wants us to flourish. As we come to the Eucharist this Sunday, let us ask the Lord to remind us of the many ways in which He is faithfully present to us. And let us remember that we belong to Him. He is our source of strength and love. Moreover, that trusting in Him at all times, we must surely be HAPPY.

# THEME 4
# REASON FOR OUR HOPE

*Deuteronomy 26:4-10, Romans 10:8-13; Luke 4:1-13*

The scriptural passages we have just heard are the oldest of Lenten readings. Their use in the Church for this first Sunday of Lent goes back nearly one thousand, seven hundred years ago. In the fourth century, the first Sunday of Lent was also the first Sunday of the Liturgical year. So it is no surprise that the Church employed these particular readings because in them we find the very heart of the Christian message. They present the core reasons we gather together as Christians, what we hope for, where we are going, and how we might get there. The first reading is from the book of Genesis. It tells of the creation of man and woman and humanity's fall from grace. It is a fascinating account from which we can learn much. In our modern arrogance, this account should not be dismissed as the mythic ponderings of ancient nomadic people.

This is not just one of many quaint creation accounts. It presents the truth of which we are as humans, where we have been, why we struggle, and why we suffer and die. Sin has its consequences, consequences for which we are responsible. While this account is often criticised for its historicity, we should remember that it was never intended to be a history in the scientific way we understand history today. But it is no less true! I would argue that what it tells us is far more profoundly true than many of the more learned and scholarly historical accounts of who we are and where we come from. The reason I say that is because this account gives precedence to our spiritual struggle as humans, something to which the scientific method is not directed. We are spiritual beings, and we cannot fully understand ourselves in any other context. This account gives us the tools to face one of the most vexing realities that we in our human condition must deal with … the existence of evil in a world that is otherwise good. God made it good, blessed it, and intended it to be good. From whence then, comes evil? This ancient biblical account is no naive account. Just look at what happens in this story and recognize how evil works against humanity. We should then think of how this same evil force is present in the world we live, in our own everyday lives. The serpent is the devil's surrogate, and his works are subtle.

He does not try to make what is evil look overly attractive. Instead, he works to pervert our human understanding of God and our understanding of what is good. He twists the divine image and deconstructs God's divine will. Instead of a loving Creator, the devil makes God appear to be a petty and jealous tyrant. God is characterised as an unjust authority seeking only His own glory by oppressing His creation and putting ridiculous demands on Adam and Eve. Satan becomes the liberator from this perceived divine oppression; he becomes the great humanist if you wish. Listen again as the serpent says "Did God really say, 'You must not eat from any tree in the garden?" By using the word "any," the serpent is changing what God said.

Eve corrects the serpent, replying "We may eat of the fruit of any of the trees in the garden; it is only about the fruit of the tree in the middle of the garden that God said, you shall not eat, nor even touch lest you die." "You certainly shall not die!" Satan mocks. "No, God knows well that the moment you eat of that fruit, you shall be like God who knows what is good and bad." In other words, you have the prerogatives of God! From this, sin and death came, from letting ourselves be tricked by the evil one who clouds our reasons and thus makes falsity look true, and truth look false.

It is said that Satan's most significant victory over the modern world happened when he convinced the modern mind that he does not exist, that he is not to be feared, that there is no longer anything sinful, nor even a hell. But don't our daily news headlines tell us that hell is real, that it is even here on earth? If we do not believe there is a Satan, how can we defend ourselves against him? And yet, even a fool can see the devil at work around us in the very same way he has always worked. Subtly and silently, Satan continues his work in our society. He suggests that the divine law is a farce. He tries to make us humans believe we know better than God, even that there is no God. He tries to make sin and death seem like a good thing. Thus we find ourselves thinking that euthanasia (mercy killing) is good. Abortion is seen as a personal right. Sexuality takes on the character of entertainment. Violence becomes a valid solution to problem-solving. And on and on it goes. In this twisting of perception, the truth must necessarily become relative … an opinion, not a fact. Because if it is a fact, then right is right and wrong is wrong, and the subtle serpent can be exposed. No, he will not let that happen!

Evil must hide behind the screen of confusion and lies. It cannot stand the light of truth. It rebels against it with all its force. Didn't Pontius Pilate have Jesus crucified after he asked, "Truth, what is truth?" In the bible, today's scripture readings continue, and there we find that God would not be defeated, nor would His creation be ruined by the devil's wiles. God's love is too strong, and His justice too perfect to be foiled by Satan's trickery. So, as we see in the second reading, God sent His son Jesus Christ to bridge the chasm between ourselves and God, a chasm caused by our disregard for God's will that was found in Adam and Eve and is found in us today as well. Jesus gives us the power to overcome our inability to think and act rightly. Christ loved us so much that He radically humbled Himself and took on our human nature and became subject to the divine law just as we humans are, so that by His obedience we might be saved, and that in His humanity, in His body and blood, we might share in His divinity.

Because of our human condition, we see Jesus in today's gospel being tempted by Satan. Again, the devil is trying to pervert and distort God's will and trying to get Jesus to choose falsehood over truth. In the first temptation, Satan asks Jesus to turn stones into bread. Playing on the hunger and weakness caused by Jesus' fasting, our Ancient Enemy tries to get Jesus to despair and complain against God like the Chosen people did as they spent their time out in the desert. He also hopes that Jesus might subvert His own identity as Son of God by inducing Jesus to use His power to turn stones into bread. Jesus resists this temptation and rebukes the devil, saying that we must be sustained by the word of God alone. In the second temptation, Satan returns to Jesus and again makes another attack on Christ's messianic identity. He says to Jesus "If you really are the Son of God then jump off this parapet and thereby prove it once and for all. God will save you if you are whom you claim to be." Jesus flatly rebukes him and says, "Do not test me; I know who I am." Angry and with wounded pride, Satan returns for one last attempt at Jesus. This time he shows Him all of the earthly power that he, Satan, has won by his deception and trickery … all of those earthly kingdoms built on the backs of man's inhumanity to man, all the power won by malice, cruelty and injustice. The souls of the unjust are but mere pawns in his wicked plan.

Jesus is shown that all of the glory of earth can be His if only He will turn His back on what is good, right and true. However, Jesus sees through these distortions in the truth and knows that in the end, it will be God who comes out victorious. Satan will be defeated, and all of those who trust in God will be saved. Throughout His life, like all humans, Jesus combated the deceptions of the devil and had to avoid the snares set to trap Him. And even though the humiliating death of the cross, Jesus did not sin but rather was obedient and thus decisively defeated the enemy. No matter what the world offered, Jesus maintained His faith in the goodness of God and remained obedient to His father's will.

Christ Jesus is now the head of humanity and calls us to be the members of His mystical body, the Church, joining ourselves into His victory over sin and death. It is from the victory of Jesus and the example of His mother, and all the saints, and the martyrs, and the countless faithful that have gone before us that we can see the truth of Christ being lived out. These people were not deceived into thinking that good is bad, and bad is good. They realised that only in adherence to God's law can we find true happiness. In His death and following Him more closely, we find that only in His life can we indeed find the meaning of our own.

Everything else falls short of the truth and cannot satisfy, and this is the core of the Christian message. It is not about some secular social work or community building, nor is it merely about being nice and kind. Instead, it is fundamentally about a battle between good and evil. In Jesus Christ, we celebrate the victory over evil and the coming of the reign of God. Every Christian is called to conform their  life to the will of God and be obedient to what He asks of us, not because our God is a power-hungry deity, but because He loves us and has made us love Him with all of our hearts and souls and strength. He knows us better than we know ourselves and longs for us to be all we can be. This Lent, may we have the faith to turn back to God with all our hearts and trust in His loving care for us. Let us trust in the great victory of Jesus over sin.

# THEME 5
# COME WITH ME

*Genesis 15:5-12, 17-18; Philippians 3:17 - 4:1; Luke 9:28-36*

Why did Jesus take these specific ones, Peter, James and John, up on that mountain top with Him? Why were they set apart from the rest to experience this astonishing revelation of the inner reality of Jesus? Furthermore, why were they, at another time, the ones to go with Him into the room of the little girl He raised from the dead? You remember that story, I'm sure. A young girl had died, and everyone was making a great din with their wailing and crying out. Jesus took Peter, James and John, along with the child's mother and father, into her room and there He raised her from the dead in front of their very eyes. And this same set, Peter, James and John, were selected to accompany Him into the Garden of Gethsemane where He sweated blood and suffered His terrible agony. Now we find them here with Him, on top of the Mount of Transfiguration.

They were with Him here when He started to change - to change from being the Jesus from Nazareth into the Risen Christ of Glory. "Come with me" He is telling them, "Come with me to a mountaintop experience. I want to show you something that's really important." Here on this mountaintop, they followed Him into a world of another dimension.

Moses and Elijah, the great experts on change and development, were there. Moses, the great exponent of change, led God's people out of Egyptian slavery to the mountaintop experience of Mt. Sinai. Elijah led those same people from their quicksand of sin into the glory of being

God's people, a glory they had never experienced before. Both Moses and Elijah were agents of total and complete transformation. And here they were on this mountain - as Jesus was beginning His transition from being the Jesus in our human brokenness to being the Christ of risen glory. They were all there on the cusp of entering a new order, of entering into God's new creation. And they were with Jesus at Gethsemane, in the garden wherein He entered upon His horrible suffering, passion and death. And there they slept. Yes, they slept! How could they sleep, we ask? How, given all that God had done for them, could they sleep, not only in the presence of Christ but also in such a moment as this when Christ so desperately needed their companionship, their comfort, their consoling presence with Him in His agony?

Well, how can we so easily go to sleep spiritually? How can we say our prayers, attend the Holy Sacrifice of the Mass, the Holy Sacrifice of Jesus Christ? How can we receive so many gifts from God and still spiritually snooze and doze our way through our prayers, our Masses and, indeed, throughout our whole spiritual life? We can be baptised, catechised, sacramentalised and yet never be wide awake, aware, and alive to the presence of Jesus all around us and even within us. We can say our prayers, do our religious duty, and take part in our religious rites, and be on autopilot throughout it all. The world would have it that way, you know. There are forces at work in our world that want us to remain spiritually asleep.

Peter, James and John, you see, are not alone in their lack of consciousness about Christ. The same Evil One who induced them into sleep is at work seducing our modern world into a state of spiritual narcosis. I deliberately use the word narcosis. We have been duped, doped up, and hooked; we live in a state of spiritual stupor. The Evil One has been quite zealous and quite effective.

Spiritually we sleep. Like Peter, James and John, we sleep with Christ right next to us. We, too, in our youth, were dazzled by His presence when we made our First Holy Communions. We felt His liberating, healing, and peaceful presence when we first went to confession way back then, in those earlier days of our youthful faith. We felt God's presence when we were confirmed. We've had, too, some mountaintop experiences of the presence of God, at sunsets and sunrises, upon falling in love, at births of babies, when parents and grandparents have passed on into the next life, when a poem, or a flower, or several other things have put us in touch with God's holy presence in us. Yet we sleep. We sleep because of routine, because of boredom, because we've been overstimulated by the narcotic of this world's "buzzes."

We sleep because we are exhausted, drained, and running on empty. We sleep because we are bloated, sated, and gorged on this world's spiritual junk food. We sleep because, well, just because we sleep. Peter, James and John, you see, are not altogether different from us. They had their mountaintop experience with Jesus. But we must never forget that when He came down from that mountain. He immediately headed to Jerusalem, to the Garden of Gethsemane, there to suffer. And what do you think caused Him the greatest suffering of all? Don't you imagine it was the fact that these three, those seemingly closest to Him, the most aware of who He was, went to sleep on Him? And we do, too. I wonder if in that garden -- wonder if there in Gethsemane as He took on His horrible agony, pain, and suffering -- He looked down through the centuries to our times and saw us too, sleeping even when we have received His Body and Blood in what we think is "holy" communion, but which is hardly any communion at all.

I wonder now if He sees my soul at some time in the future more alive and attentive to Him? I wonder if tomorrow my soul will wake up and pay attention to Him? The great mystery of it all is that only I can make that happen, and only you can make that happen - He cannot. He can't because He will not. He wants us to choose to love Him. He does not want to force us to love Him. Only I can shake off the narcosis and the stupor and the sleep in which my soul wallows.

Thank God for this holy season called Lent.

# THEME 6
# CALL TO REPENTANCE

*Exodus 3:1-8a,13-15; 1 Corinthians 10:1-6,1-12; Luke 13:1-9*

On the third Sunday of Lent, the church invites us to reflect on the urgency of repentance in an attempt to enhance our Christian lives. During this time of Lent, there is great emphasis on examining our lives and changing for the better through repentance. There is an insistence on the need for a change or transformation of the heart. One of the recurrent themes throughout the Lenten season is the compassion and mercy of God. It is something that we continuously need to be reminded of. Repentance entails the recognition of areas of unfaithfulness in our lives and is ready to make reparations. Repentance demands that we become honest with ourselves and recognise our unfruitfulness. Once we have accepted this change in our lives, God has a ready mission for us. He wants us to fulfill His mission on earth. Thus today's readings are directing us to take a good look at ourselves. In the parable in today's gospel, Jesus speaks of the tree that is alive, but it bears no fruit. There is a demand that it should be cut down. The man responsible for the tree asks the owner to give it one more year to fulfil its purpose. If, after that, there is still no fruit, it should be cut down. In the Book of Exodus, Moses is told to forget his weaknesses and fright and go perform the task of freeing people from slavery. In the second reading, Paul tells us that we are all God's people chosen ones and called upon to live purified lives for Christ.

While reflecting on today's First Reading taken from the Book of Exodus, we hear of God's concern towards His people in Egypt. He sees the hardships of His chosen people and observes their misery. He had heard their cries on account of their taskmasters and took the initiative to liberate them from the Egyptian masters. At the same time, the passage narrates Moses' awesome experience at the Burning Bush. When Moses encountered God in the burning bush, he was just an ordinary shepherd caring for his father-in-law's sheep. He had run away from Egypt, and he was very conscious of his own shortcomings. He had no great gift to talk about God or anyone, for he had a speech defect.

Moses had his own way of life, plans, preferences, and ideas that determined his course of action. But once he confronted God, He never hesitated to respond to His call. God places before him the fresh situation of Egypt and that He is fully aware of His people's untold suffering. God wants him to go, and now, being touched by God, Moses is more than ready to help them. God revealed to Moses in the burning bush as He reveals to us even today. He told him to go to His people for whom He cares so much. God showed him His power in the fire, the fire that burns and does not consume. Fire is the image of God and expresses His divine presence. Our "burning bushes" could be the poor, the needy, the sick, and prisoners in need of our visitation. This is how God makes use of His instruments to prepare them for their mission.

The Second Reading taken from the First Letter to the Corinthians provides us with more information about God's people; we learn that God did free His people from slavery. They were all baptised into Moses in the cloud and the sea. They all ate the same spiritual food in the desert. They all drank the same spiritual drink which God gave them. But, even though they were God's people, He was not pleased with most of them for their behaviour. He struck them down in the wilderness, tested them, and they remained there for forty years. These things occurred as examples for us so that we might not desire evil as they did.

And we should not complain about this righteousness of God. The Destroyer destroyed those who complained in the days of Moses. As St. Paul said, these things happened to serve as a lesson. And they were written down to instruct us. So He admonishes us, if we think we are standing, we better watch out that we do not fall.

In today's gospel, some people approach Jesus and tell Him how Roman soldiers killed some Galileans in the Temple sanctuary. It was said that Pilate had built the much-needed aqueducts in Jerusalem using the Temple money. The Galileans were angry at this, and they protested. Pilate sent the soldiers to mingle among them during the festival and had them killed for their revolt. Jesus seems to be aware of the tragedy. History, of course, says nothing of Pilate's act here mentioned. Pilate's rule was marked by cruelty toward Jews and contempt for their religious views and rites. Now Jesus responds by taking another track altogether. Instead, He mentions another incident, apparently a pure accident when a building fell on innocent people and killed many. Jesus asks His questioners whether it is their sin that brought the innocent people to death. He indeed wants us to think of the many accidents that take place daily. He wants to clear the common belief that such events are acts of punishment by God. Perhaps even more frequently, one meets people who ask why a loving God does not prevent such things from happening.

The response of Jesus is built around the event, where people are taken away by sudden death. Of this instance, namely the Tower of Siloam also, there is no other historical mention. It, too, was a small incident among the accidents of the day. Towers that are built for safety often prove to be men's destruction. Jesus cautioned His followers not to blame great sufferers, as if they were great sinners. When on earth, no place or employment can be considered secure from the stroke of death; we should consider others' sudden removal as warnings to ourselves.

On these accounts, Christ founded a call to repentance. The same

Jesus bids us to repent, for the kingdom of Heaven is at hand; or again He bids us repent, for otherwise, we shall perish. This also brings to our mind the problem of suffering, why God allows people to suffer. Jesus answers: "No, I tell you; but unless you repent, you will all perish just as they did." He calls on them to be always ready to face God and face the eventualities of life. The point is clear. Tragedies occur, whether intentionally by oppressive governors such as Pilate or accidentally by imperfections in the kind of world we live in. In neither case must one conclude that tragedies are necessarily an indication of divine judgment against sinners. Rather, given the uncertainty of life and the unpredictability of the future, one must be warned to examine one's own life and repent in order to be perfect before the Lord.

The gospel reading presents the parable of Jesus about the fig tree. This parable immediately follows after Jesus explained that sin is offensive to God, that it deserves severe punishment. Sin is understood as missing the mark and a negation of His presence. In the parable that Jesus told, a man had a fig tree planted in his vineyard. When the man went to look at it for fruit, he found none on it. The tree had now been without fruit for three consecutive years. Finally, tired of that useless tree, the man told the gardener to cut it down. Upon hearing this, the gardener asked the owner to patiently wait another year, during which time he would dig around the tree and put manure on it in the hope that it would bear fruit. If that helps after one year and there are fruits on it, good; if not, it should be cut down. The fig tree was a favourite tree of the Jews. It was a tree of peace where a happy Jew sat for his regular prayers. Here is the fig tree that had taken so much nourishment from the soil. At the same time, there is not much arable land in Israel. So the fig tree had to justify its existence.

In the parable, the master had already waited for three years, and the gardener asked for another year where it would receive extra care. The fig tree reminds us of two kinds of human persons, those who give and those who take. Those who give symbolise the sacrifice they make and fulfil the purpose of their existence. They give what they have without holding back anything for themselves, and this is in generosity. Those who only take have to justify their existence. They have to fulfil their purpose of existence. To accept Christ's message is to be open for conversion and change of heart. It invites the person to bear fruit and fulfil the purpose for which it has been created, namely, to give. Repentance or conversion means to respond to God's care for us.

We should surrender ourselves to a life of vigilance day in and day out and continuously renew our cooperation with God's grace. In cooperating, we must be confident about what we ought to do and how generously we have to perform. The unpredictability of the end and the urgent need for preparedness is a theme of today's gospel. Jesus' reply would have shocked all. One would expect that Jesus would at least lash out against Pilate and call down curses on such a cruel man. However, no such venomous vindictiveness is pronounced against Pilate. Instead, He tells the reporters: "unless you repent, you will all perish." They need repentance, implying that Jesus is more concerned about hatred and a vengeful attitude.

We ask the grace to live in a continual spirit of renewal and repentance during this Lent season. Repentance demands that we become honest with ourselves and recognise our unfruitfulness and change ourselves to bear the right fruit for God. Moses was asked to change his view and do his mission. Each fig tree is expected to bear fruit that represents the good works and virtues of those who help to build the Body of Christ. Each must answer his calling according to where God has sent him. The fig tree is called upon to be generous in the fulfilment of the mission. We have to recognize our nothingness before God and be ready to receive Him during this season of Lent. It is only after such a serious reflection that we shall have that remorse for our failures. Let us ask ourselves whether God is using this Lenten

Season to shower His abundant graces upon us through Jesus Christ so we will repent and transform our lives.

John D. Rockefeller built the great Standard Oil empire. Not surprisingly, Rockefeller was a man who demanded high performance from his executives. One day, one of those executives made a two million dollar mistake. Word of the man's enormous error quickly spread, and all were scared to meet the boss. One man did not have any choice, however, since he had an appointment with the boss. So he straightened his shoulders and walked into Rockefeller's office. As he approached Rockefeller's desk, he looked up from the piece of paper on which he was writing. "I guess you've heard about the two million dollar mistake our friend made," he said abruptly. "Yes," the executive said, expecting Rockefeller to explode. "Well, I've been sitting here listing all of our friend's good qualities, and I've discovered that in the past he has made us many more times the amount he lost for us today by his one mistake. His good deeds far outweigh this one human error. So I think we ought to forgive him, don't we?"

# THEME 7
# CHRIST MAKES ALL THINGS NEW

*Joshua 5:9a, 10-12; 2 Corinthians 5:17-21; Luke 15:1-3, 11-32*

The theme that pervades through today's readings is that Jesus Christ makes everything new. God tells us that everything old has passed away and will pass away, and we have anew creation. This is our initiation into the life of Christ. Once we are baptised in Christ, we become His new creation, the members of God's own family. Today, as we enter the fourth Sunday of lent, we are called upon to renew ourselves and experience the loving invitation of our Lord to be renewed in Him. Those to be baptised and public sinners are called upon to understand this new life. There is a great search for happiness and fulfilment in life here and now. This search for happiness and fulfilment is symbolised by the image of the younger son in our gospel parable of today who went away with all his wealth in search of happiness. The only problem was that he thought he could find happiness in what the parable calls a life of debauchery. We would say now he tried to find happiness by satisfying every desire of his no matter whether moral or immoral. However, he did not know that true happiness is not found within oneself but in our hearts. The first reading tells us of God leading the people to the Promised Land, where people received happiness as they ate the land's produce, the fruit of their hard work. St. Paul tells us that we find happiness in Christ who makes all things new.

The first readings tell us that Israelites reached the Promised Land under the leadership of Joshua. Their arrival was made possible by a miracle of the Lord. Just as the sea opened up for them as they escaped Egypt, so the water of the Jordan opened up before them so they could cross the Canaan. They encamped on Jericho's plains and discovered that with God's help no earthly obstacles could stand in their way. God tells Joshua that Egypt's slavery and the reproach of being serfs under a pagan dominance are removed at last. The Israelites now can live freely in their own country. The reading tells us that they happily ate the produce of the land. The manna, which was their food for forty years, ceased to come from heaven and they had the new products of the land for themselves. The people could now enjoy the abundance of the Promised Land. God had tested them and had all things new for them. God tells that on His day, He has taken away from them the disgrace of Egypt. They could now celebrate their new life in the Passover that recalls the beginning of their journey.

In the Second reading, St. Paul tells the Corinthians that if anyone is in Christ, he is a new creation: everything old has passed away; see everything has become new! Paul tells them that everything is from God, who reconciled them to Himself through Christ, and has given them the ministry of reconciliation; that is, in Christ, God was reconciling the world to Himself, not counting their infidelity against God, and giving them the grace of reconciliation. Jesus is the mediator in the process, and our part is to accept God's gift of reconciliation. However, such a call imposes a sense of responsibility for them. Henceforth they are to be the ambassadors for Christ since God is making His appeal through them. He asks them to become the righteousness of God in Christ. He invites them to remember that for our sake, God made Christ to be sin who knew no sin so that in Christ, all might become the righteousness of God. In other words, our sins are forgiven, and we share the very holiness of God.

Today's gospel is the family story of the Prodigal son, generally understood as the greatest short story in the world. The context of today's parable is very important. The Scribes and Pharisees, who considered themselves followers of the law and self-righteous, grumble that Jesus is the friend of sinners and eats with them. So, He tells the story that the younger son is the bad boy, a favourite of the tax collectors and sinners who are listening to Him. The elder son, the good boy matches up well with the Scribes and Pharisees who are also in his audience. What unites the story and makes it powerful is the abundance of love the father shows towards his sons.

By the end of the story, we see that both of them, in different ways, prove themselves to be obstacles to family unity and harmony, which the father desired more than anything. That younger son reminds us of the struggle in society at this time to be successful. He convinces his father to give him his share of the inheritance and squanders the whole thing in an irresponsible way of living. He shames his father and family name. He degrades himself by living in a gentile country and working for a gentile employer. This son is not dumb, and he knows that to survive, he must do something to change his life. Therefore, he plans to return to the father not as a son but as an employee, hoping for some work, food and shelter. This is the interior change and repentance. He is also aware that such a plan may not work since he has disgraced the family, and the father may disown him. But on his return, there is a surprise for him when the father receives him back and restores him to his former dignity as a son. Perhaps in the present-day situation when we look for changes and new life, we visualise ourselves as the younger son living with the pigs in need of returning to our father. Therefore, we have someone waiting for us with open arms to welcome us and receive us in such a situation. There is always hope and restoration of the dignity of man.

The elder son despises his younger brother for leaving and his father for accepting him back. He is now seen as an angry and hostile person. However, again the father breaks the social custom and pleads with the elder son to join the celebration. This is not being polite. The father truly wants his elder son there because he loves him. The elder son cannot understand this, and the story does not tell us whether he went to the celebration. However, the story tells us that the father loved both sons beyond every possible human level and broke all cultural boundaries. He does not care what society will say to him. He accepts his sons. This is the love proclaimed by God for us in Jesus.

The entire problem began with the younger son. Without waiting for his father to die, he asks for his share of the inheritance. Usually, the property was divided only after the death of the father. Then he abandons his duties and responsibilities in the family estate and goes abroad to live a life of fun. His reckless lifestyle drains his fortunes, and he finds himself reduced to abject poverty and misery. That a Jewish prince like him should condescend to feed pigs, which Jews regarded as unclean animals, shows the depths of degradation in which he finds himself. A life away from the divine quickly enough leads people to a situation where they lose all sense of shame and decency. However, no matter how far sinners move away from the father's house, the father's loving heart always follows them, gently whispering in their hearts.

"Come home! I want you. I am waiting for you." The Prodigal son decides exactly that when all is lost and chooses to go back to the father.

In the parable, we are given the most beautiful description of our Heavenly Father. He is outside of the house waiting for the younger son to return. And when he does return his father moves close to him, claps him in his arm and kisses him tenderly, and he brings him in and throws a party for him. When we return to God, he throws a party for us too.

Not only does he come out of the house once when he sees his older son angry, but he comes out a second time to try to persuade him to come into the house. In the same way, our Heavenly Father comes out to welcome each of us to his party. The most beautiful thing in the parable is what the father says to the elder son, "All I have is yours." Our Heavenly Father also says to us, "All I have is yours." This is the most beautiful promise and a stunning invitation. At the end of the parable, we are not told whether or not the elder son went into the party. After reading the parable, we also have a choice to make, whether to stay outside or to go in to enjoy the father's party. But the best offer of happiness is from God our Father, "All I have is yours."

The prodigal son did not get the opportunity to fully express to his father that he wants to become a paid servant.

The father immediately readmits him as part of the family and gives the order to bring the robe, the ring and sandals and to kill the fatted calf for a celebration. The younger son, in reality, had a warped notion of his father's forgiveness. He had no understanding of what mercy means. However, now he had learned the depth of the love of the father. The elder son also did not know what forgiveness and love meant. He did not and could not forgive his younger brother for his misdeeds. In this parable, Jesus teaches us the depth of the generosity of God and His mercy. God, our Heavenly Father, is always waiting at the door, waiting for us to come to Him. At every Mass, we receive the same invitation from Jesus, to share His body and blood and, hence, forgiveness. The younger son needed to turn back from his frivolous lifestyle and return to the father's house and be responsible and obedient. In our life, we often regret that others are more privileged than we are and get more benefits than us. Often we are hurt and indignant like the elder brother in the parable. We indeed have missed the point. It is not about who is more or less deserving in a given situation. It is about our ability to love unconditionally and to believe in the fundamental dignity and equality of all people.

A pastor hears that one of his parishioners was going about announcing to everyone that he would no longer attend church services. This rebellious parishioner was advancing the familiar argument that he could communicate with God very easily, out in the fields with nature as his setting for worship. One winter evening, the pastor called on him for a friendly visit. They both sat before the fireplace making small talk but studiously avoiding the issues of church attendance. After a while, the pastor took the tongs from the rack next to the fireplace and pulled a single coal from the fire. He placed the glowing ember on the hearth. As the two watched in silence, the coal quickly ceased burning and turned ashen grey, while the other coals continued burning in the fire. The parishioner then turned to the pastor and said: "I'll be back for the service next Sunday."

# THEME 8
# IN HIS TIME,
# GOD MAKES ALL THINGS NEW

*Isaiah 43:16-21; Philippians 3:8-14; John 8:1-11*

Today's gospel places before us an episode that emphasises the need to examine ourselves and avoid passing any judgment on others. Generally, there is a tendency within us to find fault in others and condemn them. Again, we maintain our long memories of the hurts, and forgiveness does not come easily. During the Eucharist, we repeatedly ask forgiveness from the Lord, and yet we hold back so much grudge in our hearts. As we approach the end of the Lenten season, we are reminded of the immense opportunity to cooperate with God's special graces. The theme that pervades through the reading is that God makes all things new. Today's gospel presents us with a sharp contrast between the cruelty and wickedness of the Scribes and Pharisees and the compassion of Jesus. The Scribes and Pharisees had no regard for the woman caught in adultery and brought her to the master. They were only interested in using her to try to trap Jesus. They had no regard for the fact that she may not have initiated the sin; she may have been led into it by their man. But Jesus is full of compassion; Jesus handles the serious offence delicately. He challenges both the accused and the accusers: he calls on both to look deep into their hearts and examine them. Jesus has final words to the woman "go away and don't sin anymore", and these words will never be forgotten till the end of times. Jesus transforms her into a new person.

Jesus places a bigger challenge before the accusers. He asks them to consider their own actions and their own shortcomings. He tells them to look into themselves before passing any judgement on others. He bends down and writes into the mud or sand. No one knows what Jesus wrote on the ground, but some people suspect Jesus wrote the sins of the Scribes and Pharisees. Notice also that it was the eldest who went away first. Perhaps the eldest had committed more sins; the persons who had lived longer had more to be sorry about in their own lives. Although Jesus has forgiven the woman her sin, he expects her to now live a life of grace and union with God by not sinning anymore. Jesus doesn't say that sin does not matter because sin does matter and damages our relationship with God. He only tells her not to sin anymore and to change her life completely. He restores the woman in two ways. He restores her spiritually by forgiving her, telling her He did not condemn her, while also insisting that she should not sin again, and He restores her to society by saving her life and grants her forgiveness. In this story, the Scribes and Pharisees are presented as sinners, perhaps worse sinners than the woman. Not in their own eyes, of course, but in the eyes of Jesus and His gospel, they lack the virtue of compassion. They intended to trap Jesus and put Him to shame, but ultimately they go away in shame. The Pharisees and the Scribes were persons proud and arrogant, and they sat in judgement on others. They had no idea how to love and forgive, but only how to observe the law externally. They do not love the people that God loves.

However, there is another element in the story that is not explicitly mentioned but is strongly implied. The woman has been dragged before Jesus as a pawn in a game. They wanted to find fault with Jesus on the observance of the law and His application to human kindness. They tell him that Moses had ordered in the law to condemn such women to death by stoning. What is the response of Jesus? They hoped to put the Rabbi who ate and drank with sinners, on a collision course with the sacred traditions coming from Moses. They hoped to condemn him from His own mouth. However, if He agreed with Moses, then He believes His own teaching and behaviour with sinners; but if He rejected the Law of Moses, He could be denounced and labelled as not a man of God.

Further, the Jews had no authority to pass a death sentence on anyone. If they did, they were punishable before the Roman law, and Jesus would be accused as a person breaking the law. Jesus knew the trap too well and refused to give them any answer. But this knowledge surpasses all human understanding that tells of love and forgiveness, and the nameless woman is the beneficiary.

Once Jesus challenged them regarding their own sinfulness, they moved away one by one, and St. John says very clearly, beginning with the eldest. They knew too well that they had to be honest regarding their sinfulness; they could not publicly accuse a person while they were sinful. The only person who could have thrown the stone at the woman is Jesus himself and being a kind person, He would rather show forgiveness. Now only Jesus and the woman are left. Her accusers were all gone, and the one person remaining is not going to accuse her. "Woman, where are they? Has no one condemned you? Neither do I condemn you. Go away and do not sin anymore." Unlike the Pharisees and Scribes, upholders of the Law, Jesus did not condemn her. Instead, He allows her to repent, to convert and change her ways. Jesus shows that He has come not to condemn but to save, rehabilitate, and give new and enduring life.

Now let us look at Jesus in this scene. First of all, Jesus does not deny the woman's sin, and before the law, this was a grievous sin. Adultery involved an intimate sexual liaison between two people, at least one of whom is already married. It is a severe breach of trust in the marriage relationship and a grave injustice to one's partner in the marriage. The seriousness is really in this breach of trust and the injustice to one's partner rather than the sexual activities, which in this case, are secondary. The story does not tell us whether the woman was married or not. What is admitted by Jesus, the Pharisees and the woman herself is that she sinned. He is the one who forgives her and gives her a new life.

During today's first reading, we heard the prophetic words of the Lord God speaking to the prophet Isaiah. Yahweh begins by identifying Himself. He says that it was He who created Israel. It was He who led the Exodus of His people under the leadership of Moses. He divided the Red Sea and destroyed the great army of the Pharaoh of Egypt. It was He who quenched the life out of the enemies of His people. Yet, He tells them to look ahead and not look back into the past. The past always closes our minds and does not allow us to see the present as they are. Therefore the Lord promises to the people "I am about to do a new thing." In other words, at every moment, He creates new things for us. He further says, "For I am about to create new heavens and a new earth, and former things shall not be remembered or come to mind." The Prophet also says that God promises to make a way in the wilderness or the desert, and put rivers in the desert, making the wild animals honour him. His presence makes all things new for the sake of humanity. The people have plenty of reason to praise God for all the gifts.

In the second reading of today, Paul tells the church of Philippi to break away from their past. Paul presents his mature reflections on how much God loves him, written some twenty years after his conversion. The purpose of his whole life has been the right relationship with God. Indeed we see Paul filling himself only with Jesus and cutting out all rubbish from his life: "I believe nothing can happen that will outweigh the supreme advantage of knowing Christ Jesus my Lord. For Him, I have accepted the loss of everything, and I look at everything as so much rubbish if only I can have Christ and be given a place in Him. All I want is to know Christ and the power of His resurrection." In his search for perfection, he observed all the rules and norms as a Pharisee, but ultimately he found meaning in Christ. He accepted the loss of all things that he might gain Christ. Knowing Christ did not mean intellectual knowledge solely, but a personal relationship with Him, the Saviour. Earlier in the same letter, Paul said, "Make your own the mind of Christ Jesus." Then all our sufferings become not a penalty but a privilege. Finally, because of these marvellous blessings that we have received from God, St. Paul urges his church to act as aliens and exiles, to abstain from the desires of the flesh. He receives the assurance from Jesus not because of his own efforts but from the fact that Jesus has taken possession of him.

Contemplating the gospel passage, we see that Jesus has won the test, and the woman has retained her life. He now tells the woman not to sin again as He does not approve of any sin and since sin is so horrible and horrific; He wants her to take steps to ensure that she lives a changed life. On His part, He forgives her, which is a divine act. In reality, the first step the person has to take is to deal with the source of sin, namely, the mind. Among the Native Americans, there is the story of the father who said two wolves were fighting within him, one bad and one good. His son asked which wolf wins, and the father said whichever wolf feeds the most. When Jesus instructs, we need to fill our minds with what is good instead of rubbish. The woman in this story is not just an isolated sinner. She represents all of us. In the word of God today, we heard the divine message that God makes all things new. Jesus gives us a basic command that helps us to identify if we are getting closer to Him. We must persevere in our living faith. Jesus said to the woman as he tells us: "Go your way, and from now on, do not sin again." Once a person is touched by God, and once he has received that divine command, he cannot remain the same.

That was the experience of Moses, Isaiah, Jeremiah, Peter, Paul and several others who came into close contact with Him and remained persons attached to Jesus. Therefore Peter in his letter tells us "We are a chosen race, a royal priesthood, a holy nation, God's own people, in order that we may proclaim the mighty acts of Him who called us out of darkness into His marvellous light." Therefore he says that we should conduct ourselves honourably among the non-believers, so that, though they malign us as evildoers, they may see our honourable deeds and glorify God when He comes to judge. In other words, the lesson we carry home is that we have to be the living examples of Christ in the world.

# THEME 9
# CHRIST, A PATH TO RECONCILIATION
# AND PEACE

*Acts 2: 42-47; 1 Peter 1:3-9; John 20: 19-31*

When Pontius Pilate decided to have Jesus crucified, he asked the question: "Truth? What is truth?" He really wasn't interested in the answer because he needed to put the truth out of the way so he could have Jesus crucified. "Truth?" he asked, "What's that? Does truth |matter?" An author once wrote: "Cowardice asks the question, is it safe? Expediency asks the question, is it political? Vanity asks the question, is it popular? Conscience asks the question, is it right?" There comes a time when one must take a position that is neither safe nor political nor popular, but one must take a particular position simply because it is right, genuinely right because it is based on truth.

We just heard about "Doubting Thomas." One wonders what questions were in his mind. We know how his questions were answered. They were answered so convincingly that he was the first of the Apostles to profess his absolute belief in the divinity of our risen Saviour by crying out: "My Lord, and my God!" Jesus presents us with the God of the Second chance. On Easter Sunday evening, the Lord signals the apostles that even though they had turned their backs on Him, He would not turn his back on them. Christ gives Thomas a convincing experience, not just for his own sake but for ours as well. Jesus forgives him for his disbelief in the Resurrection and out of Thomas' doubts comes the best news of Easter for all of us. God starts all over again. Through forgiveness, He gives us another chance. St. John, the writer of this gospel account, is anxious for us to know that all of this took place on the first day of the week, the first day of God's New Creation. If you do a computer scan, you will discover that "the first day of the week" is mentioned in the New Testament a remarkable seven times. St. John wants us to understand that Sunday had become the Lord's Day. So, our gathering at Liturgy on Sundays as a 'Jesus community' is no accident. We have taken our clue from the apostles. We gather so that Christ can again be with us on the first day of the week. As He gave Thomas, he gave us another chance to encounter him on the first day of his new creation.

For many of us, Thomas is our man. Belief and doubt have the nasty habit of co-existing uncomfortably in our hearts and minds. We have our beliefs while at the same time we have our doubts. If that is a problem for you, do not be too upset with yourself. You are in the best company. All of us are a mixture of fear and doubt, pessimism and trust, belief and unbelief. All of us are in search of certainty. "Seeing is believing," we tell ourselves. However, with what degree of self-deception do we see things? How easily we can fool ourselves! And this is why we need to have others, trusted others, with whom we can verify things. Thomas, we must note, was with others. Thomas stands at the border, standing as he does between those first eyewitnesses of the risen Christ and those of us who are blessed because even though we have not seen, we nevertheless believe. Thomas moved from his isolated independence into interdependence with the chosen witnesses, the apostles. It was when he was among them that he passed from disbelief into life belief. It was there among them that he found and touched the risen Christ. The same can likewise be true for you and me. Christ is here for you and me in our shared Holy Communion. These points to our own need for the Church, our own need for its "Cloud of witnesses," our own need to see and experience the many other signs our risen Saviour works among His followers. This also points to our world's need for us to bring the risen

Jesus to them in what we say, in what we do, in how we regard others, and in how we present ourselves to them.

Sunday, as we note, is the "first day of the week," not Monday. It is on this first day of the week we, with the others who know Christ, have gathered together in this special room where he appears among us and confirms our faith by giving us His body and His blood. We receive our knowledge from others. Is there anything you know that you did not receive from others? So, too, with faith, love, and knowledge, we share all gifts because others have first given them to us. The question may be asked: "If Jesus Christ is risen from the dead, then where is he?" That is a wonderful question. The answer is that the reality of Christ resurrected is found wonderfully in the lives of those who, touched by God's Holy Spirit, have shared His compassion and mercy in His healing forgiveness, in His care and concern for outcasts, and His loving embrace for all of God's children. How can we be such a Christ-filled family of faith? There are four essential features found in early Christian communities that we need to find in ours: (1) devotion to the teaching of the apostles, (2) living together in a community of caring and love, (3) sharing in the breaking of the bread, and (4) prayer. Without these, our Church would waste away, break up, and eventually disappear. Without these, we would fall into the most deadly and modern form of atheism, the atheism of being so busy that we think God does not matter. Without these four essential elements, Jesus may as well still be in His tomb.

Finally, we should not forget that the first thing Jesus did when He rose from the dead was to go to His apostle and give them the gift of healing forgiveness, the gift of reconciliation. He put them at peace with Himself. Is it not what our torn-apart world needs the most right now?

# THEME 10
# NEVER GIVE UP

*Acts 5:27-32, 40-41; Revelation 5:11-14; John 21:1-19*

All of us face judgment at one time or another in life. Some regard us as loyal, constant and steadfast friends. Others think of us merely as stubborn, inflexible and unable to adapt. The most painful critic, each of us must face is our own selves. How do we see and judge ourselves? Indeed it is good to be determined and steadfast. Surely it is good to hold to singleness of purpose and never lose sight of our ideals and goals. But just as surely it is good to adapt, to be willing to listen to reason, and to change course when necessary. The problem, of course, comes in distinguishing between the two. All of this, of course, different from merely "giving up". Giving up is surrendering to weakness or even despair. Do we give up merely in order to take the easy way out? Do we give in to despair? The temptation to give up comes to us in many forms and on many occasions, often appearing to us as a good thing to do. Giving up can be the work of the devil.

Giving up was found in each of the three temptations Satan presented to Christ when He was out in the desert preparing to embark upon His public ministry. Giving up was the last temptation, Satan hurled at Jesus as He hung dying on His cross. When do we give up on others? I've known parents, and you have too, who have given up on their children. We've known spouses who gave up on their marriages without going through the effort of counselling and working for reconciliation. We've all known family and friends who have given up on the Church, or on religion, or on their spirituality, or even on God.

God, however, never gives up on us... even when we've turned our backs on Him and betrayed Him.

That's what today's gospel account is all about. Here we find Jesus encountering some of His disciples after His resurrection. The encounter is situated on water's edge, reminding us of the water of chaos in the Book of Genesis. The Creator brought out an order, creating all things, and eventually creating us from the slime of the earth. The water of the Red Sea, the water of the River Jordan, and the water of baptism are all hinted at by this location. The disciples were all gathered there together on the shores of the Sea of Galilee. Jesus came to them in their midst, foreshadowing how He would come to us thereafter. There were overtones of the Last supper there along with all future celebrations of the Eucharist. At that encounter, Jesus asked Peter those three famous questions, questions that recognised the triple denial of Peter during Christ's passion. Implicit in the questions, however, was the fact that Jesus had not given up on Peter.

Jesus' love for him and commitment to him were still there, even after all that both He and Peter had gone through. We need to reflect on what might have happened had Judas not despaired and stayed with Peter and the Apostles. Would Jesus have forgiven Judas? We know, of course, that He would have. It was not Jesus who had given up on Judas. It was Judas who had given up ... given up on Jesus and given up on himself. From beginning to end, the entire Bible presents us with the truth that God offers Himself to us and then waits for our response.

The most marvellous and awe-inspiring truth lying deep within is that God has offered Himself to us and will never withdraw His offer! His love is everlasting, and His mercy endures forever. His love and His commitment to us stay forever, no matter what sort of distinguishing and horrific sins we may have committed. God never, ever gives up on us. Any thought of "giving up" is on our part, not God's. "Unconditional love" is something we've all heard about. Theologians tell us of God's unconditional love. We want to give unconditional love to our children, our spouses, and our family members. We all, however, have our moments when we've abandoned unconditional love and slapped others with conditions on our love, telling them we'll love them or forgive them "if ..."

Each one of us has our own set of "ifs." And to be honest, we all must admit that we have had our moments when we've felt that unconditional love is impossible for us to give. This is why we need to seek God's forgiveness, not merely to save our skins but so that we, in His forgiveness, might have the power to forgive others as He has forgiven us, so that we will not give up on them. Without God's power, unconditional love is most likely impossible. But with God's love and power, all things are possible, even loving others unconditionally... even not "giving up" on them. Do you think that you have loved God more than Peter? Do you think that you stand in better shoes than Peter's? Maybe, in the last analysis, we should all stand before God as he did. Maybe we should all stand in his shoes, and have his power to forgive, the power that Jesus gave him, there on the shores of the Sea of Galilee.

# THEME 11
# THE LORD IS THE SHEPHERD

*Acts 13;14, 43-52; Revelation 7:9,14b-17; John 10:27-30*

Good Shepherd Sunday is the fourth Sunday of Easter in our new Catholic liturgical calendar. The name derives from the gospel reading on this day, taken from the 10th chapter of John. In recent times this day has also become known as Vocation Sunday, a day on which prayers should be said for vocations to the priesthood and religious life. The image of the shepherd and His sheep is very old in scripture. We have the beloved images of Jesus the Good Shepherd. In some, we see Jesus holding a sheep/lamb over His shoulders, holding the two front legs of the lamb/sheep in His right hand and the two rear legs in His left hand. Or we have a smiling Jesus sitting under a tree, with a cute little lamb on His lap. This image of the shepherd appeals to us because of the tenderness of Jesus, His care for the lamb/sheep and His compassion. In those days, a shepherd did not walk behind the flock beating them with a stick to keep moving. He walked in front of them, seeking out a safe path to food, water and shelter. The sheep followed him because they recognised his voice, and they trusted him. Jesus tells us the kind of good shepherd he is. He leads, and we follow.

During today's gospel reading, Jesus uses the image of the Shepherd and the sheep. The relationship between the shepherd and the sheep is so intimate that it is an extension of the relationship between the Heavenly Father and son. We heard the words of Jesus: "My sheep hear my voice and follow me." In this particular passage from the gospel of John, Jesus was speaking of His divine title as the Good Shepherd. The sheep listen to and recognise the voice of their shepherd, and that is why they continue to follow Him rather than another. It is essential for us also to recognise the voice of Jesus as it comes to us in our daily life. Earlier in the same chapter, Jesus had said, "I am the Good Shepherd. The Good Shepherd lays down his life for the sheep." Since Jesus is the Good Shepherd and not a hired hand, He does not run away when the wolf comes. Instead, He is ready to give His life for His sheep. On the other hand, the hired person runs away when the wolf comes, leaving the sheep in danger. Jesus, the Good Shepherd, to the point of giving His life for His sheep, died on the cross for the sake of humanity. The Good Shepherd became the Lamb of God to take away the blemish of the world.

Jesus, as a shepherd, shows a deep sense of commitment and responsibility towards His own. He is a leader who is concerned about the other, and hence there is attractiveness in Him. Secondly, there is the knowledge of the shepherd. Every good shepherd knows that his sheep knows him and he knows his sheep. There is a mutual understanding and love between them. This mutual bond of love and intimacy is often compared to the mutual relationship between Jesus and His father. The shepherd knows his sheep, and the sheep acknowledges its shepherd. Thirdly the Good Shepherd deeply desires that many other sheep should come to identify themselves with him. This is the call of the kingdom of God that there may be "one flock and shepherd." In this sense, an invitation for the universe to be united together with its God and Lord.

Finally, the good shepherd wished to lay down His life for the sheep. We have a God who is ready to die for others, and Jesus emphasises that, in giving His life for His sheep, He is doing so of His own will. His death is to be the living proof that "the greatest love a person can show is to give one's life for one's friend." This is proof that Jesus truly is a good shepherd. As we celebrate Good Shepherd Sunday, let us pray to the Lord that we may be His good sheep, listening attentively to His voice, and follow His example of self-giving love. Let us also pray for all our shepherds, especially our religious and political leaders. May they follow the example of Jesus who was willing to serve and lay down His life for His sheep. Jesus, our shepherd, is the way, truth and life. He is the one who goes after the lost sheep leaving the ninety-nine to bring it back to the fold. Today let us pray for vocations to the priesthood and religious life, that many will be inspired to show true love, to the point of sacrificing many other attractive options to become Priests of Jesus, to follow Him in religious life.

# THEME 12
# LOVE ONE ANOTHER
# AS I HAVE LOVED YOU

*Acts 14: 21b-27; Revelation 21: 1-5a; John 13:31-33a, 34-35*

The theme that dominates the readings of today is love and service. Jesus tells His disciples to love one another as He has loved them. He shows the type of love He carries with Him: He serves them and washes their feet. During the last supper, He tells them that there is no greater love than one giving his life for his friends and He gives His life for us all, calling us His friends. He also defines for us the meaning of God's love which is sacrificing and self-emptying love. God emptied Himself and gave His only son for our sake that we may have life in Him. The first reading tells us how the apostles who had deep and personal experience of Christ are willing to suffer for the love of Him. The second reading tells us of the new heaven and new earth prepared by the Lamb out of love for us. The love of Christ in the Church is received as a precious gift. It also needs to be demonstrated in accordance with Christ's command to love one another. Love will be the mark of the community left behind after Christ has departed. He promises the gift of the Spirit, but that is a gift of empowerment to fulfil His mission on earth. All this is based on love. Love is the basis of Christian discipleship and the motivation of Christian action. Love makes a Christian a distinct person. Above all, as St. Paul says, Christ is Love. Viewing the images coming out of Haiti, pictures of little children suffering terribly, some with arms and legs hastily and excruciatingly amputated, pictures of desperate people struggling for a mouth of water or bit of food, along with other images of terrible and painful human suffering. We see a need for service, a need to show love, a call to the service of the other person.

John says, "God is love; those who abide in love abide in God, and God abides in them." He reminds the disciples that

> "Those who say, 'I love God,' and hate their brothers or sisters, are liars; for those who do not love a brother or sister whom they have seen, cannot love God whom they have not seen. The commandment we have from Jesus is this: those who love God must love their brothers or sisters also."

The season of Easter reminds us of the resurrection of Jesus. It is the celebration of new life that has come to us through our Risen Lord. John tells us that God loved the world and sent His Son to save us. However, man rejected the Son of God and killed Him. But God raised Him up and gave Him back to us out of greater love. That is the resurrection. It is the extension of the love of God. Love is to wish each other well. It includes affection and service, as is explained in the gospel of today. Love is the union of minds and hearts and wills. Love is compassion, support, healing, missionary and service. Today's psalm tells us that love is gracious, merciful, slow to anger and rich in abounding mercy. Above all, God's love is kind, compassionate, sacrifice and reaches out to all. Resurrection is this love of God shown to us in Jesus.

Today Jesus calls us to love like Him, a love of service. He calls us to love like our Heavenly Father, who shows no partiality. He calls us to love as He loved, meaning to be filled with love for one another. The disciple of Christ is not primarily an individual person but an inter-person. He is always at the service of the other. Hence Jesus gives us the new commandment to love other people as He has loved us. The divine command is to love God with our whole heart and soul and to love our neighbour as ourselves. Jesus has added a new element in telling us that the true test of discipleship is to love other people in the same way that He has loved us. His love was the sacrificial love where He gave His life for us. God has given us a world in which people are necessary for Him to get things done. To be sure, God gives us guidelines; to be sure, God gives us prophets and priests; to be sure, God gives us vision and purpose. But having given us His manifold gifts along with His offer to be with us, He, in turn, waits for our response. God offers, we respond. Everything depends upon our response.

St. Teresa of Avila lived during the 1500s, a tumultuous time in our human history. She wrote a beautiful reflection that applies to us today just as much as it did to the people of her day. She wrote:

> Christ has no body but yours,
>
> No hands, no feet on earth but yours,
>
> Yours are the eyes with which He looks with
>
> Compassion on this world,
>
> Yours are the feet with which He walks to do good,
>
> Yours are hands, with which He blesses all the world.
>
> Yours are the hands, yours are the feet,
>
> Yours are the eyes, yours are His body.
>
> Christ has no body now but yours,
>
> No hands, no feet on earth but yours,
>
> Yours are the eyes with which He looks with
>
> Compassion in this world.
>
> Christ has no body now on earth, but yours.

# THEME 13
# REMAIN IN MY LOVE

*Acts 15:1-2, 22-29; Revelation 21:10-14, 22-23; John 14:23-29*

All of us have had to face moments of departure and loss. Was it when we were desperately in love, and then the one we loved left us? Was it when we graduated from school and then suffered separation from our dear friends? Was it when we had to take a job in a city far away? For those leaving, it is a wrenching experience. For those left behind, it is equally wrenching, perhaps even more so. The moments and days approaching departure are filled with terrible anxiety. Our hearts are filled with fear and sorrow. Such a time, experienced by Jesus' closest friends, is presented to us in today's gospel account. The scene is set during the Last Supper. Jesus' words are a part of His last discourse, thoughts and words He was sharing with them immediately before His passion and impending agony and death. The break-up was just about to occur, and He was giving them His last words of love. What was going through Jesus' mind? I imagine He felt much like a parent feels when his or her child or children will be left on their own. They will have to fend for themselves. They will have to find protection and security using whatever devices they learned while at home. So, too, while they were with Him, Jesus had protected them. Who would protect them now? Who would guard them, care for them, and provide for them?

The Church gives us this setting as she prepares us for another departure, namely the Ascension of Jesus and His going back to His Father in heaven. "Do not let your hearts be troubled," He tells them. He promises them God's presence will be given them in a way. The Holy Spirit will be with them to comfort them, empower them, and inspire them. However, they will have to see God and experience God in a new way, in a spiritual way, in an inner way. God's presence will no longer be tangible and visible to them and immediately available to them, as a close friend embodied in a human body. The Jesus they had known was about to become someone new and different for them. There is no life experience that is more frightening, sadder, and more tragic than the experience of not belonging. To not belong to anyone is a terrible and terrifying experience for any one of us. We are, after all, made to belong. We are made in the image and likeness of God; the God whose very nature is three divine persons totally belonging to each other. Therefore, to not belong strikes at the very ground of our existence… our reason for being. To be left alone is a frightening thing. It directly contradicts the way God made us to live. We are, however, not left alone. God has not left us, nor will He ever.

We have his powerful, loving, caring and life-giving presence in His Holy Spirit, the one who dwells in His church. The first reading, taken from the book of Acts, gives us a glimpse into where we will find God after Christ's resurrection and Ascension. We find God in belonging. The urge to belong, the drive for community grounds all of creation. I say "grounds" because everything is built upon God. We, precisely as persons, mirror God's very own existence, namely the being of God found in the total and infinite union of the Father, the Son, and the Holy Spirit. We are divine, Revelations tells us, made in the image and likeness of God. We are created to live in God's very own way of living. Our existence and our lives are made for living in community, in communion and love, with others. The Church exists for a purpose. The Church exists to bring us to union with God, with and in Christ and by the power of the Holy Spirit. But the Church also exists to bring us into communion with each other. Holy Communion not only unites us with the risen Christ, but it also unites us with each other in Christ's very own life, the life He gave to share with us, the life in which we are taken back to our father in heaven.

The Book of Acts, from which today's first reading was taken, is a book that's all about that. It is in that communion, in that community or family of faith that we call the Church, it is in that Holy Communion, that God comes to us in Christ and we return to the Father, by the power of the Holy Spirit, in the risen Christ. The very life of the Church is expressed in its actions. The Church's concern for the family is all about that. Parish life is all about community. Catholic charities are about community. Catholic schools are all about community. The urge to belong, the drive for the community, is deep within the very nature of the Church, the expression of the mystical Body of the risen Christ. The terrible thing about sin is that it isolates us. It tears apart the bonds of communion. It attacks belonging; it sets the individual against all others, including God. I cannot imagine a hell worse than having only myself to live with and love without anyone else to live for and love. Hell, it seems, is to live forever in infinite isolation, cut off from any sort of belonging. Sin is the diabolical opposite of living in communion with others and with God. Perhaps this helps us realise why the main pastoral efforts of the Church are that forgiveness brings God's healing and loving reconciliation and forgiveness to everyone, no matter how depraved, no matter how steeped in sin they may be. This, after all is said and done, was the chief ministry of Christ Jesus, the ministry of reconciliation. It was His first gift to us immediately after He rose from the dead. His Ascension into heaven is our gift in order that we, in Him, might return to our Father, the one who made us in the first place to belong to Him forever in love. May you and I, all together, live in God's love with each other.

# THEME 14
# CHANGE IS POSSIBLE

*Acts 16:16-34, Psalm 97, Revelation 22;12-14, 16-17, 20-21,*
*John 17:20-26*

As we draw closer to the season of Pentecost, we are constantly reminded of the power of God to change human hearts, minds, and attitudes. On the eve of Pentecost, we pray that the presence of the Holy Spirit will help to inform and direct the course of our lives as members of a Christian family.

Our meditations for the seventh Sunday in Easter include a well-known passage from the Book of Acts in which Paul and Silas were imprisoned and caused to suffer a great deal because of their faith and their steadfast proclamation of the Good News of Jesus Christ. Despite their mistreatment and false arrest, Paul and Silas slowly transformed the minds and hearts of their captors and others who were imprisoned through their deep sense of faith and, especially, their behaviour. Our text notes: "About midnight, Paul and Silas were praying and singing hymns to God, and the prisoners were listening to them."

In our world today, we hear very distressing and painful stories of abuse, misconduct, man inhumanity to man. While this shameful conduct does not reflect or mirror the pattern of behaviour by the vast majority, these incidents do reveal the potential for human beings to act inhumanely towards others during times of overt hostility. Unless we are centred with strong value systems and identify with a faith tradition that affirms every human being's dignity, the difference between oppressor and oppressed remains less a matter of substance than context.

Paul and Silas behaved differently because they truly believed in

Almighty God's power to positively change hearts and minds. Their captors were overwhelmed, not so much by how a violent earthquake freed the chains and opened the doors of those imprisoned, but by the desire of those imprisoned to wish their captors no harm. Indeed Paul and Silas told their jailors, "Believe in the Lord Jesus, and you will be saved, you and your household." Furthermore, the jailor and his whole family came to know the love of God as they were baptised in the name of Jesus Christ.

This passage reveals the magnitude and degree of change that is possible in human life and how intentional we must be as Christians in working to be agents of change. As Christians, we are called to a ministry of reconciliation, transformation, and renewal. Our behaviour and willingness to effect that change are defined by our relationship to the risen Christ.

The capacity to be different and act differently because Christ is the centre of our being is one of the best ways to share the Good News. Our commitment to recognizing and appreciating the best that is possible in others reflects the best qualities of what it means to be truly human. As disciples of Jesus, we all find ourselves captive and imprisoned by things that separate us from Christ and one another. We may be imprisoned by fears, prejudices, attitudes, anger, and a multitude of other feelings that swell up during times of stress.

At times like this when we are unable to manage the complexities of life or circumstance, may we be drawn to the power of the Holy Spirit to help us deal with those areas of life for which we find ourselves ill-equipped, uninformed, or unprepared. In all things may the mind of Christ, through the Holy Spirit, direct us to fulfil God's work during our lives. May the Holy Spirit work within us to bring a sense of joy, centred peace, and a deep sense of compassion in our work and witness with others, in the name of Christ. Come Holy Spirit, fill the heart of your faithful, and enkindle in us, the fire of your divine love.

# THEME 15
# UNITY IN DIVERSITY

*Acts 2:1-11; 1 Corinthians 12:3-7 & 12-13; John 20: 19-23*

It is said that Pentecost is the birthday of the Church. If so, it was a birthing out of human frailty, the Apostles having locked themselves up in the Upper Room in fear. But it was there and then that God unleashed an unheard power upon them. For there the Apostles courageously burst out of their private little room into the public square, driven by the Holy Spirit's wind and fire to spread throughout the world the particular Presence of God that had come to them from the Father of Jesus Christ. I would suggest that we in our way are very much like the pre-Pentecost Apostles, huddled together in fear of what's going on out there in the world's marketplace. Today we face daunting experiences from child abuse, sexual abuse, and divorce, to name only a few. We have a culture in distress; it is a "culture" coming apart.

Moreover, while we rejoice in our diversities, we are at the same time finding unity to be something that's more and more elusive. Our Church is called the Catholic Church precisely because it encompasses so many diversities. But when either unity or diversity outweighs the other, we experience an imbalance that can be quite destructive. Individuality is something dear to some people. We cherish our right to privacy. Personal empowerments, individual rights, and the promotion of personal lifestyles are very much in vogue these days. Some would suggest, however, that our living together in a shared community is being lost. Whoever talks these days about the Common Good? Or about the rights we should have as a community of people? Have individual rights, rights to privacy, and personal lifestyles trumped our security, the peace and the security of living while respecting the rights of others?

The coming of the Holy Spirit brought a sense of unity to those fractured eleven Apostles. More importantly, it brought one faith, one baptism, one God and Father of all in Jesus Christ. God's Holy Spirit spoke one commonly understood word that was heard in a diversity of languages. The Church was endowed with unity and universality so that the hearts of all could be touched. In their unique individualities and in all of their diversities, the lives of all could be shared in the one Christ, in the one bread and in the one cup, in the one church that was at the same time one and yet many. This Christian unity subordinates all elitist and particularistic pretensions to supremacy. Precisely in our unity and shared community, we find universality, a catholicity, without which individual diversities can only war with each other for dominance. We should celebrate the diversities we have here in our parish family. We should rejoice in them and be grateful that our loving heavenly Father is endowing our worldwide Catholic Church with rich and wondrous multiculturalism. At the same time, we need to be fully committed to remaining Catholic, committed to keeping the core of what it means to be one, holy, catholic and apostolic. It is only in the strength of that richly composed reality that we can forge the bonds that allow us to express our diversities and our individualities in loving ways that are not threatening  and do not seek to dominate others. For if we have no unity, no commonly shared mission and purpose, how can we, as the particular Christian people that we are, endowed by our Church with the Holy Spirit given her at Pentecost, confront and engage the world around us and the culture in which we are immersed?

When John F. Kennedy was campaigning to become the first Catholic President of the United States, he was asked how he could be a loyal American. In other words, he was asked whether or not Catholicism is compatible with being an American. I want to suggest that today the real question is rapidly being turned the other way around. Is our so-called "progressivism' compatible with being a Catholic? How, then, can we challenge our culture, one in which individuality and privacy are exalted over the unity of commonly shared values and the common good? How can we challenge the fracturing that eats away at the reality of our living together in a community? Indeed, what does the "Community" really mean where we live apart from a commonly shared national arena in which so many ideologies combat with each other for dominance in our civic lives?

What do we mean by the term 'civility' when public discourse is so often anything but civil? I can't help but wonder about the impact of television talk shows on our youngsters – talk shows that are more shouting matches than rational discussions. We stand 2,000 years distant from the pre-Pentecost Church huddled together in the Upper Room. Perhaps we would do well to gratefully receive, along with those Apostles, the Advocate, the "lover of the poor, the light of human hearts, the kind guide and giver of gifts, the gracious visitor who eases our toils, the consoler with cool grace in heat and light in darkness, the warmer of our hearts and healer of our wounds, the gift of joy and absolver of sins.

Dear loving Father, with your only-begotten Son whom you consecrated and raised from the dead in the power of your Holy Spirit, send your Holy Spirit yet again upon us to renew us and to renew our troubled world. Renew in us, loving Father, that wondrous life that You gave to the Church 2,000 years ago, so that with fresh vigour we may join ourselves into the mission of your Apostles and live together in that organic and holy communion that we know of as one, holy, Catholic and apostolic church – in order to accomplish your work. Refresh us and bless us once again with your life-giving Holy Spirit.

# THEME 16
# THREE PERSONS IN ONE GOD

*Proverbs 8:22-31; Romans 5:1-5, John 16:12-15*

When you recite our profession of faith each Sunday, do you realise you're making a statement about the Holy Trinity? Well, you are. Notice that it is divided into three sections, each one setting forth our beliefs about the Three Persons in the one God.

The first section is, of course, about God the Father and Creator of all exists. We Christians take that for granted, but others not of our faith do not … atheists and agnostics, for instance. Christian thinkers down through the past two thousand years assert that nothing can only produce nothing. Nothing comes from nothing. Chaos can only produce chaos. Order can only be produced by intelligence, finds structure, and purpose. In that way, our world and nature are both assembled and functional. Christian thinkers attribute that reality to a purposeful Creator, whom we call God, the Father and Creator of heaven and earth. The second section of our creed or profession of faith devoted to God reveals His mind and heart to us. St. John, at the beginning of his gospel, puts it this way:

> "In the beginning was the Word, and the Word was with God, and the Word was God. He was at the beginning with God. All things came to be through him, and without him, nothing came to be. What came to be through him was life, and this life was the light of the human race; the light shines in the darkness, and the darkness has not overcome it. Was in the world, and the world came to through him, but the world did not know him." (John 1:1-5, 10)

Some Christian preachers teach that God loves us and so we should love everyone, and then they stop there. Other Christian preachers teach that God loves us, we should love others in turn, and we should obey God's commands, follow His way, and then they stop there. We Catholics believe that God loves us, that He sent His son to tell us about God and how much He loves us, and how to live in God's ways according to His commands. But then we say that we believe all that about God and God wants to share His very life with us. Not only that, but also that God wants His very own life to fuse with our lives deep within us. What Jesus is giving to us is God's marriage to us, God entering into us and joining our lives into His life.

Our profession of faith, our creed, set forth our belief that God the Father sent His Son to us as Christ Jesus in order to overcome the gulf between God and us, in order to build the bridge between God and us, so that He can live with us and we can live within Him. How can that happen? Well, we go now to the third section of our profession of faith, and there we set forth our belief in the presence of God that comes to us in the Holy Spirit.

He is the Person of the Blessed Trinity that shares God's energy, God's power, and God's love for us in such a way that He, the Holy Spirit, "makes it all happen." Not only that but He, the Holy Spirit, guides us and helps us when we are mystified, confused, and simply do not understand. He is the expression of God's presence, power and love for us. It was through the Holy Spirit that Jesus was conceived in the womb of the Blessed Virgin Mary. Dying on the Cross, Jesus handed over to us His spirit. It was by the power of the Holy Spirit that Christ Jesus was raised from the dead. At Pentecost, God the Father and God the Son forever gave us their Holy Spirit in the Church. Our triune God saves us through all three Persons of the Blessed Trinity.

The three Persons are together at work whenever one of them is at work. No one of them works apart from or separate from the others.

Whenever God acts, He acts triune. One thing that is at the very core of God is His urge for and drive toward unity. We are made in God's image and likeness, and so we feel that powerful urge and drive deep within us. It is a divine fire that burns in our hearts and souls. Love, communion, community and unity are at the very core of our Catholic religion. The drive for love and union is a divine fire He has placed inside us. They shape and form the very soul of our Church. They are the ground upon which we live out our lives. All of this perhaps helps to explain why our Mass is put together so that we recite our Profession of faith, our beliefs in the nature of God, at the end of the Liturgy of the Word and the beginning of the Liturgy of the Eucharist. After reading about God and talking about God, we are driven to share Holy Communion, receive the very life of God in and through Jesus Christ, and then share it with ourselves and all the others we will meet in our daily lives in the coming week.

May the blessing and love of God the Father, God the Son, and God the Holy Spirit be with you both now and in all of the days of your life. Amen.

# THEME 17
# I AM THE BREAD OF LIFE

*Genesis 14:18-20; 1 Corinthians 11:23-26; Luke 9:11-17*

Today's celebration of Corpus Christ brings us joyful good news of God's wondrous gift of himself to us in the Body of Christ, a reality that we encounter in celebrating the Eucharist, in receiving Holy Communion and in adoration of the Blessed Sacrament. There is a great mystery here; how is it that God's love has brought Him to be so deeply immersed in our sinful humanity? We will never plumb the depth of that wonder. At the same time, we should never cease rejoicing in the fact that He took on our humanity at its best and in its worst. There will be many homilies preached around the world this Sunday, which will focus on the sixth chapter of St. John's gospel, where we find Jesus declaring that He is the Bread of Life, that His flesh is true food and His blood true drink. "I am the living bread that came down from heaven," He declared: "Whoever eats this bread will live forever; and the bread that I will give is my flesh, for the life of the world. This led to a dispute among many who asked, "How can this man give us His flesh to eat?" To which Jesus declared: "Amen, amen, I say to you, unless you eat the flesh of the Son of Man and drink His blood, you do not have life within you. For my flesh is true food, and my blood is true drink." Upon hearing these words of Jesus, many of His very own disciples left Him.

Many Christians around us today do not accept the truth of Jesus' words about His body and blood. For us as Catholics, however, along with Eastern Orthodox Christians, this teaching of Jesus is central to the very nature of the Church. Without the body and blood of Christ, the

Church would not be what it is. The Eucharist makes the Church and the Church makes the Eucharist. Without Christ's sacrifice of His body and blood, there would be no priesthood. The Holy Sacrifice of the Mass is central to the very existence of the Church. Likewise, it is central to our life as Catholic Christians. Because of it, we can access heaven, whereas before Christ gave it to us, heaven's doors were closed. The Eucharist and the Church are God's marvellous gifts to us. They are not of our making; Jesus Christ saves us from our sins by offering the totality of Himself to our Father in heaven, offering His body, blood, soul and divinity. Jesus continues this one sacrifice of Himself down through the ages of human history in the Holy Sacrifice of the Mass. In the Mass, Jesus takes us into himself, "Through him, with him, and in him" He then returns us back home to our Father in heaven. It is a dynamic act, a continuing act, not something that happened only once over 2,000 years ago, outside Jerusalem's walls.

When we celebrate the Holy Sacrifice of the Mass during the offertory prayers, the priest takes a cruet of water and mingles a few drops of the water in the wine. As he does so, he will pray, "By the mystery of this water and wine, may we come to share in the divinity of Christ, who humbled himself to share in our humanity." Moments later, during the Eucharistic Prayer, the priest calls down the Holy Spirit, asking God to consecrate the mingled water and wine into the Blood of Christ. It is in our mingled humanity with Christ's divinity, that the life of God the Son comes to us in the Eucharist, in His Mystical Body. The Church is never more Church than at that moment. In the Eucharist, God's life and our human life are fused together. Hopefully, when we spend time in Eucharistic adoration outside of Mass, we make the proper connection between the body and blood of Christ in the Eucharist, with the Mystical Body of Christ that is present and active in the world. After all, when we receive the Eucharist in Holy Mass, the idea is to take the true and real presence of Christ within us out into the world. We celebrate Mass not merely as a private devotion to save ourselves and enliven individual holiness within us. Yes, we do that, but with the greater purpose of carrying out our Father's mission. He sent his Son into the world not to condemn it, but to save it. Christ's mission is our mission. All Eucharistic devotion is quite central to that mission, an active mission, not passive, in the world, not separate from it.

Many centuries ago, theologians spoke of the Eucharist as the Mystical Body of Christ. The phrase is often used today to identify the Church. Once again, we need to realise that to make real in our lives and those around us, the reality that the Church is the Mystical Body of Christ because the Eucharist constitutes the Church. In their Constitution on the Sacred Liturgy, the Fathers of the Second Vatican Council taught us

> "... the liturgy is the summit toward which the church's activity is directed; at the same time it is the fount from which all power flows. For the aim and objective of apostolic work is that all who are made sons of God by faith and baptism should come together to praise God amid of His church, to take part in the sacrifice, and to eat the Lord's supper."

The Body of Christ takes us into Jesus' entire life, a life given over to God in every way at every moment. His death on the cross was the culmination of His life among us as Jesus of Nazareth. Christ's resurrection was the beginning of His life as the Spirit-filled Christ is risen in glory. This is what we mean when we enter into the "Paschal Mystery" when we receive the Body of Christ, and we enter into His life to its fullest extent. We do not enter it merely because we will to do so, we enter into it because we are called and empowered to do so by the Holy Spirit. Mass (the Eucharist) is not something we watch; it is something we do. God calls us to Himself, not in some remote and distant heaven, but here on earth. His call is to us now; His call is present. Our response is not some future response; our response is now, here on earth. The bread and wine we offer at Mass symbolize the sacrifice of ourselves. Our giving thanks in the Eucharistic Prayer is our surrendering ourselves to God, in Christ's Communion; we enter into the totality of Christ incarnate life among us.

There is an intrinsic interconnection between the Holy Sacrifice of the Mass (which we call Eucharist), Holy Communion, and the Blessed Sacrament. In this sense, "receiving Holy Communion" is a dynamic reality: we receive Christ, and in so doing, Christ receives us, by the power of the Holy Spirit presents us to the Father. The intended result of our active participation in the offering of the Mass, will be found in an ethic of life that participates in Christ's active life in our world, a life that is sent into the world "so that the world might believe" in God's caring love for us all as His children. We are here at Mass in order to be sent, sent with God's enterprise, with God's meaning and purpose for our lives. We come to Mass to join ourselves into Christ in His Mystical Body and into His mission among us. The purpose of Mass is not to be seen as an action wherein the priest simply consecrates hosts; some people think their participation in the Eucharistic Prayer is all about watching the priest and then receiving Holy Communion. Indeed it is much more. Our Holy Communion incorporates us into the Body of Christ, but our incorporation is not something that we simply receive. We are taken up into the totality of what Jesus Christ is all about so that through Him, with Him and in Him, all honour and glory will be given our Father in heaven. May you fully, actively, and intentionally participate in that reality, a reality summed up in the dynamism of Corpus Christi.

*May the Body and Blood of our risen Lord Jesus bring us together into eternal life.*

# THEME 18
# CALLED TO LOVE

*Samuel 12:7-10, 13; Galatians 2:16, 19-21; Luke 7:36-8:3*

When we read bible passages or hear them read to us, we glean more if we pay attention to who wrote them, why they were written, and what their authors are trying to convey. Today's gospel passage comes to us from St. Luke's gospel. St. Luke was a physician; he had a special concern for those who were hurting and needed healing. Therefore, by no accident, St. Luke in his gospel included today's episode about the sinful woman. In other parts of his gospel, we learn of outcasts, people who have been shunned and hurt by others, and people who were ill-treated. In his writing, St. Luke pays special attention to women and their role in the life of Jesus. In St. Luke, we find Jesus giving women attention, respect and the honour they would not otherwise receive in the culture in which they lived back then. In reading sacred scripture, we need to see ourselves in the various characters presented to us. For instance, in the Parable of the Prodigal Son, we need to see ourselves as the younger son, see ourselves as his elder brother, and see ourselves as the prodigal son's father. We need to picture ourselves in their attitude and in their behaviours. Looking at St. Peter, can we see elements of his character and attitudes on our own? The same for St. Joseph, as another example. Perhaps above all other saints, we can find our Blessed Mother's characteristics, her attitudes, and her relationship with her son in our own personalities. How are we similar to them? How are we not at all like them?

The images of humanity within our Saints are made available to us to know what real humanity is. With that in mind, we turn to today's gospel and give our attention to two important characters that come into focus; one is the Pharisees, the other the sinful woman. Early Christian writers viewed them as allegorical characters, the Pharisee representing the Jewish religious establishment and the woman representing us, the church, and the followers of Jesus. Theologians and preachers in the Early Church (the Church Fathers as we call them) saw her as his type, an icon. That being so, the members that constitute the body of the Church, should likewise recognize ourselves in this woman.

As we begin to glean things for today's passage, I want to point out to you that it was the custom in those days to offer water to those who entered homes for a meal, water to wash the dust and dirt off their feet, and water to wash their faces and hands. This was a common and expected courtesy. Here, in this episode, the Pharisee offered no water to Jesus even though He was a guest. It was a snub, a snub that in effect, said, "You are dirt as far as I'm concerned." Usually, a warm greeting with a kiss on the cheek was tendered. You see that today in the Middle East when people first meet and greet each other. Upon Jesus' arrival into the Pharisee's home, He was given no kiss, no sign of closeness or friendship. In other words, He was told He was an outsider. The message was: "You'll get no respect here!" Anointing with oil was another gesture of hospitality. The ointment was a kind of perfume. In those hot, dusty regions of the world, you can imagine the smells that must have accumulated in the travellers' clothes. Perfumed oil was a way of making the guests more comfortable. Anointing with oil also had a healing quality to take care of muscle aches, pains, and weakness.

What about the woman who appeared at the dinner? Was she invited? Probably not. After all, she had a bad reputation and had most likely been sexually promiscuous. We don't know how she got into the party, but that doesn't matter. What we do know is that she was conscious of her sins, very conscious of them. She knew she needed forgiveness and acceptance. Quite obviously, she knew who Jesus was and that He was an extraordinarily holy man of God. Boldly she approached Jesus, washed His feet with tears, wiped them clean with her hair, and then covered His feet with her kisses. These actions were very intimate… but then she knew a lot about intimacies. The guests at that dinner must have been shocked.

Apparently, she also knew a lot about Jesus and the forgiveness that overflowed from His heart. She could recognize love when she saw it, and she fully recognized all of the love in Jesus' heart. In her faith, she humbly laid claim to His love and forgiveness. Her many sins were forgiven. She loved a lot; she was forgiven a lot. Love motivated this woman. Love did not motivate the Pharisee. She knew what was in the heart of Jesus and, acting in faith, she placed her hope in Him and gave Him her love. The Pharisee being distant from Jesus, cold in his aloofness, didn't receive any forgiveness - he didn't even want it. This raises a question for you and me. Just how close are you and I to Jesus? Can you see yourself on intimate terms with Him, just as this woman saw herself? Do you approach him as humbly and boldly as she did? This leads to another question: How do you approach not only touching but receiving the Body and Blood of Jesus? Many around us are indifferent. Many regard receiving Holy Communion as if it is just another religious gesture. Do they think Holy Communion is only a piece of bread and a bit of wine? We need to ask ourselves if we can capture some of the woman's fervour, some of her love. If we think of the Pharisee's house as representing the world around us as we find it in our day, can we see ourselves and see our church as this woman, sinful and in need of healing and forgiveness? Can we have hearts as warm as hers and boldly anoint His feet with our own devotions? Indeed, we are all too aware of the sinfulness in the world today. Much penance is called for, and much forgiveness is needed. What Jesus declared is our hope: So I tell you, her many sins have been forgiven because she has shown great love.

May you and I be a part of the great love that is needed both for our church and in our church today, the wounded Mystical Body of Christ now so profoundly in need of healing.

# THEME 19
# CLOTHED WITH CHRIST

*Zechariah 12:10-13:1; Galatians 3:26-29: Luke 9:18-24*

They come here all clothed in white, many times wearing long white garments, passed down through family generations, white baptismal garments that dress up baby boys and girls with no gender distinction except for their names. For as we just heard in St. Paul's letter to the Corinthians: For all of you who were baptized into Christ have clothed yourselves with Christ. There is neither Jew nor Greek; there is neither slave nor a free person; there is no male and female; for you are all one in Christ Jesus. Thus, they come to baptize, to put on Christ, to be clothed in Christ. Their families, too, parents, Godparents, relatives and friends, come dressed in their Sunday finest. Guests at a wedding show their respects by wearing their finest. Brides, of course, clothe themselves to appropriately display their new identity. It's not a fashion show neither should it be. It is a sign, a sign of recognition, the beginning of a new family, the family that they and their bridegrooms are about to bring into our world. They come dressed in their best. And finally, they come to church again, borne this time in caskets, caskets that are covered with a white garment, a pall, to proclaim that now, clothed in Christ, they are entering into the final new life, eternal life, life clothed in Christ as He brings them home to God our Father in heaven. Our culture has turned clothes into a fashion industry, an industry that uses clothes to show off, distinguish and make statements about who is "in" and who isn't. Equality is not scorned. The fact that we are clothed with the best, does that make us better than the rest? After all, only clothing, pieces of fabric artfully stitched to reveal the curves in the human body. The clothing that matters is our coverage of others with our caring, compassion, and love.

When it comes, however, to baptism and entrance into the Christian family, status is unimportant. One's rank in society doesn't matter when one processes to God's altar. The symbols of status, power and wealth, are meaningless when it comes to being clothed in Christ. Each one of us is loved by God with all of His love. In God's eyes, the nuns who serve the pope in his Vatican apartment are as important as the most exalted of the princely Cardinals. Outside in St. Peter's square, a street sweeper with his straw broom, stood before God with the same status and rank as the Vatican's Cardinal Secretary of St. Paul had to press that idea upon St. Peter and the early Apostles of Christ. St. Paul championed the Gentiles, the non-Jews, insisting that they, too, along with the first Disciples of Christ, were baptized in the Holy Spirit and that because of Christ's passion, death, and resurrection, they were the recipients of God's gifts and love as Christ's brother and sisters. They were in the family just as much as anyone else and were entitled to the same inheritance. In Christ, there is no distinction between Jew and Greek. Privilege based on status meant nothing in the eyes of the dying Christ who, on His cross, looked out upon us all and saw us with the loving eyes.

Self-aggrandizement is when someone stands at the foot of the Cross absurdly. When you look at the crucifix here in this church, you see the naked and powerless humanity that is Christ's, and you see it while standing with others in only one shared status, the status "of a being loved sinner." No matter how we clothe ourselves, with our own self-satisfied opinions about ourselves, we have, in reality, only one shared status—that of being a loved sinner. So in our private fancies, how do we dress ourselves up? With what jewels of power, privilege, and prestige do we bedeck ourselves? In what ways do we consider ourselves to be "better" than others? The remedy needed, the spiritual medicine we must swallow, is to die to self. To be sure, we have our differences. We are created equal but not the same. We have our unique identities. Being Christian doesn't cause our human differences to disappear and vanish. Baptism, however, and sharing in all of Christ's Sacraments does make our differences irrelevant and without meaning when it comes to living together in the life of God given to us in Jesus Christ.

Our Holy Communion's significance is that our union in Christ is found in simple, ordinary bread and in common – not vintage – wine. He was born among us in simplicity and powerlessness; He died among us without the trappings of prestige but in utter powerlessness, clothed only with His faith in His Father's love. If anyone wishes to come after me, declared Jesus, he must deny himself and take up his cross daily and follow me. For whoever wished to save his life will lose it, but whoever loses his life for my sake will save it. In today's gospel, Jesus speaks of His identity. If we identify ourselves by the clothes we wear, then we cheaply sell ourselves short. If we cover ourselves with outer garments without girding our souls with the strength of character, then we are weak. But if we are clothed in the power of the Christ who rose victorious over sin and death, then we have the power to face the world and the chaos that surrounds us. We have strength and stability in a volatile world where weak people think they can control others only through dominance and force. Those who are insecure use the trapping of power and dominance to try and control those around them. It is the coward who worships brute force. They sold their souls in order to acquire the marks of superiority and status. However, those who have put their souls in the hands of Christ, stand secure in the certainty of Christ's victory over all that is phoney, fraudulent, self-aggrandizing and evil in our world.

When you were baptised, clothed as you were in your baptismal white, you put on Christ. When you die, you will once again be covered with the white funeral pall as you make your journey into the next life. May you live all the days in between clothed in the love of Christ, all the while covering others with your caring compassion, your hope, your faith, and your love for all of God's children. Remember always that God loves each of us with all His love, and that is the only status symbol we can wear that matters.

# THEME 20
# FACING LIFE-CHANGING DECISIONS

*1 Kings 19: 16, 19-21; Galatians 5:1, 13-18; Luke 9:51-62*

We have all faced life-changing decisions, some forced, most made by our own free will. The death of a parent, suffering a divorce, the collapse of our business, floods, fire, a terrible accident, are all examples of forced changes on our journeys through life. Some decisions are our own: choosing a college, proposing marriage, having children, changing career, joining the church, entering the seminary or joining a religious community, are examples of choices we make of our own free will. The readings today present us with the reality of decisions, life-changing decisions. We are called by God to be decisive. Decisions bring consequences with them, and we have to live with the consequences of our decisions. Nobody can undo them for us. We want to make our own decisions, and we want to have the freedom to make them. This is God's will, His plan. God wants us to freely choose. He wants us to freely choose to have the freedom in which to make them. This is God's will, His plan. God wants us to freely choose to love him. That's why He made you and God, too, must live with the consequence of our decisions.

Take a look at that crucifix. It tells us the price God paid for living with the consequence of our decisions. In today's first reading, we find the need for security being challenged by the Prophet Elisha's decision to move into an unknown future. In the second reading, we are presented with a false sense of freedom, the freedom of license and anything goes, the true freedom of living for other's sake, particularly the other that is God. Finally, in the gospel, we find the challenge to move beyond the ties of family loyalty and affection into commitments outside the pale of our immediate families. The consequences involve our movement into decisions and responses consistent with making God central in our lives. We are called to make hard, tough decisions in life. It's not easy to leave one's childhood family to cling to a spouse in marriage and start a new family. We all know of husbands and wives who have been arrested emotionally. They remain fixated without further development. Not only that, but when we marry, we quickly learn that there are things we cannot do, our freedom to do whatever we want is gone. So, too, when we have children, we soon learn that our freedom to do many things is severely restricted.

Many folks never come to the full realisation that sacrifice is not merely a nice idea; it is a fact of life. Life forces us to make choices. The question is not whether we are willing to sacrifice. After all, life is filled with sacrifices. It's always a question of how much are we willing to sacrifice... and for what are we sacrificing? We cannot have things of value and at the same time, live footloose and carefree lives. All commitments involve sacrifice. So does growth. To be sure, some try to live free and unfettered lives, but what becomes of them? To say "yes" to anything special requires saying "no" to many other things. For instance, one cannot be "a little bit religious" for very long. You commit, or you end up saying that you don't go to Mass very often anymore because of this, that or the other things. To say "yes" to everything means we cannot say, "yes" to anything in particular. One cannot both commit and keep all of one's options open at the same time. "No man can serve two masters," Jesus said. Keeping all of one's options open is another way of avoiding full commitment. It's another form of denial. That's true in our close and intimate relationships with others. Moreover, that is true in our relationship with Jesus Christ. Commitment, love, marriage and friendship all impose things upon us. They require an uncluttered "yes." A "yes" that is life-changing. The same is true in the commitment to enter into religious life. However, while love demands sacrifice, paradoxically, it also lets us find freedom.

True lovers give each other the gift of freedom, freedom to be the very best persons living deep down inside of them. True lovers give each other the freedom to become the best they can be. A true lover gives us the joyous freedom to say "yes", "yes", to something greater and far more wonderful than just living for ourselves in our self-centred world. The greatest life-changing event in human history occurred when God, moved by His infinite love, bridged the unimaginable chasm between us and became man, that moment in cosmic history when God took on our humanity and became one of us. That moment was given to us when Blessed Virgin Mary responded to God's glorious messenger, the Archangel Gabriel, with her profound "yes, be it done unto me according to your word." In her "yes," God the Son forever opened the way for us to return home to our father in heaven. We need to recognise the truth that freedom is found indecisiveness. You and I all know of indecisive people; we find them among our friends and acquaintances. They can't make up their minds. They're paralysed and imprisoned in their lack of ability to make decisions. They get hung up on a hook called "the paralysis of analysis" and suffer from their indecision.

Finally, we need to give ourselves the freedom to focus on where we're going in our lives, along with the freedom not to be held captive by continually looking back at our past. Do you drive a car looking through the front windshield or do you drive looking through the rear window? If you drive your car by looking through the rear window, you will undoubtedly crash! If you are always living in your past, you are not going forward in your life. We grow by focusing on our future, not the past. Jesus said to His disciples: "No one who sets a hand to the plough and looks to what was left behind is fit for the kingdom of God." He was talking about fitness and abilities, as well as vision. We can be crippled and disabled if we're constantly dwelling on our past mistakes, if we're always feeling sorry for ourselves about what's happened in our past, or what we've given up. To be truly free, our eyes must be fixed on what's ahead, not what was in the past. When I was a little boy, my mother taught me "True happiness is something to do, someone to love, and something to hope for." We need to have things to hope for to know what to do and how to love. To find happiness in true freedom, we need to keep in mind for just what it is that God has given us -freedom. Hope and freedom are joined together. For me, my hope is always to walk in "the glorious freedom of the sons and daughters of God." I am never freer than when I am doing what God wants me to do. Nor do I find greater happiness.

I leave you today with a beautiful prayer, a prayer composed by a famous Trappist Monk, Fr. Thomas Merton. In moments of doubt and wonderment, it has given me greater comfort. Perhaps it will work for you, too. In his book, Thoughts in Solitude, he wrote:

Lord God, I have no idea where I am going. I do not see the road ahead of me. I cannot know for certain where it will end. Nor do I really know myself, and the fact that I think I am following your will does not mean that I am actually doing so. But I believe that the desire to please you does, in fact, please you. And I hope I have that desire in all that I am doing. I hope that I will never do anything apart from that desire. And I know that if I do this, you will lead me by the right road, though I may know nothing about it. Therefore will I trust you always though I may seem to be lost and in the shadow of death. I will not fear, for you are ever with me, and you will never lead me to face my perils alone.

# THEME 21
# SENT ON MISSION

*Isaiah 66:10-14c; Galatians 6:14-18; Luke 10:1-12, 17-20*

In the gospel account, we heard that Our Lord did not send only His apostles into the world to reveal God's kingdom. He sent others as well. The opening sentence was, "At that time the Lord appointed seventy-two others whom He sent ahead of Him in pairs to every town and place He intended to visit." There were times in our history when we thought that only Bishops, Priests, Deacons, and Nuns could authentically, and with proper authority, present the face of the Church to the world around us. The Second Vatican Council put an end to that sort of thinking. The Bishops of the world had a different vision. In their Decree on the Apostolate of the Laity they declared:

> "The laity derive the right and duty to the apostolate from their union with Christ the head; incorporated into Christ's Mystical Body through baptism and strengthened by the power of the Holy Spirit through Confirmation, they are assigned to the apostolate by the Lord himself." (Documents of Vatican II, Decree on the Apostolate of the Laity, Chapter 1, # 3)

This leads many to think of the emerging role of the laity as more of a matter of pragmatic necessity than a renewed vision and understanding of the nature of the Church. I want to stress now the point that the role of the laity is a matter of theology. It is not a matter of personnel management and deployment of resources. It is by your Baptism and by your Confirmation that Christ sends you into our world. This is not merely a matter of pragmatic necessity. Some may be asking what it is they are supposed to be doing. There is no one simple answer to such questioning. This is because there is so much to be done, in so very many areas, in so very different ways. Said the Bishops at the Second Vatican Council:

"There are innumerable opportunities open to the laity for the exercise of their apostolate of evangelisation and sanctification. The very testimony of their Christian life and good works done in a supernatural spirit have the power to draw men to belief and to God... since, in our times, new problems are arising and grave errors are circulating which tend  to undermine the foundations of religion, the moral order, and human society itself, this sacred synod earnestly exhorts laymen - each according to his gifts of intelligence and learning to be more diligent in doing what they can to explain, defend, and  properly apply Christian principles to the problems of our era in accordance with the mind of the church." (Documents of Vatican II, Decree on the Apostolate of the Laity, Chapter 2, #6)

If we ask the question: "What needs to be done?", we could well spend most of the rest of this day setting forth what Christians need to be doing in our time, along with the methods they need to employ in facing the challenges that are out there in the world around us. Let me suggest that we also need to pay some attention to how we should be conducting ourselves when we engage the world around us. First and foremost in my mind, is the Spirit of kindness that ought to mark the Christian in dealing with folks around us, in our neighbourhoods, places of work and in the volunteer association in which we find ourselves. I want to offer you some thoughts on kindness that appeared on a holy card printed over fifty years ago, by the Trappist Monks of Our Lady of Gethsemane, Abbey in Kentucky. Some of you will remember the name of its most famous monk, Thomas Merton. Back then, we heard the term "apostolate" frequently used. The term denotes the fact that we all share in the Apostle's duty and responsibility, to bring Christ's love and values to bear on the world in which we find ourselves.

KINDNESS: Of all the apostolate open to all of us, the most effective, the most far-reaching, the most consoling is kindness. Kindness is one of God's best gifts to the world. It drives gloom and darkness from souls. It puts hope into our hearts. It sweetens sorrow. It lessens pain. It discovers unsuspected beauties of human character. It calls forth a response from all that is best in souls. It purifies, glorifies, and ennobles all that it touches. It opens the floodgates of children's laughter. It gathers the tears of repentant love. It lightens the burdens of weariness. It stops the torrent of angry passion. It takes the sting from failure. It kindles bold ambition. It lifts the unfortunate. It leads back the wayward. It walks in the steps of Our Saviour. Let us become apostles of kindness; it is exalted; it is sublime; it is Christ-like.

In addition to the twelve apostles, Our Lord appointed a further seventy-two to go into the world and be about the task of revealing God's kingdom here on earth. No matter what we do, and no matter how we do it, let us always be conscious that nothing will be accomplished unless we do what we do in the Spirit of kindness.

# THEME 22
# MY NEIGHBOUR

*Deuteronomy 30:10-14; Colossians 1:15-20; Luke 10:25-37*

The Samaritans lived in the northern part of the original territories of the Jews. History records that the Persians conquered the Jews in war and carried them off in captivity to Babylon, leaving behind Samaritans, Jews who lived in the northern parts of Israel who collaborated with the Persians to stay in Samaria. Later, when the Jews returned home to Promised Land from their Babylonian captivity, they despised the Samaritans. The hatred lasted for centuries. This was the context Jesus faced when He travelled through the northern parts of Israel. Remember that Nazareth is in the north of Israel and so Jesus had frequent contact with Samaritans. And do you remember the account of Jesus meeting the Samaritan woman at the well when He requested a cup of water from her? There were other incidents, too, recorded in the bible, in which Jesus found Himself dealing with Samaritans.

We have now turned to the lawyer we heard about in today's gospel. He was uneasy with the teaching of Jesus. The lawyer's conscience was beginning to bother him, and so we find him today coming to Jesus to ask Him a tricky question. The lawyer was not so much trying to trap Jesus with foolish questions, but he was trying to weasel out of what his conscience was trying to tell him. Being very familiar with the Law of Moses, he knew what the Jewish Law required of Jews concerning aliens and foreigners. It required Jews to care for them. Our friend, the Jewish lawyer, had his defence mechanisms engaged just as much as we do. He knew respect and all that. He had memorized the words about loving God and loving our neighbours as we love ourselves. The problems the lawyer was giving to Jesus and the answer that Jesus gave him are our problems as well. Whom do we consider to be our neighbour? Today, tomorrow and the next day, spend some time asking yourself who your neighbours are. How much care would you give these people? The answer tells us how close we have let our faith come to us.

Our faith is not some nice, abstract theory, somewhat ideal that perhaps we might someday try to reach when we have more time. It's all very close to home; very near to each one of us. We don't have to cross any ocean to be religious or go off into some monastery or convent. We don't need special, holy people to be religious for us and send them up into the heights on our behalf.

God wants the love of ordinary people, not just saints. And God wants to work through just plain folks, like you and me. And so we are confronted by God – challenged by him. Living in the kingdom of God isn't some nice theory, some ideal that we can't reach in our everyday lives. Religion isn't something that just happens on Sunday so we can put it away for the rest of the week. It is something very close … too close for some of us… and we all have moments when we squirm just like the lawyer in today's gospel account. So, then, just who is our neighbour and how close to our hearts are they? Our neighbour is anybody we identify as "those people," people we call by ugly names, people we want to go away and get out of our lives. However, we need to remember that one day they might pick us up out of our ditches. They might care for us, spend their resources on us, people we identify as "those other people" may be Samaritans for us. Will we let them? Will we let them get close to us? The Word of God is a two-edged sword. It not only protects us and helps us; it also has moments when it confronts us. God's word at times comforts the afflicted, and at other times afflicts the comfortable. Who, then, do I care for? Who do I allow to care for me? Who do I go out of my way to really help, to bind up their wounds?

To whom do I give my time? Giving money is easy compared to giving our time and attention.

Recall that the Samaritan gave more than just money in caring for the stricken man lying in the ditch. The question "Who is my neighbour?" is important both for me as well as for you. It is also an important question for us to face as a people. The answer is a gauge of how close we have let religion come to us and how close to the kingdom that Jesus bids us to reveal in our everyday lives.

"For this command that I enjoin on you today is not too mysterious and remote for you. It is not in the sky that you should say, 'Who will go up in the sky to get it for us and tell us of it, that we may carry it out?' Nor is it across the sea, that you should say, 'Who will cross the sea to get it for us and tell us of it, that we may carry it out?' No, it is something very near to you, already in your mouths and in your hearts; you have only to carry it out."

# THEME 23
# INVITATION TO CLOSENESS

*Genesis 18:1-10; Colossians 1:24-28; Luke 10:38-42*

It is difficult for us to imagine the importance of hospitality in the culture in which Jesus lived 2000 years ago. Being invited to eat in one's home was of tremendous significance. It was not only a sign of honour; it also was a statement about closeness, a closeness that amounted to saying, "you're one of family." Inviting someone into your home today is very meaningful, but back then, it had the greatest significance attached to it. Martha was engaged in very important service. Because it was Jesus who was the guest, it was even a holy service. We need to see that Jesus was certainly not criticizing Martha or her efforts. As a matter of fact, we should note that Martha's love was more fervent than Mary's. Why? Because before Jesus had even arrived at their home, she was ready to serve Him. And remember that when Jesus came to raise their brother Lazarus from the dead, it was Martha who ran to Him and came out first to welcome Him.

Along with all of this, we need to see that virtue is not found in only one aspect; it is expressed in many ways. In the gospel account just read, we see St. Luke presenting Martha and Mary as two sisters who both want to please the Lord. And in fact, both did please him. The difference between them is that Martha's path, hospitality and caring for others, does not have consequences, consequences that pass beyond human life here on earth. Martha takes the way to service, the path of working for the Lord. Mary takes the path of relationship – being with the Lord.

One path involves doing; the other path involves being. Service of God is transitory; listening to and taking in the word of God is eternal. The former is not as necessary as the latter. Only one thing is necessary: union with the Lord. There's much to be done for the Lord, and there's much to be done for God's people. Caring for the hungry, the homeless, the neglected, the underprivileged, and the marginalized are very much a part of what we, as the followers of Christ, should be all about. After all, didn't Jesus set the example? To reach the soul, one must begin with the body. The one necessary thing, however, is union with God.

To return to St. Luke's gospel, recall an earlier event in Christ's life when He was invited to a Pharisee's house and was snubbed by His host. It was customary in those days to receive dinner guests by washing their feet, giving them a welcome kiss, and perfuming them with sweet-smelling oil. The Pharisee did not honour Jesus with any of these gestures. We can only surmise that the snub was deliberately an indirect statement of disrespect. During the meal, a woman "with a bad reputation in town", approached him. Washed His feet with tears, wiped His feet with her hair, covered them with her kisses and then anointed Him with precious oil. It shocked everyone, while at the same time revealing the hypocrisy of His host. Jesus said to His host:

> "Simon, do you see this woman? I came into your house, and you poured no water over my feet, but she has poured out her tears over my feet and wiped them away with her hair. You gave me no kiss, but she has been covering my feet with kisses ever since I came in. You did not anoint my head with oil, but she has anointed my feet with precious ointment."

Do we, with Martha, welcome Jesus into the house of our hearts? In today's gospel account, we need to see that Jesus is not asking us to choose between being a Martha or being a Mary. To be a full disciple of Jesus, we need to be both Martha and Mary. Furthermore, we need to see that to be a good Martha; we must first be a good Mary. It is absolutely necessary to see who we are, what we're doing with our lives, what our lives, filled as they are with so very many activities, are all about. What does God want me to be doing? What should I do to please God? Quiet times, time of reflection and times spent in "sitting at the feet of the Lord" while listening seems to be regarded these days as luxuries. In truth, they are not; they are absolute necessities. Some translations of the bible have Jesus saying to Martha, "Only one thing is necessary. Mary has chosen it, and it will not be taken away from her." Be honest with yourself now; ask yourself these questions: Is my life focused? Do I have singleness of purpose in my life? Am I leading a holistic life, a life directed clearly toward a purposeful goal? If you have trouble answering those questions, then you need to put some time to reflect on your life. You need to "sit at the feet of the Lord," so to speak, and recover 'the one thing that is necessary' and that is missing in your life. Otherwise, you will be worried and concerned about many things", doing all sorts of things, and feeling as if you're accomplishing little, if anything. Fear may perhaps be holding you back; fear that God may be angry with you. Try as best as you can to set that fear aside. Find a place of solitude and silence. Begin by simply telling God that you love Him and want to do what He wants you to do. Have the courage to do that based on the knowledge that God loves you and wants you to experience His love. We know that is true because that's the core message of Jesus Christ – and you can rely on it. Then in that silent solitude, let your conversation with God begin.

Years ago, back in 1954, one of the greatest Christian writers of our time, Romanio Guardinji, wrote a wonderful book simply titled "The Lord." In it, he said, "For the greatest things are accomplished in silence not in the clamour and display of superficial eventfulness, but in the deep clarity of inner vision; in the almost imperceptible start of decision, in quiet overcoming and hidden sacrifice." Light, God's light, is overcoming the darkness that surrounds our souls. Peace, God's peace, is overcoming the fear in our hearts. Love, God's love, can overcome our inner loneliness. His presence, power and love, patiently waits for us to come, sit at His feet, and let Him speak His words, His life-giving words of love deep within our hearts. Two Mary's have shown us the way --- Mary, the sister of Lazarus, and Mary, the mother of Jesus, our Mother Mary. Ask them to help you.

# THEME 24
# STEWARDS OF THE KINGDOM

*Ecclesiastes: 1:2; 2:21-23; Colossians 3: 1-5, 9-1; Luke 12:13-21*

"You can't take it with you". That familiar bit of homely wisdom isn't confined to Christian thinking; it's wisdom that's repeated in all religions. The ancient Jews had it in their scripture, as reported in today's first reading from the Hebrew book of Ecclesiastes; and yet few people take this wisdom seriously.

Jesus knew it needed repeating, and so He gives that thought to us again in today's gospel parable. He knows quite well what's deep within the human heart; He knows that despite the pieties we utter with our lips, our hearts are captivated by our lusting after flesh, money, power, fame, and prestige. Jesus knows our rapacious hearts that given a chance, we will seek to acquire more and more things. So in today's gospel, in yet another parable, we find Jesus telling us about ourselves. He begins by informing us: "There was a rich man whose land had produced a good harvest..." To begin with, we need to remember that the earth and its resources, the lakes, rivers, and seas that surround us, and the very air we breathe are all God's gifts to us. Our legal system may give us title to a piece of the earth, but we did not put our plot of land there in the first place. The land we live on is not ours --- it is God's, we hold it only as God's stewards. The crops that God gives us are, strictly speaking, not ours. No, they are given to us by God to care for and feed His people. Whatever human contribution we make to the enterprise of farming, it is to produce a yield for God's purpose, a purpose greater than our own. Whatever we produce in any work in which we engage is not just for our benefit but also for the benefit of others.

The Jewish law of forbidding work on Sabbath was to remind us not only that the Sabbath belongs to God, but also the land, and along with it whatever that land produces. God doesn't need our labour in order for His earth to be productive. But God has given us the dignity to co-labour, to collaborate, with Him in causing His creation to be fruitful and to grow bountifully. Losing touch with why we don't work on the Sabbath causes us to lose touch with our creator and His purposes in using our labour to benefit others – not just ourselves. The Sabbath is for contemplation and reflection. It reminds us that God has His time in the days of our lives. Time is also His gift to us. Sabbath time is our gift to God. "What shall I do?" the rich man asked. "I have no place to store my harvest." Those words reveal that the rich man is out of touch not only with the land, and why he is producing crops, but on a deeper level, he is out of touch with his reason for being – out of touch with his purpose in life. He is no longer aware of the meaning of his life. It never occurred to this rich man that he didn't need to build bigger barns. God already provided him with plenty. The barns that he needed to fill were the empty barns that are the stomach of those neighbours who had experienced drought or other crop-destroying tragedies. He needs to fill the empty stomachs of the poor and the hungry, all of those less fortunate than he.  The goods of the earth are given to us so that we might meet the needs of all, not just to satisfy the desire of our own hearts, not just to meet the demands of our own self-interests. Our self-concerns are revealed in the farmer's thoughts; thoughts filled with "I", "Myself", and "Me", with no thought of anyone else. Not only were his barns filled with grain, but his heart was also filled with self. Consequently, he was facing a crisis in what financial advisors phase "personal assets management."

Remember now, we're not speaking of some mythical man. In using parables to teach us, Jesus is giving us lessons about you and me. Jesus was never talking about abstract people; He's always frightening, concrete and specific. He is always speaking about what He sees in our heart, in your heart and in my heart. The rich in today's parable plunges ahead declaring,

> "This will I do: I will pull down my barns and will build greater barns; and into them will I gather all things that are grown to me, and my goods. And I will say to my soul: Soul, thou hast many goods laid up for many years take thy rest; eat, drink, make good cheer."

You and I know there are many people who live as if they really believed that the purpose of humans living is to "eat, drink and be merry, for soon we will die". There's no thought of others in that philosophy of life! No thought of why we are given land, why we are given talents and abilities, why God has given us what we have, or our purpose in living. The offices of psychiatrists are filled with sick people who are so filled up with nothing but themselves that they want to throw up. This farmer's interior monologue is not a dialogue with others or with God. No, not at all, it is self-talk – talking in isolation, with no one else listening, with no one there to hear the words. Then God said to him, "You fool! This very night your life shall be required of you. To whom will all this piled-up wealth of yours go?" Have we forgotten that what we do with our lives is our gift back to Him? Today's parable causes us to stand revealed as people who have allowed greed and lust for more and more things to fracture our relationship with God. The result of our broken relationship with God is that we live in broken relationships with each other.

Once again, questions are raised: "Why was I born? What is the purpose of my life? Why has God given me the things that I have? What am I supposed to do with them? What is my life all about?" These questions are open to our answers, so that we may have eternal life.

*May your love be upon us oh Lord, as we place all our hopes in you.*

# THEME 25
# LOOKING AT THE FUTURE

*Wisdom 18:6-9; Hebrews 11:1-2, 8-19; Luke 12:32-48*

Today's scripture readings put the question to us: "What does the future hold in store for us? What awaits us when we die? Is what's in front of us determined by what we did or didn't do in this life?" These are the big questions we face today and in all of the days of our lives.

Jesus talked with His disciples (and we are His disciples) about the future, telling them they were to face it not with fear but with hope and in a spirit of positive expectancy. He spoke to them in terms of making investments, investments in their future.

> "Sell what you have," He told them, and buy into the sort of retirement plan I am offering you, a never-failing treasure with my Father and with me in heaven. For, He said, "…wherever your treasure lies, there your heart will be."

But how can we live in a world and with a future that is not yet here? Only by living it in faith. St. Paul tells us "Faith is the confident assurance concerning what we hope for, and conviction about things we do not see." It is counter-cultural to live that way. The world tells us not to have faith in anything, to accept only what you can touch, taste, smell, measure and control. Suspend your beliefs and don't accept anything else. What we can control is the big issue as far as this secular world is concerned.

Faith is not something that belongs only to religion - it belongs to everyday living. Every day we take risks and act on probabilities. Hardly ever do we act on certainties. We take risks in depending upon the decisions of others, never knowing with certainty what the outcomes will be. Even scientists operate on theories, the Theory of Evolution being just one of them. Rarely does science give us proof.

What I am saying is that to live out life on this tiny little speck in the cosmos, this little blue dot in the Milky Way is to live in faith, to live in a wondrous adventure. To graduate from school, having chosen a career and to enter into it with all your heart and all your wit is one of life's great acts of faith. To get married and have children is a profound act of faith. To enter each day that God gives us with hope and expectancy that we will do good and make the world a little bit better for those around us is a tremendous act of faith. And to die, going forth from this life without knowing exactly where we are going except into the hands of God, is our ultimate act of faith. Throughout life, people live in the confident assurance that what they hope for will one day come to be. Each day we live with convictions about things that are not yet seen.

To be realistic, however, we must pay attention to the fact that a good deal of our recent history attacks our faith. We have been betrayed and betrayed often by people in our lives, people we trusted, all of which erode our basic need to believe in others. Life is unfair and bad things do happen to good people. And yes, many people are unreliable. But, for all that's wrong in life, in our world, and in others, we cannot afford to give up, stop believing, and lose faith. Jesus knew that back then, and He knows that right now, which is why Christ presents Himself to us in the Bread of Life. He comes to us, after all, in faith, placing Himself in Holy Communion inside us with the belief in His heart that we will accept Him in love, and with a firm purpose to live as He would have us live.

Yes, this world belongs to God. And yes, God has given us the dignity and the responsibility of working with Him to bring the world to completion, to wholeness, and to that unity in which He made it to exist and us in it, in the first place. For God, you see, has made a tremendous act of faith in you. God believes in you enough to give you the freedom to choose His love, the freedom to choose to accomplish His work, the freedom to do good. For God, you see, finds it necessary to love us and to live in His faith in us.

How comforting it is to know that others have faith in us. How tremendously comforting it is to know that God trusts us, has high hopes for us, and believes in us. It is a fantastic honour to realise that when we receive Holy Communion, God our Father believes in us enough to put His only begotten Son into our hands. Faith is forever an adventure in living, an adventure in which God Himself lives and wants to share with us.

# THEME 26
# THE MOTHER OF JESUS

*Rev. 11:19, 12:1-6, 10; 1 Corinthians 15:20-27; Luke 1:39-56*

Throughout Christian history, it is clear that those who seek Mary's love and care find something that only a Holy Mother can give. Of all the women who have ever lived, the mother of Jesus Christ is the most renowned, celebrated, venerated, and honoured. Millions of newborn babies have been given the name Mary, along with countless churches, shrines, and holy places. The world's greatest musicians and artists have lavished their considerable talents upon Mary with prodigality unknown for any other woman in human history. Eastern Orthodox and Roman Catholic Christians maintain that she remained ever a virgin, that she was born without sin, and that she shared in the redemptive suffering of her Son for our salvation. Several commentators in recent history, along with our two most recent popes, maintain that Mary played a significant role in the ending of Communism throughout Poland, Eastern Europe, and even within the former Soviet Union itself. In her appearance at Fatima, Portugal, in 1917, the Virgin predicted the rise of Soviet totalitarianism. Shortly thereafter, that happened when the Russian Revolution ushered it in. Furthermore, in the Fatima vision, she requested that the pope and the Catholic bishops consecrate Russia to her Immaculate Heart for the conversion of Russia.

Perhaps there remains a powerful connection between those events and the Virgin's appearances during this century, particularly at Fatima. You can be sure that almost everyone in the first century thought that all of the important and significant things were happening in Rome or

Athens, or other centres of political power and commerce in our world. But God was doing something far more important in the womb of an unknown little Jewish girl in the backwaters of the world's arena, just as He was at work in the womb of an old and apparently sterile woman, Elizabeth, Mary's cousin. The determining event in history was not taking place in Rome, with all of this world's might and power, but in Mary. Rome's power now lies in the dust of history, but the so-called insignificance of Mary still exerts tremendous influence on the lives of countless men and women today, 2,000 years later. Whenever we hear something about Mary, we should quickly consider what such a statement tells us concerning ourselves. Every statement, every dogma and doctrine about Mary is a statement about the Church, and consequently about us since we are the Church. First, there is the matter of our destiny, a destiny found in death and the purpose of human life.

Clearly, Mary's Assumption into heaven is a recapitulation of the Resurrection and Ascension of Jesus Christ. We face in these two events a statement by God that human life has a destiny beyond death. Humanity can look, says God, to Mary as an archetype; she sums up what God has in mind for you and me. The Assumption of the Blessed Virgin Mary into heaven is another way of stating the last part of the Nicene Creed: "We believe in the resurrection of the body and life everlasting. Amen." We can have genuine and reasonable hope in a future that cannot be outdone by death. Why? Because the first instalment of that hope has been given to our mortal human nature in Mary, a mere mortal like us. It may be said that Mary was something special, a very significant person, a magnificent and extraordinary human being created specially by God. We might think we can never hope to be like her. She is too "different", too "extraordinary" for us to identify with her. But the testimony of the New Testament will not allow us to sustain that interpretation for too long. Why? Because the evidence of Salvation History forces us to conclude that God tends to work with small and insignificant things, with little and forgotten persons. God reminds us that He makes very significant what is ordinarily insignificant. And that applies directly to you and me. Think of your relationships with the ones whom you love. Think of the events and moments and think of the people who have shaped your life. Most of them, I dare say, entered into your life in hidden insignificance, smallness and in silence.

Mary's Magnificat is a very consoling prayer for me because it gives me hope. A little Jewish peasant girl responds with a message of hope to an old and seemingly sterile woman in a backwater part of the world. Both are pregnant, strangely pregnant, by the power of God. The tiny fingers on the hands of their babies taking form in their wombs will shape and mould human history. That ought to fill us with a genuine sense of expectancy, even for us in today's world we should stop and ask ourselves: What tiny little hands are with us today. This explains why the Church has picked today's first reading from the Book of Revelation. It is a book of death and destruction – it is a book of hope and life. It tells us that at the end of this world, God's goodness and love will prevail over this world's violence, hatred and evil. Everything is headed towards His ultimate victory. Mary was born and lived in evil times. Women in the various cultures of her day were treated as men's property, useful for men's pleasure. They were without rights except in that so far as they belonged to men. The poor and lowly were oppressed. Mary's place in God's grand scheme of things can hardly be overstated. The centrality of her role in the history of our salvation is found next to her son and joined with God's saving plan for us all. Her Assumption is joined with her son's Ascension. Together their lives make a statement that we are all headed toward a certain point, that ultimate point when we are destined to be joined with God and the whole world is returned to God because of the saving work of God's only son who was joined with our humanity through His mother and our mother as well. "The woman" is a title assigned to the church as well as to Mary. Both have given us spiritual birth. God protects both, and the gates of hell have not, and will not, prevail against them. Both of them are our refuge and strength. Both of them invite us to see Christ Jesus as they see Him. Both of them hand Him over to us, inviting us to take Him to ourselves just as Mary did at the foot of His cross. Does our Church's dogma of the Assumption of the Blessed Virgin Mary into heaven have meaning for you and me? You bet your life it does! Through Mary and His Church, God has offered His saving love to us. He waits for us to respond. May Mary's Magnificat be your response - and mine as well.

*May your love be upon us oh Lord, as we place all our hopes in you.*

# THEME 27
# MANY ARE CALLED
# BUT FEW ARE CHOSEN

*Isaiah 66: 18-21; Hebrews 12:5-7, 11-13; Luke 13:22-30*

We just heard the prophet Isaiah proclaim:

"Thus says the LORD: I know their works and their thoughts, and I come to gather nations of every language; they shall come and see my glory. I will set a sign among them; from them I will send fugitives to the nations: to Tarshish, Put and Lud, Mosoch, Tubal and Javan, to the distant coastlands that have never heard of my fame, or seen my glory; and they shall proclaim my glory among the nations."

In St. Matthew's gospel, we heard Jesus put it simply: "*Many are called, few are chosen.*" Added to that, we have all heard the adage: "The road to hell is paved with good intentions." So today, I want to share some reflections on these teachings.

In living out my life, I have had more trouble with myself than with other people. My biggest problem is with my missed opportunities, my lost chances. When I look back over the landscape of where I've been, I see it littered with lost opportunities. So many times I've been "a day late and a dollar short," as the saying goes. In all the years I've spent studying in school and reflecting on life, the most challenging subject to master has been myself.

Today's gospel reading has in it one of the least remembered of the parables of Jesus. Many misinterpret it. And those that do remember it are likely not sure of what it means.

Is it a lesson in good manners, telling us to be on time? That would be a good thing for many folks to take to heart. Habitual tardiness is very inconsiderate, even arrogant. It is a means of control. I can control you by making you wait for me. My failure to show up on time sends a message saying, "My time is more important than your time." What I have to do is more important than what you are doing."

But Jesus' parable isn't about good manners. It's about the world we live in, a world of closing doors. The week you have just lived is a week that will never return to you. The decisions you have made are decisions that will always be a part of your history.

Where is yesterday? And what did you *not* do in it? The door is closed forever. If you ignored your spouse or neglected to hug your children, you'll never, ever, be able to go back and do what you failed to do. The time God gave you slipped away and will never return. With each tick on the clock that measures the passing of time, there is also the click of the lock on the door that's forever closed. Whenever you watch the sunset, a moment comes when there is a silent "click" and that day's door is now closed to you forever.

Our loving Father in Heaven litters the landscape of our lives with opportunities to love Him and to love Him as we find Him in the hearts and souls of others. He pours out opportunities to join with Him in making our world a better place, to bring His redeeming love to the world around us. Sympathy, compassion, forgiveness, caring, quality time and attention for others... God gives them all to us in an inexhaustible supply of these opportunities. God is forever replenishing them in the wells of our souls. It is what we do with them that matters. Decisions have consequences, even though we live in denial. We can only blame ourselves for our lost opportunities, not God.

We have opportunities to read, to study, and to develop our minds. We have opportunities to invest in the stock market and make lasting investments in the hearts and souls of others. We have opportunities to speak to others about our Faith, God, and how important it is for us to pay attention to God.

And then there is prayer. We are all called to it, but few of us make the cut. Think about all of the time we have wasted, time not spent in prayer and in contact with God.

God intends that every one of us will be saved – that we spend eternity with Him. But how can we spend eternity with Him in heaven if we never spent any time with Him here on earth? After all, heaven is entered here on earth, not in some sort of dream world that we will find when we are no longer capable of finding anything at all.

God has showered you and me with limitless gifts, gifts that are opportunities. The outcomes of our lives are not His responsibility; they are ours. Everyone is called to share life with God; few make the choice. And we must never forget that the choice is ours! God has made His choice. What remains is our response. God doesn't have to waste a lot of time casting people into hell; we do it for Him.

All around us, doors are slamming shut… and we hardly notice, our heads and our eyes so full of the glitter, clutter, and concerns of this world. But we also live in a world of open doors. A sunset follows every sunrise. The sun will rise tomorrow morning, and you will be gifted with another supply of opportunities by God. But while we are hopeful for tomorrow, we must remember that one day the sun will rise on the last day of our life. When it arrives, we'll never have another day in our lives. A final day is coming to you and me just as surely as I'm standing here before you.

Some will claim that Jesus' teaching that many are called but few are chosen is harsh. After all, wasn't Jesus always optimistic, kind and forgiving? Well, yes, He was. But He was also a realist. And it is a reality we need to see and not live in wishful thinking about all of the things we're going to do but never seem to quite get around to doing.

The road to hell is indeed paved with good intentions. The door is wide, but the path is narrow. Many are called, but few make the necessary choices.

Once again, it remains true even now that I've had the most trouble in life with myself... far more trouble than I've ever had with anyone else.

# THEME 28
# THE PRICE OF CHANGE

*Wisdom 9:13-28; Philemon 10:12-17; Luke 14:25-33*

We hear a lot of talks these days about "change." It has been one of the big words in the recent history of our Church, and we are hearing about it again with next year's publication of the 3rd edition of the Roman Missal with its changes. Change is one of the buzzwords in today's business world. Economists are talking about it a lot. As we all know, it is the word "change" that swept Barack Obama into the White House. Change is the in-thing which is talked about everywhere.

Jesus ushered in change; He brought with Him His own revolution. The gospel of today speaks of the radical change in attitude Jesus sets in front of us. What Jesus is really doing is giving His disciples a reality check: Are they willing to pay the price? Do they know the price of the change Jesus has in mind? Jesus well knew the costs involved in change. We find Him here in today's gospel episode on the way to Jerusalem. There He would be spit on, laughed at, humiliated, tortured, and put to death in the most excruciating of ways. It would change everything in our relationship with God.

Here we find Him wheeling around and confronting those who were following Him. He stopped them dead in their tracks and asked: "Do you REALLY know what you're doing? Are you sure you are willing to follow in my footsteps? Did you count the costs? And are you willing to pay them?" Jesus wanted change. And so did His followers. And so do us. We find ourselves in the same old patterns; we treat our wives, our husbands, and our children in the same old ways, all the while being upset with ourselves for doing it. We never seem to pray well. And when we pray, it's always in the teeth of misfortune, never when things are going well for us. And how often do we thank God? Praise God? Give to God's causes? It's always the same with God, our spouses, our children, and our families. When will we ever change?

Change, as I say, is costly. It hurts. It demands energy, time, and what's deep down inside us. There's a country not far from ours that once had a terrible dictator. He was sucking the blood out of the poor. The farmers of that country got upset. They organised themselves and shot the old dictator. They appointed a new leader. And after a few years that new leader turned into a dictator. He too ended up sucking the very blood out of the poor. The farmers got upset. They organised themselves and, well, you know the story. It's the same old repeated story that's found in human history, found in our own families, and that's found in our own personal lives. Will you pay the cost for real change? Don't try to build a new city or a new world unless you have counted the cost. Don't try to raise an army and fight a revolution unless you are willing to pay the price, a terrible price. Unless you do, nothing will be won. Two chapters ahead of today's gospel account, St. Luke report Jesus declaring: "The law and the prophets lasted until John, but from then on the kingdom of God is proclaimed, and everyone who enters does so with violence." (Luke 16:16) He is saying that one has to take harsh measures in changing our old comfortable self with its old comfortable and oh so familiar ways. Comfort and change cannot both exist in the same person or the same people at the same time. Do not say that you are going to change anything, your government, your political loyalties, your amount of body fat, your drinking patterns, your smoking habits, your ways of relating to those around you, *or your spiritual life*, without giving up all that offers you comfort and security. Change costs.

Do not try to change anything at all, and most especially do not try to change your relationship with yourself, with others, or with God, unless you are willing to pay the real costs. If you're not willing, then you're not willing to change anything at all. And nothing will happen; nothing will be won. Being a real disciple of Christ is a way of life that is demanding. It can cost you the loss of friendships. Others will ridicule you, laugh at you, and scorn you for our values. Jesus came to establish one church, not many churches. As they come to us in the Bible, His teachings are meant to be understood and applied equally to all, not merely accepted and interpreted individually. In our Catholic Church, we worship as a 2,000 year-old community in a shared communion, not simply as an aggregate of individuals, each with their own private relationship with Jesus Christ. We are a family of faith, united, whole, and under one roof led by the successors of St. Peter and the college of Apostles. We have schools, hospitals, and social service agencies that cost but we give generously to support them because Jesus taught, healed and cared for the poor, the marginalized, the sick, and the outcasts among whom He lived. What I am saying is that discipleship costs, it costs us in terms of comfort, popularity, time, energy, and treasure. Being a disciple of Christ is, when you stop and think about it, a radical calling. It goes to the root of who we are, how we understand ourselves, and how we appear in the eyes of others. Jesus ushered in change, a radical change in how we relate to ourselves, others, and God. There's nothing automatic about our salvation; it makes demands on what we do, what we value, how we see ourselves, and how we relate to others. The demands are not easy, but the rewards are out of this world.

# THEME 29
# UNCONDITIONAL LOVE

*Exodus 32:7-11, 13-14; 1Timothy 1:12-17; Luke 15:1-32*

We just heard one of the most famous of all the parables employed by Jesus in His teaching, the parable of the prodigal son. It opens with:

"A man had two sons, and the younger son said to his father,' Father give me the share of your estate that should come to me.' So the father divided the property between them. After a few days, the younger son collected all his belongings and set off to a distant country…"

We rarely, if ever, pay closer attention to that part of the parable, namely the son's decision to leave his father, probably because we want to focus on the father's forgiving love or the elder son's icy coldness. But today, let's consider the son's departure and what it tells us.

First of all, the younger son asks for his share of the inheritance that will come to him upon his father's death. By demanding his inheritance right away, he's telling his father that as far as he is concerned, his father is dead. The only thing the son is looking for is for his father to die. However, that will not happen right away, he is demanding his inheritance now. This is self-centredness at its height. Nevertheless, we've heard of young men and young women who have walked out on their parents, left their homes and have in the meanness of spirit, put great distances between themselves and their parents and their childhood homes. They may as well consider their parents to be dead as far as they are concerned. Fortunately, we don't hear that story too often, but when we do it causes us to feel sad, very sad indeed.

We ought to consider what happens when people cut themselves off from their parents, families, and homes. That tearing asunder may at first give the younger person a sense of freedom, but it's a freedom that comes at a terrible price. The price paid is a loss of grounding, a profound loneliness in this world, a world that is often hostile. Without the grounding of a home, we can find ourselves to be in a sort of foreign land, surrounded by foreign people in the sense that we do not know them or understand them. Thereby we become vulnerable to being used. Spiritually and emotionally, and perhaps financially as well, we can become emptied and bankrupt. That's one of the points being made in Jesus' parable. The younger son ended up penniless, his self-respect in tatters while living among pigs, starving not only for food but more importantly, for love.

Life is all about relationships. We are made in the image and likeness of God; the God whose very nature is to be Persons totally in love and existing for each other in infinitely deep relationships. We came from that God, and our destiny is to find ourselves in living out that reality. Leaving home, separating ourselves from our parents and families is lethal; it is death-dealing, a form of slow suicide.

Now, all that I have put in front of you so far is situations in which people of their own choice cut themselves off from their fathers and their mothers and families. Consider now the terrible truth that most men who populate our nation's prison systems are fatherless men. From the time they were babies until they grew into their teen years, they had no fathers, either physically or emotionally. The terrible cost of being fatherless is found in many young men (not all, thank God) who have turned to gangs to find their self-worth. In joining a gang, they have found a sense of identity, of who they are. It's always a twisted image; it always results in hate-filled hearts and souls; it causes them to become anti-social and commit terrible violent crimes. Being fatherless, homeless, and alone in our hostile world exacts a dreadful toll on the individual souls involved and a terrible cost to our society.

As Catholic Christians, we place a heavy emphasis on God's plan for us to be born and raised in what today's media calls the "Traditional Family," as if it is simply one option among many living arrangements. Of course, we recognize, that many wives and children lose their husbands and fathers because of death, disease, or other causes and go on to successfully raise their children and keep their families intact. I am in no way dismissing the roles of mothers and other women in raising children. But fathers and adult male figures are important along with the roles of women, and they need to be recognised. May God bless each one of them.

Today's gospel account with its parable involves situations in which a son or a daughter leaves home and family due to their own choice. Such a choice brings with it great peril, peril to one's soul and peril to one's relational life with all others. As Catholics, may we do all in our power to build up all families and likewise do all that we can to cherish, care for, and support youngsters who have lost either their fathers or their mothers.

The family is the cradle of our culture and life, and of peace and harmony in the world that surrounds us. Certain voices in our world sneer at that, but the family, after all is said and done, is the building block of our society.

Finally, I ask you to consider that the key figure in today's gospel account is not the prodigal son; it is his father. May we have a father's love for all children, a love that comes from the love of our Father in heaven.

# THEME 30
# THE BEAUTY OF RICHES

*Amos 6:1a, 4-7; 1 Timothy 6:11-16; Luke 16:19-31*

Three Sundays ago, we heard Jesus teaching us that we must not let our possessions possess us, that we must set them aside in favour of putting God first above all else. Two Sundays ago, we were presented with the parable of the prodigal son. He demanded his share of his father's estate immediately and thereupon went out and spent it all ending up in poverty with the pigs. Last Sunday we looked into the parable of the crafty steward who cooked his master's books to win favour with his master's debtors. Today we have before us the story of the rich man sitting at his table eating his sumptuous feast while Lazarus, a destitute man, sat at his front door covered with sores while dogs licked them.

Jesus used all of these parables to teach us that the love of money and the love of possessions, that is to say, any form of greed, corrupt our souls and blinds us to the vision of what God wants us to be. The poor man at the rich man's front door was hideously burdened and in obvious need, a need the rich man could not even see or acknowledge. He was simply unnoticed. Interestingly enough, the poor man's name was Lazarus, the same name as Martha and Mary's brother whom Jesus, just before His entrance into Jerusalem to suffer and die, raised from the dead. The poor man in today's parable may as well have been dead. As the parable unfolds, both the rich man and the poor man have died. In his own torment, the rich man addresses Abraham as "Father," in effect claiming he is Abraham's son. Was he hoping to claim an inheritance from his Father Abraham just as the prodigal son claimed and received his inheritance from his own loving father? Maybe those who are rich are used to giving instructions to be carried out by others, and so we find the wealthy man today instructing Abraham to send Lazarus to him with some cool water to ease his torment. Notice that the roles are reversed. The rich man, while dining sumptuously ignores poor, sore-covered Lazarus who was sitting on his doorstep but he wants Lazarus now living in paradise to come to him and comfort him.

How does the saying go? "What goes around comes around?"

Abraham does not necessarily refuse the request. He notes the reality of the great chasm of destiny, a destiny in the next world determined by the choices we make in this world. This should cause us to sit up and take notice. The lesson to be learned is that we shape our destinies by the choices we make as we move through life. To put it more starkly, God doesn't have to damn us because we do that for Him by our own free-will choices. Those who clamour for "freedom of choice" perhaps do not realise what they really want. God, it seems, really respects the choices we make; He won't cancel them out. We determine our destinies. To go further in today's parable, we need to recognise that the rich don't know how to take "no" for an answer. So the rich man makes another request of Abraham, asking him to send Lazarus to his house where his five brothers live and warn them of what they face. Abraham denies his request while noting that they already have access to God's prophets and everything they need to know about what God expects of us. Ignoring God now brings its consequences later.

Note, too, that the rich man's vision of who his brothers are is a narrow vision, confined only to his blood brothers. So we should ask ourselves: Who are my brothers and sisters? The answer God expects us to give is this: The children of Abraham are my brothers and sisters. All of God our Father's children are my brothers and sisters. We are all His family. Apply that now to the world around us as we find it today and ask yourself: How should I be treating all of God's children? All of the members of our family? In that context, what attitudes do I have? Whom have I let go unnoticed? What sort of decisions have I made when recognising others around me who are in dire straits, who are being picked on, bullied, or thrown out?

There is, in fact, a chasm between our human ways and God's ways. Jesus, the bridge-builder, has come to us from across that chasm, providing us with a way, with truth, and a way of living that will allow us to cross that chasm. How can we claim that God hasn't given us a choice? While we may not be financially prosperous, we have opportunities that engage our attention, living as we do amid the Internet, TV programs, text messaging, Twittering, and sports -- a sumptuous table of things to which we can help ourselves. We are very rich in things to do, places to go, and things to which we can give our time and attention. In the midst of these riches, we should ask ourselves what we give to God? How much time and attention we give to notice Him, to notice what He wants us to do?

The poor, the oppressed, and the outcast are with us, children of Abraham, our father in faith, children of God our Father. They are also our brothers and sisters and belong to us as God's own family. How we relate to them and how we treat them is the bridge that overcomes the gap. The chasm between our world and God's world is not unbridgeable; it can be crossed. It only becomes a fixed chasm when we, at the end of our lives, add up the sum total of all our decisions. We need to notice all of those who are at the front door of our consciousness. To ignore them is to put our souls in peril.

# THEME 31
# HIS GRACE IS ENOUGH FOR YOU

*Sirach 35:12-14, 16-18; 2 Timothy 4:6-8; Luke 18:9-14*

The gospel account we just heard is famous. It tells the well-known story of the sinner who sat in the back of the Temple seeking mercy while the Pharisee sat up in front, reminding God about what a great person he was. His "holier than thou" argument is often used today by those who don't go to church to criticize those of us who do. But the story goes much deeper than the comparisons we make between others and ourselves. The parable deals with our perception of who we are in the eyes of God.

This parable reaches to the core of our relationship with God. The basis of that relationship is that God chooses us. He establishes the relationship. We have not won this relationship with our prayers or our actions. No, it's the other way around. It is God who chooses us. This truth has not been easy for many to accept. It has taken an endless struggle on God's part. Taking on our humanity and becoming one of us in His Incarnate Son, His effort has been directed toward all of us. The extent of His love for us is proven through His sacrificial love for all of us on the Cross. The struggle also includes our Lord's continual effort to win each one of us into His love.

So often, however, you and I have run from Him. Perhaps we fear that His love for us is too demanding. Maybe we're afraid that getting close to God means we have to give up all of the fun things in life. Maybe we're afraid that He will ask us to give up things that we feel we just can't give up. Or, maybe it's a control issue. Do I control my life, or does God control my life? In our relationship with God, each one of us has been gifted with God's love, a love flowing to us through our family of faith, the Church. At the same time, His love is unique since we are individuals. God loves us all, and at the same time, He loves each one of us individually. While I am a member of His Church, I nevertheless stand before God's eyes all by myself. Each one of you has his or her own unique and individual relationship with God. But we must always remember that in the eyes of God, no one person is better or worse than another person. Take, for example, your relationship with your children. Each one of your kids is not better or worse than the others. To be sure, they are different. However, all of your children receive your love. And so it is with God. We are all God's children. Yet God sees us and loves us individually. He doesn't judge us as better or worse than another person. He does judge, however, our actions.

One way that we tend to avoid accepting responsibility for our actions is to contrast ourselves with those whose deeds appear to be worse than ours. The Pharisee's thought: "Look at that guy; he is a sinner and a tax collector. "At least I'm better than him" is a judgment that is no different from thinking to myself: "Look at that guy, he's a drug addict. At least I'm better than him." Comparisons are usually both sad and bad. But when it comes to comparing ourselves with others, well, we either come off being arrogant or else we end up with a huge inferiority complex. Teenagers struggle with comparing themselves with other teens – which, I suspect, accounts for their frequent and unpredictable mood changes. And, if the truth were told, all of us are making comparisons every day. Do we find Jesus making comparisons? No, we don't! What we do find is Jesus associating Himself and giving His best gifts of love to those whom everyone else has shunned, those whom everyone else has considered being inferior.

No matter who you are or where you find yourself, give thanks to God for your own good, but at the same time realise that God sees into the heart and soul of each of His children. He looks into our hearts, and

He sees all those hidden forces that have pushed us in one direction or another. God sees the times He has directly intervened in our lives, offering us His presence. Moreover, He sees the times that we have accepted His presence and the times that we have told Him, "Not now… not in this matter… maybe later. You are asking too much." He judges us as individuals. He is not concerned with who is better than whom. He is only concerned with how well each of us has individually responded to His love. Catholicism is often accused of putting people on guilt trips. That is not true. Catholicism puts people on reality trips. Catholicism dares to speak about unpopular topics like sin. Catholicism dares to invite people to consider their own participation in sin, to admit the truth, and seek forgiveness. Is that a guilt trip? Or is it a real trip? I firmly believe that Catholicism fosters a realistic approach to living. It recognizes that our salvation is a process in which we are engaged. We are not saved, yet we are being saved. It recognises that we are human beings and that we can give in to the temptation to sin. It tells us that the Lord was one of us. He experienced temptation, and He understands our need for mercy. He gives us the sacrament of mercy, penance, and reconciliation because He wants His mercy directing our lives, not our guilt.

Catholicism is not so much concerned with guilt as it is concerned with mercy. So many times, I have had people tell me how much they need the loving mercy of God. They are realists. We all need the mercy of God. As we come to a deeper understanding of all that God has done for us, we also come to a deeper understanding of how much we need His mercy and forgiveness. The greatest saints are people who saw themselves as great sinners because they had a profound realisation of the extent of God's love for them, and the many times they had not returned His love.

The pilgrim's prayer is a prayer that we all have to say within our hearts throughout our days --- "Lord Jesus Christ, Son of the living God, have mercy on me, a sinner."

# THEME 32
# YOU ARE THE CHANGE THAT YOU SEEK

*Wisdom 11:22-12-2; 2 Thessalonians 1:11-2:2; Luke 19:1-10*

In last week's gospel, Jesus presented us with the parable of the Pharisee and the tax collector in the Temple. Do you remember them? Today's event is no parable. It is an account of an event in Jesus' life. Tax collectors were hated, and Jews hated Jewish tax collectors most of all. They were puppets of the Romans and considered traitors. They were given a quota of taxes to collect and had the power of Roman soldiers to assist them in collecting taxes. All the Romans expected were their quotas. The tax collectors could collect more than was owed and could unleash the Roman soldiers upon Jews who didn't pay the amounts set by the tax collector. Not only were these tax collectors, traitors to the Jewish people, but they were also traitors to the Jewish religion.

In today's gospel account, Zacchaeus was the chief tax collector in Jericho. This very wealthy city was famous and envied by all for its economic privilege and very well-off citizens. All of which meant that Zacchaeus was indeed a very wealthy and powerful man. Now you see the shock that electrified the Jews when Jesus called out to him and said, "Zacchaeus, come down. Hurry, because I am coming to stay at your house." Not only was Jesus going to dine at Zacchaeus' table, but he was also going to stay in his house! It was unthinkable that a rabbi would do such a thing yet it was true. Not only was Zacchaeus wealthy at the expense of others, but he was also friendless. No one would associate with him. No one, that is, until Jesus came down the road. Suddenly he had the greatest friend anyone could ever have. Two things need to be seen. One was that the Jews had wholly misjudged Zacchaeus. The second was that as a result of his encounter with Jesus, Zacchaeus was completely changed. Not only would he make good on any fraud or extortion he had committed, but he would also see to it that his victims were more than repaid. He went beyond simple restitution and in effect put those whom he had oppressed into standards of living they had never known before.

Well, so what? What's the point? The first point is to ask ourselves just who it is that we condemn and harshly judge? By what standards do we judge them and condemn them? And how do we think we know how God judges them? Do we think we know what's in their hearts, and do we know their intentions better than God does? More importantly, when we judge ourselves, why do we apply such rigid and perfectionist standards to ourselves? Perhaps we have such an idealistic image of ourselves that we set ourselves up with impossible standards to meet and frustrate ourselves. Two evils flow from that. One is despair which allows us to excuse ourselves from prayer, going to church, or keep away from any sense of closeness to God. Despair is a terrible evil. It leads to a complete giving up on ourselves. It leads to self-punishing behaviour that certainly doesn't please God and forces others to live with a miserable person. They don't deserve that, God doesn't, and neither do you. The other effect is to rationalize one's self by coming to Mass. It provides a convenient excuse for not participating in the Sacraments and in the life of the Church. "I'm such a terrible sinner," we say, "that even God couldn't forgive me." Therefore I don't need to go to church anymore.

Pride and egoism lurk behind such a sentiment. Why do we think our miserable little sins can restrain Almighty God and keep Him from giving us His loving mercy and tender forgiveness? What arrogance it is to declare that you are the worst of all sinners, so bad that God Himself stands powerless in front of you! As the Son of God ignored the judgments and opinions of the local populace concerning Zacchaeus, so also God ignores our judgments and opinions about others and particularly about ourselves.

Finally, observe that Zacchaeus is much like the prodigal son who lived among the pigs and came home to find his father to be even more prodigal in forgiveness. In contrast, the elder son stood aloof in icy condemnation and furious judgment. The story of the prodigal son and the story of Zacchaeus are stories of God's unbounded prodigality in sharing His forgiveness and His all-powerful, life-changing love. Do you find yourself to be up a tree and distantly observing Christ as He walks by? If so, be prepared to hear Him call out to you and tell you that He wants to come to your house today and stay with you. Hopefully, your response will be as holy as Zacchaeus' response. For it is God who justifies us; we can never succeed in our own self-justifications. It is God who sanctifies us; we can never succeed in making ourselves holy. It is God who saves us; we are total failures when it comes to saving ourselves. If you want to have your life changed, give up the self-delusion that you can change your life on your own. Only God can change your life. And He can do it just as easily as He changed the life of Zacchaeus, that hated and the traitorous Jewish tax collector who found holiness simply by responding to God's invitation.

# THEME 33
# MARRIAGE AND ETERNAL LIFE

*2Maccabees 7:1-2, 9-14; 2Thessalonians 2:16-3:5; Luke 20:27,34-38.*

Two weekends ago, we heard about a powerful group called the Pharisees, and last weekend we heard about Zacchaeus, the tax collector representing oppressive and controlling government officials. Today we hear about another powerful group called the Sadducees. The Sadducees' chief concern was about money, power and control, not about religion as such. Politics and profit were their big concern. Life after death didn't matter much to them because they didn't believe in the immortality of the soul and the soul's resurrection into everlasting life. There are lots of Sadducees around today. They are the pushers of pills, pot and all that's marketed under the Pleasure Principle. They set the standards of what's "cool" and "uncool" on MTV labels. They want to be in control of fashions and fads, setting the pace, the standard, the norm of what's "in" and what's not. I suspect they don't have what it takes to make themselves important among their peers. But maybe they have other motives, like a profit motive.

In today's gospel account, we find the Sadducees confronting Jesus with their ridiculous story of an unfortunate woman who had married and then lost seven husbands. They did not start with the real issue, namely belief in life after death and the consequences of our daily decisions in determining how we would live in that life after death. No. Instead, they started with the question of whom the woman would belong to in the next life. They were, no doubt, laughing before they finished with their crazy question. What a fool Jesus would look like, they thought, answering their clever little question! Jesus wasn't laughing. He ignored their stupid question and, instead, asked them a question about their national heroes, namely Abraham, Isaac, Jacob and Moses. Did they think that God created these giants only to blot them out into nothingness upon their death? Do you think that all the beautiful people you know are strong, loving and wise? Are they compassionate and kind, and care passionately for life and love? Do you think that when they die they simply go poof, and disappear into clouds of nothingness? The secular atheists of our day do.

There are a lot of silly questions that the world puts to us. Many questions divert our attention and take us away from the most fundamental and, therefore, the most important question of all. And that question is: Why do you exist? Why were you brought into being? What is the meaning of your life? We have an answer; they do not. It is absurd to imagine that all of the love, all of the beauty, all of the compassion, care, concern, goodness, and hunger for justice and decency that you find in yourself and admire so much in others is there only to be blown away at death. And it is absurd to hold to the position that all of the goodness, love, and pursuit of justice that we have in our hearts and souls and have shared with others is only good for the few short years we live here on earth and that it simply disappears into nothingness at death. That truly is absurd.

When we deceive ourselves about Jesus, we deceive ourselves. When we play games with God, we play games with ourselves. Furthermore, we play games with those around us. Ultimately we play games with the life we are destined to live after death, for there is no such thing as a small decision in life. All decisions have consequences. Our life after death, who we are, and what sort of character we shall take with us into the next life is shaped and formed by the questions we answer in the way we live our lives right now, tomorrow, throughout the coming week, and the remaining days of our lives. There's no such thing as a sinful life that doesn't matter. Nor is there an act of love that's of little or no consequence. Wasn't that one of the main points of Jesus' teaching?  I believe that the reason why you were born, the reason why you are living here among us today, and the reason why you will die is *to love God face to face*. And I also believe that the face of God is found in those around us who are hungry for love, goodness and decency. I believe the face of God is seen in those who are imprisoned in addictions and compulsive behaviour patterns, in those who are lonely and have no one to love them, in those who are sick with self-hate and with self-loathing. And I believe, too, passionately believe, that God has fallen in love with ordinary humanity, has fallen in love with you and me, not just saints and that we celebrate here on the altar the Wedding Feast of the Lamb so that God's Body and Blood can mingle with and become yours. And I firmly believe that we only have a glimpse here on earth of what love and marriage will be in the everlasting life that awaits us.

To my way of thinking, it is silly to think otherwise --- to believe that a beautifully lived life disappears into nothingness when we die. The Sadducees had nothing of substance to offer at the time of Christ. And the Sadducees of today likewise have nothing of lasting value to provide us with. But God, being a God of the living and not of the dead, has everything to offer you and me. May we now and all of the days of our lives respond fully to His loving offer of Himself to us here on our altar in the Wedding Feast of the Lamb when with His Body and with His Blood He joins Himself to us in a marriage that will last forever.

# THEME 34
# LOYALTIES

*2 Samuel 5: 1-3; Colossians 1: 12-20; Luke 23:35 – 43*

Today's Mass challenges us with the question: "Who or what exercises power over our lives?" We all know, don't we, that it should be Christ our Lord -- He should be the One in whose dominion we should live. Here on earth even though we are citizens of the City of Man, we should first be citizens of the City of God. Other things can cause divided loyalties in our lives, causing spiritual conflicts that are quite emotional within us. We can, and often do, fall down and worship strange gods. In our examination of our moral consciences, we need to pay attention to the First Commandment, the one that states: "I am the Lord thy God – thou shalt not have strange gods before me." Take, for instance, the ancient god known as Mammon. Mammon is a term used in Biblical literature to describe greed, avarice, and unjust worldly gain. A Mammon worshipper is any person who gives the first place in his or her life to the acquisition of more and more money and power – money beyond what is necessary to care for his family and provide for his children. There are people whose main objective in life is to acquire more and more wealth. They are driven by it; they are controlled by it; they are held captive by it. They want more and more money, as much money as possible to exercise power and control over others, sometimes even members of their own families. They threaten to cut their children out of their Wills; they control their children by telling them that they are paying the bills and that unless their kids do exactly as they are told, they can get out of the house. Mammon worshippers use the money to control everyone except themselves.

Consumerism is another form of Mammon worship. Let's be honest with ourselves – how often are we controlled and driven by those who manipulate our desire to purchase the newest and latest gadgets, fashionable clothes, and the baubles that are dangled in front of our hungry eyes? Advertisers are the priests in the temples of that false god. They want to control the money we spend and capture us as their customers. Don't get me wrong; there's nothing wrong with money itself. It is a useful tool we can use in our lives to provide for others and give our families decent lives. But there is something disordered when we are held under its dominion and control or when we use the money to manipulate and control others. That's something to think about on this Christ the King Sunday. Moloch is the ancient name of the God who seeks human sacrifice. It was to him that ancient pagans sacrificed human lives, even the lives of their own children. It is to Moloch that some people even today seek to build themselves up and promote their interests by destroying those around them. Some put others down and even destroy the careers of others to advance up the ladder of corporate power structures. Lust isn't a vice that is confined to sexual exploitation; lust for power is likewise a false god that can exert power and control over us as well. Modern-day Moloch worshippers determine to do whatever is necessary at all costs, even at the cost of human sacrifice, in order to advance themselves. That, too, is something to think about on this Christ the King Sunday.

Perhaps there are other false gods to which we give sinful allegiances. If there are, they will eventually bring us pain, inner conflict, and a hellish life to those around us, and ultimately the eternal hell of our own loneliness. We have to realise that after we die, our false gods won't be there for us. Also, we need to see that after we die, we will be the persons we have shaped and formed for ourselves. When we face God's judgment, we will see ourselves in the eyes of God, the God of the living and of the dead, in the eyes of the God of the way we should have lived. Christ came among us to show us that Mammon, Venus, Moloch and our other false Gods only bring us pain, inner conflict, and a hellish life both for ourselves and for those who must live with us. Their power is the power of manipulation and control. They may bring us temporary pleasure and a false sense of well-being, but they are utterly incapable of giving us lasting happiness and genuine peace. Christ is among us to show us that if we live in His kingdom, with Him as the Lord of our lives, we can find the only form of lasting and genuine happiness, namely the charitable mission of making other people happy. For happiness is not something that we can buy, win, or achieve; it is a gift given to us. It comes only as a gift that is a by-product, a result of living the way Jesus lives. And what are the principles that should guide us in that way of life, the life of Jesus? My pleasure is in your pleasure; my happiness is in your happiness; my treasure is the money I spent to build you up; my rewards are your rewards; my life is for you. For what is mine is ours together. All of the powers of Christ were expended for others so that in His kingdom all might have freedom, dignity, and happiness both in this life and in the next. All that is Christ's He gave to us to be shared.

Human pride keeps many away from God, holding them in bondage and causing them to bow down to false gods that replace the Living God. Human pride understands power as that which is to be acquired, kept, hoarded, and possessed to be used solely for one's own advantage. It was a shocking scandal to human pride to witness Christ die, revealing that God thinks in just the opposite way. Thus, Jesus had to be done away with; He had to be rejected, shoved aside, crucified and buried. Many are still about that task, even in our day. A God who empties Himself? A God who sacrifices Himself – limits Himself and shares His very substance with others? No! Never! We want a different king and god, they shout. We have no king but Caesar, no God but Mammon, no God but Moloch, no Goddess but Venus!

Just what kind of a God is God, and what does He expect of us? How we answer those questions will shape what we desire in life, what we want to control us, and what we know will give us genuine happiness, true love, and lasting peace. That's the challenge of this Sunday on which we honour Christ our King.

# THEME 35
# GIVE ATTENTION TO GOD

*Isaiah 2:1-5; Romans 13:11-14; Matthew 24:37-44*

Through our numerous daily affairs, God seems distant for so many of us. Let's face it; we're just too busy for God. More often than not, we are giving our attention to our concerns more than we are about giving our attention to God. That sounds harsh, doesn't it? But isn't it true?

You and I are here at Mass to give our attention to God now and in doing that we hear today the voice of one of God's ancient prophets, the prophet Isaiah. In the first reading, we heard him calling us to climb to the top of the mountain and look for the Lord's Advent, and the Lord's coming into our lives. He's calling us to rise above the mountains of our daily worries, problems, and anxieties to take a look over the whole of our lives and examine our lives with all of their peaks and valleys. As Christians, we do that in the vision of Christ, the Light of the World, God's gift to us.

The problem you and I face comes not from the fact that we are unconcerned or apathetic or lazy. We have the opposite problem. We're far too concerned about so many things, things that divert us from being aware of God's presence. We are so caught up in all of the events of our days that we ignore our souls, our inner spirits, and our inner selves. In biblical language, this spiritual blindness is spoken of as darkness. Our darkness is not one of sleep; our darkness is that we are blinded by the flashing lightning bolts of the dark storms that come upon us.

When through accident, through chance, or in some other unexpected event, we become aware of God's activity in our lives, we suddenly pay attention -- we wake up. And in that moment of spiritual awakening, we likely think that God's coming to us is sudden, unexpected, startling. However, the truth is that God has always been there. He is actively present to us all the time, every day. It's our awareness of Him that changes. God hasn't changed even in the slightest way. He is constant. It is we who are inconstant and changeable.

We often speak of Advent as a season in which we prepare for the Lord's coming into our lives. Perhaps we should see it as a season of our heightened awareness, for the truth is that we should be looking for God already at work in our lives each and every day. God is always offering Himself to us – we are not always responding. Advent is a time to conscientiously, deliberately, and with awareness, responds to His offer of Himself to us. How about beginning each day of Advent by giving God some early moments of reflection and awareness of His presence to us along with a commitment to go about accomplishing His purposes, His tasks? What better way to begin our days?

It's all a matter of seeing eternity in every season of our lives. It's all a matter of paying attention to God's presence to us in our lives as children, as teens, as young adults, in our middle age, and in the final seasons of our lives when the leaves fall from their branches, and the world goes to sleep under a blanket of snow. In each of those seasons of our lives, God's ever-present and everlasting love can break in upon us. Each one of us feels it to be unexpected. But what is so unexpected about it? God is always calling us to climb to the top of the mountain, look for His coming, and take a look over the broad range of our lives. Our lives are cluttered with too many things demanding our attention, draining us of our energies, and blinding us to the big picture. Money only goes so far. Technology can only do so much. Medicines have a short shelf life. All of our human resources are limited. Only God has what we need, and He has it in an inexhaustible supply.

Can we look ahead? Yes, we can, if we take the time and make the space to do so. Can we track the writing of God's finger as He sends us His message? We can. Can we seize the opportunity to make time during Advent to come to some daily Advent Masses? Attend parish communal penance services? Read from the bible? Spend extra time in thoughtful reflection and quiet prayer? We can. But that is not the issue. The big question is not what we can do. It's what we will do. It's our will that is controlling, not our abilities or our wishes.

As your teachers taught you in school, the Greek philosopher Plato (who lived four hundred years before Christ) declared: "The life which is unexamined is not worth living." Every Advent, and indeed every time you come here to Mass, Holy Mother Church bids you to examine your life. I, as your priest, have always had that purpose in mind every time.

Once again, we enter into and begin our journey through Advent, hopefully looking for the coming of the Lord into our lives. And so I invite you to read again the passage of St. Paul, words you just heard in his letter to the Romans, and in the words of Jesus you just heard on today's gospel account:

"Brothers and sisters: You know the time; it is the hour now for you to awake from sleep." "So, too, you also must be prepared, for at an hour you do not expect, the Son of Man will come."

# THEME 36
# PATH OF CONVERSION

*Isaiah 11:1-10; Romans 15:4-9; Matthew 3:1-12*

A gift can only be received, fully received, according to what is in the heart and soul of the one who receives it. That being so, we hear today John the Baptist preaching a message that asks us to prepare, to prepare to receive the gift that God wants to give us. John wasn't so interested in assigning blame and finger-pointing at the moral bankruptcy of the Pharisees and Sadducees as he was in touching those who were listening to him with sincere hearts, hearts fully aware of what human sin can do but likewise fully aware of God's merciful promise of a Saviour who would, through our own conversion to His ways, deliver us from the power of evil. John wanted us to convert and with expectant faith to receive God's gift to us. If we give any attention at all to human history, we can't help but realise that our humanity is weakened by our lust for power, money, and sexual exploitation of others, even children. Vice abounds. Is that God's fault or ours? Some blame God for everything that has gone wrong both in their own lives and in our human history. But, we must ask, did God create us to live in misery?

The Book of Genesis gives us a different picture, a picture in which God created us to live in happiness, His creative purpose symbolised by the Garden of Paradise. God's primal intention was that we live in love, peace, and harmony, harmony with our world and harmony in our human relationships with others. It goes on to present us with all that has gone wrong. And what has gone wrong? Our desires to decide for ourselves what is good and evil, what is right for us and what is wrong for us. We decide for ourselves, apart from what God wants.

It's important to bear in mind that sin has weakened us, sickened our souls, and diminished our love, both our love of God and our love for one another. That condition is known in theology as "Original Sin," our sinful rebellion that is in our origins. We are born into human history and bear its weakness, a weakness so inherent in us that we cannot save ourselves. This offends our human pride. This bruises our egotistical belief that we can justify ourselves, save ourselves, make ourselves whole again. The truth is that only God can save us; only God can justify us; only God can restore us to wholeness holiness. The only way up and out of the quicksand in which we find ourselves thrashing about is to reach up and take hold of God's hand, God's saving presence that comes to us in His Christ, the One who stands on solid ground, on a rock, the One who offers us His healing strength in His Anointed One, Christ our Lord. He offers, nothing happens unless we respond. It is not the will of God to allow evil to triumph over us. God's will is just the reverse. Evil has no more power over us other than what we allow it to have. Evil has no power over us when God's love in His Christ abides within us. God has limited evil's reach. Satan's power is not limitless, it is limited and more than limited, it is negated when we choose not to eat of the tainted fruit from the tree that stands in the middle of our world. What John the Baptist calls us to see is that religious persecution and systemic evils, as symbolised in the Pharisees and Sadducees, will beset us so long as we fail to recognise Christ our Saviour living now among us. We need to recognise that Jesus Christ didn't come among us 2,000 years ago and then leave. No. God would not play that dirty trick on us. We need to see that God sent His Son among us to abide with us, not only among us but live within us. With Him, we can overcome what our Original Sin has done to us.

The path out of our mess is the path of personal repentance and conversion, where we change our ways. These prepare the way for us to receive God's Christ, God's gift to us. Repentance isn't simply saying: "I'm sorry" and then moving on as if nothing has changed.

Repentance involves recognition, becoming aware of our sins, something quite beyond simply feeling bad about what we have done. Nice sentiments are not the stuff of repentance. To be sure God offers us His forgiveness, but nothing happens until we respond --- respond with changing patterns of behaviour. That is true repentance. Recovery is hard work; you can't just talk the talk, you've got to walk the walk. That is what John the Baptist is telling us. The wonderful thing about Advent is that at the end, we are given the certitude of God's loving presence in our lives, God's Holy Spirit abiding deep within our hearts and souls. Advent is all about expectant faith and hopes found in the Gift of God who loved us so much that He sent us His very best, His only Son. And if we receive Him in our hearts and souls, receive Him not simply with good wishes and nice thoughts, then the changes that we enter into will take us out of our weakness and into the certainty of God's love abiding deep within us, empowering us to deal with our wounded selves and enjoy life as He would have us enjoy it.

He is our Saviour; we are powerless to be our own Saviour --- and that is good news!

# THEME 37
# KEEP FAITH IN YOUR DOUBT

*Isaiah 35:1-6, 10; James 5:7-10; Matthew 11:2-11*

Life is full of questions. How do you feel about them? How do you regard them? Not being comfortable with mysteries, some of us don't like unanswered questions and are annoyed by them. Others of us ask questions because we have doubts and use questions to express our doubts. Many students want answers and want them immediately handed to them on a silver platter. Isn't that something we all experience?

Along with instant gratification, don't we want immediate answers to our questions? But life isn't a problem to be solved, it's a mystery to be lived. To be sure, lovers like to pursue each other; they like to be pursued, sought out, to be found in love's great game of "catch me if you can." Love can't be engineered. Love can't be proved either scientifically or in a court of law. Love can only be lived and found in the mystery of the one we love. Love is pursued in many, many questing.

Jesus continually pushed His disciples with questions. "Who do people say I am?" "Who do you say I am?" Using parables in His teachings, He asked His disciples to tell Him what those parables meant. He allows us to experience questions; questions like: "What is the meaning of my life?" "Who am I?" "What does God want me to do with my life?" "Why is there suffering?" "What does evil exist – where does it come from?" "Why did Jesus have to die a horrible death on His cross of agony?" Religion leads us into questions. It should! Our faith takes us into a quest for God, for His truth, for His love. Some preachers think religion should provide us with all of the answers. Nothing could be further from the truth. Religion should lead us into searching out the meaning of life, particularly the meaning and purpose of your life and mine. That requires many questions to which the answers are not simple.

So, turning to today's gospel account, we find John the Baptist sending his disciples to Jesus with the question: "Are you the one who is to come, or are we to look for another?" John was not asking the question because he doubted or was denying that Jesus was God's Anointed One, the Christ. After all, when he baptised Jesus in the River Jordan, John the Baptist proclaimed: "Behold, the Lamb of God!" Later in his preaching, John declared: "After I, comes He who is mightier than I, the thong of whose sandals I am not worthy to stoop down and untie. I have baptised you with water, but He will baptise you with the Holy Spirit." John knew very well that Jesus was the Promised Messiah. He didn't need to hear Jesus' answer to the question: "Are you the one who is to come, or are we to look for another?" But evidently, he knew his disciples did. Many of Jesus' contemporaries expected the Messiah to deliver them from their enemies, particularly the hated Romans. Many expected God's Messiah would solve all of their problems. People in our own time still expect Christ to be their ultimate problem solver. They reject Him when they find that they have to work at solving their problems, failing to understand that God works with us, not for us. We have our responsibilities – God is not going to relieve us of all that we have to do to work with Him to make our world a better place. God isn't going to take care of everything for us.

Jesus answered the question put to Him by John's disciples, saying:

"Go and tell John what you hear and see: the blind regain their sight, the lame walk, lepers are cleansed, the deaf hear, the dead are raised, and the poor have the good news proclaimed to them. And blessed is the one who takes no offence at me."

He knew His answer would disappoint John's disciples because they were hoping for a warrior king, and instead, they got a shepherd. He also knew that this was good news, joyful news, for all who experienced oppression and suffering, both physically and spiritually. All of the prophecies found in the Old Testament were about to be fulfilled. All of Israel's prophets foretold the advent of the Messiah; John stood at the threshold and was privileged to usher in the very presence of the hoped-for Messiah. Many people around us are looking for easy answers rather than for good questions. Preachers and pundits are given to offering us simplistic slogans and simple solutions. We need to continually remind ourselves that finding the right answers depends on asking the right questions.

The most important of those questions is the one Jesus asked of His disciples: "Who do you say I am?" Rather than answering by producing a list of things we expect from Christ, we should continually, each and every day, ask ourselves: "What God expects of me?" "Am I listening to God?" "What is God telling me?" Perhaps we don't have answers that are immediately apparent to us, but asking the right questions is undoubtedly better than having a false set of expectations of God.

What do you expect from God is a good question. A better question is: What does God expect from you? Can He find your wholehearted love, or should He look for another?

# THEME 38
# THE PROMISED MESSIAH

*Isaiah 7:10-14; Romans 1:1-7; Matthew 1:18-24*

Christmas is for families, we are told. That is quite true. Certainly, you have received Christmas cards depicting Mary, Joseph, and the child Jesus in lovely settings, usually painted in a holy, heavenly light emanating from the Star of Bethlehem beaming down its light from heaven above. The Church celebrates the Feast of the Holy Family on the Sunday immediately following Christmas thus emphasising the fundamental importance of the family. Yes, Christmas is for families and for their bonding together. That's the truth, but not the whole truth. Christmas celebrates the birth of our Saviour, God's promised Messiah. That's true. In celebrating it, however, we should not think of His birth as the beginning of His existence. Having said that, I want to go a bit more deeply into our belief that God the Son existed from all eternity, along with the Father and the Holy Spirit without a beginning. Because that is so, what we are celebrating is the fact that God Himself became human flesh and blood, became one of us, and thus entered into our human nature and human history. That's stupendous, so astonishing that the theologians refer to it as the miracle of the Incarnation. The miraculous birth of Christ is the incarnation of God the Son in human flesh and blood.

It makes a whole lot of sense when you stop and think about it. After all, how else could God make Himself known to us? Oh, He could send us angels, He could raise prophets and holy men to tell us about Him, or He could let Himself be known to us in awesome events taking place in nature. Actually, He has done all that, but we just didn't get it. So God went the whole distance and in doing so removed any distance between Himself and us – He became Man. I realise full well that this fundamental belief of Christians is heavy fare coming to you amid your preparations for Christmas. You are busily concerned with buying gifts, preparing for parties, and trying to get a whole lot done in your pre-Christmas preparations, but when else am I going to have the opportunity to share these ideas with you? The truth that God comes to us in our humanity is vital and essential to how you and I think about God and His fundamental relationship with us. Matthew, Mark, Luke, and John give us their reports about who Jesus Christ is and what He is all about. Each uses his own particular techniques in teaching us. With that in mind, we need to see how St. John begins his presentation of Christ to us. The way he begins his gospel, his good news about Christ, points up my message for you today.

St. John begins with a prologue –an introduction to his testimony about Jesus Christ. John was a teenager when he became one of Christ's closest disciples. He went on to live until his early nineties, which means he gave much thought to his message, to what we know of as the gospel of St. John, a gospel account he wrote in his old age. With that in mind, listen now to the first part of his prologue. It goes to the heart of what Christmas, what incarnation, is all about. It sets the stage for everything St. John has to say about Jesus Christ.

*In the beginning, was the Word, and the Word was with God, and the Word was God. He was in the beginning with God. All things came to be through him, and without him, nothing came to be. What came to be through Him was life, and this life was the light of the human race; the light shines in the darkness, and the darkness has not overcome it.*

You have all heard that before, many times. But how many times have you stopped to consider what it is saying? That's what we are doing right now. St. John tells us that Jesus Christ is the human expression; no more, the human reality of God's Word made flesh,

God's self-expression and self-revelation of who He is. God has something He wants to say to us, something He wants to give us, namely His love and His very own life. In His love for us, God wants to share His life with us. Why? For no other reason than He loves us and wants to be united to us. You know as well as I do that there is distance between ourselves and God. This distance is not God's doing; it is not His will. It is our doing. Sin and the evils we have perpetrated are the cause of the distance. And there's nothing that we can do by ourselves to close the gap. We need God to do that. And so He sent us a Saviour to bridge the chasm between God and us. Before that Saviour came to us, we were powerless to bridge the gap. With God's gift to us, with the Saviour He has given us, we can bridge the chasm. Most marvellous of all is the fact that God sent His Saviour to us not simply to live among us but actually to become one of us in our very nature. That is the astounding miracle that happens each and every time we celebrate Mass, and you receive Him in your own humanity in Holy Communion. God becomes one with your body and blood with His Body and Blood. Because of the Incarnation, God becomes one with you. Each Mass is another Christmas. That's the truth, the whole, and nothing but the truth.

# THEME 39
# THE DIGNITY OF THE HUMAN PERSON

*Isaiah 49:3, 5-6; 1 Corinthians 1:1-3; John 1:29-34*

In all of God's creation, what is His most significant, His most important one? Is it not the human person? When we go back to the beginning, to the Book of Genesis, we find God creating light out of the darkness and order out of chaos. We find God creating the sun, the moon, the stars, the seas, mountains, and animals. Then toward the end of the first chapter of Genesis, we read:

> "And God saw that it was good. Then God said, 'Let us make man in our image, after our likeness; and let them have dominion over the fish of the sea, and over the birds of the air, and over the cattle, and over all the earth, and over every creeping thing that creeps upon the earth.' So God created man in His own image, in the image of God, He created him; male and female He created them. And God blessed them, and God said to them, 'Be fruitful and multiply, and fill the earth and subdue it; and have dominion over the fish of the sea and over the birds of the air and over every living thing that moves upon the earth.'"

The most important point to note is that God made man and woman in His own image and likeness. Among all of the things that God has created, none except the man and the woman were made in God's own image and likeness. The significance and importance of that cannot be overstated. Because the human person is made in God's own likeness, we are of supreme importance and possess a dignity that is high above all else in God's creation. The human person must be respected above all else.

In the Baltimore Catechism, we find the famous question: "Why did God make you?" The answer known worldwide by Catholics is: "God made me to know Him, to love Him, and to serve Him in this world, and to be happy with Him forever in the next." Yet, in human history, that answer is almost universally ignored. The world has, for the most part, treated human persons as merely useful.

Holy scripture gives us a different perspective, one telling us that we are deliberately and intentionally made. King David in one of his psalms (Psalm 139) sings of God's purposes.

What I want to say to you today is that you, too, each one of you here, is significant in God's great scheme of things. Let me point out two things about each one of you. Each one of you has his or her own unique DNA coding. No one who ever was, or who is living now, or whoever will live in the future can have your DNA coding. You are wholly one of a kind. No one else will ever be exactly like you. Even if you are someone's identical twin, your twin will not be who you are.

Moreover, there are your fingerprints. No one who ever was, or who is now, or who will yet be born will ever have your fingerprints. They are fully unique to you. They identify only you.

That said, let me go on to point out that only you can love God just as you. While God has brought millions and billions of other people into existence, He has never made anyone else just like you. This means that everyone's love for God is different. If you don't love God as who you are, then He will never be loved like that by anyone else. You are special.

See how significant you are in the eyes of God and in the heart of God? You are very special to God, very important to Him. Let me repeat it: there will never be another you, and if you don't love God just as who you are, He will never be loved like that, *ever!*

Here's another thing. You play a significant role in the lives of those around you. Your example in dealing with life is significant and important for those around you who know you. Life is unfair. Life is difficult. Life brings suffering, a lot of suffering. How you deal with it will be very significant to any number of people who know you. But life has its joys, too. Life brings good fortune and happiness to us. How you handle success, along with the generosity in your heart, can be of great significance to people who know you. How you handle both success and failure has a significant impact on others.

The great prophet Isaiah had to deal with failure, even near despair. At times he sounded as if he were amid burnout. Said he: Though I thought I had toiled in vain, and for nothing, uselessly, spent my strength, yet my reward is with the LORD, my recompense is with my God. (Isaiah 49:4) However, the same Isaiah whose words we just heard in today's first reading who said: The LORD said to me: You are my servant, Israel, through whom I show my glory. Now the LORD has spoken who formed me as his servant from the womb that Jacob may be brought back to him... I am made glorious in the sight of the LORD, and my God is now my strength!

Let me point out that each one of you here was formed by God in your mother's womb. Each one of you here has a destiny that God has given you. God knew you in your mother's womb.

This brings me to the matter of your faith, your spirituality, and religious devotion. You may never know what significance you have in the hearts and souls of people who know you. You may never know how your faith has built up the faith of those around you, especially members of your family and your close friends. You may not realise what God is doing with your life. But God knows of your importance even though you may not realise it yourself.

Have faith, then. Have faith based on what Jesus said of John the Baptist: Amen, I say to you, among those born of women there has been none greater than John the Baptist; yet the least in the kingdom of heaven is greater than he. (Matthew 11:11)

# THEME 40
# LIGHT IN THE DARK

*Isaiah 8:23-29; 1 Corinthians 1:10-13; Matthew 4:12-17*

When Jesus heard that John the Baptist had been arrested, He withdrew to Galilee. He left His hometown of Nazareth and went to live in Capernaum, in the region of Zebulun and Naphtali, that the prophecy of *Isaiah might be fulfilled:* land of Zebulun and land of Naphtali, the way to the sea, beyond the Jordan, Galilee of the Gentiles, the people who sit in darkness have seen a great light, on those dwelling in a land overshadowed by death light has arisen. From that time on, Jesus began to preach and say, "Repent, for the kingdom of heaven is at hand."

In our times, what forms of darkness do we live in? The theme of light and darkness runs through the entirety of the Bible, starting with the Book of Genesis to the crucifixion and death of Jesus on His Cross. What is God's word calling us to see in His light, not only in the history of our salvation presented to us in the Bible but in our own particular and individual histories? What forms of darkness overshadow us in our own lives?

What is the importance of the light that comes from God, the light that shines in the darkness that surrounds us? When you look into the lives of great people, you will come to discover one common golden thread that weaves throughout them all. They all did not allow adversity to flatten them, to drain them of their courage, to empty them of their faith and their hope. None of them was deadened by the dark spirit of defeatism, that evil spirit that is one of the devil's most effective weapons. The Light of God of which I speak of is God's Holy Spirit, the One who was present in God's creation when God overcame the darkness and uttered His creating command: "Let there be light." Everything that exists originates in the energies found in God's Light.

When one loses hope, one thrashes around in real darkness. When one loses courage and simply gives up, one's soul is deeply darkened. Our great heroes and heroines did not allow themselves to yield to defeatism. The stories of Washington, Lincoln, Joan of Arc, Mother Teresa, Florence Nightingale, Pope John Paul II, Mahatma Gandhi, and the stories of our other greats all share one common theme – they never allowed the flame of faith and hope to be extinguished within them, in the face of total darkness, there burned within them a fire that we Christians call the flame of the Holy Spirit, that Spirit that raised Jesus from His dark tomb into the light that was the dawn of God's New Creation.

Jesus confronted the forces of darkness by turning Satan's victory into everlasting defeat. The Bible personifies the forces of darkness in giving them a name -- the Prince of Darkness, Satan, or Lucifer. As members of Christ, we must do the same confronting in our lives. St. Paul reminds us that we, in Christ, carry on that epic struggle against the forces of darkness arrayed against us.

It is the intention and goal of the Prince of Darkness to disable you from revealing God's presence here on earth. He accomplishes that purpose by filling us with thoughts of inferiority and inability by filling us with a sense of failure and futility. The Prince of Darkness likewise presents you with seductive opportunities or with concerns that captivate your attention and keep you from considering the presence of God within your heart, mind, and soul. You can identify Satan's presence when you encounter doubt, discouragement, disillusionment, depression, defeat, despair, and finally, death --- the death of God's life in your soul. When we encounter those works of Satan, you and I need to expose them to God's Light, the Light of the Word that we receive from Christ. That is why coming to Mass and receiving Our Blessed Lord in Holy

Communion isn't something that is simply "nice," it is essential. It is truly the Bread of Life that nourishes and sustains us, particularly when we feel weak.

And so today I leave you with this vision of St. Paul who was writing to the Roman Christians who were suffering in dark persecution:

What then shall we say to this? If God is for us, who is against us? He who did not spare his own Son but gave Him up for us all, will He not also give us all things with Him? Who shall bring any charge against God's elect? It is God who justifies; who is to condemn? Is it Christ Jesus, who died, yes, who was raised from the dead, who is at the right hand of God, who indeed intercedes for us? Who shall separate us from the love of Christ? Shall tribulation, or distress, or persecution, or famine, or nakedness, or peril, or sword? As it is written, 'For thy sake, we are being killed all the day long; we are regarded as sheep to be slaughtered.' No, in all these things, we are more than conquerors through Him who loved us. For I am sure that neither death, nor life, nor angels, nor principalities, nor things present, nor things to come, nor powers, nor height, nor depth, nor anything else in all creation, will be able to separate us from the love of God in Christ Jesus our Lord. (Romans 8:31-39)

Do not allow the work of the Prince of Darkness to separate you from the love of God that comes to you in Christ Jesus, our Lord. Along with Jesus at your side, snatch victory out of defeat.

# THEME 41
# YOU SHALL BE CALLED BLESSED

*Zephaniah 2:3, 3:12-13; 1 Corinthians 1:26-31; Matthew 5:1-15*

Today's gospel account in which we find Jesus giving us the Beatitudes provides us with a good background to look at winners and losers.

As in so many things, a lot depends on your viewpoint and the angle from which you are looking at things. St. Paul puts that issue into sharp perspective in today's second reading, which was taken from his letter written to very cosmopolitan and sophisticated Greeks living in Corinth:

> "Consider your calling, brothers and sisters," writes St. Paul, "Not many of you were wise by human standards, not many were powerful, not many were of noble birth. Instead, God chose the foolish of the world to shame the wise, and God chose the weak of the world to shame the strong…"

So much of our spiritual life depends on how we see things. I daresay that everything depends on how we see people and things. It's all a question of having eyes to see and ears to hear so that we may rightly understand. Do we see things in God's light as God sees them – from above? That's hinted at with the Star of Bethlehem guiding the wise men to Bethlehem and the Christ Child. It is no accident that Jesus teaches His disciples on the Mount of the Beatitudes. Mountain-top experiences allow us to see things from above, from God's perspective. What a worldly person sees is not what God sees. What the worldly judge to be desirable, God does not.

The Beatitudes provide a dizzying new vision of the world, a perspective designed to turn upside down the political and social world of our time. Jesus describes those who are truly fortunate, the lucky ones of their day. However, it is not emperors, conquerors, priests, and the wealthy who enjoy this favour. Instead, the common people, those whom earthly success has largely passed by the poor, the meek, the persecuted, and the peacemakers. How can this be? The answer is that even though they may have been denied worldly success, what cannot be taken away from them is their potential to live rightly by one another. It is all too easy for those who enjoy the pleasures of this world from their hilltop mansions to float above such obligations. Jesus says that so long as ordinary people stand for the right things and do not retreat in their rightness before those who seem to have more power, what is right will prevail. It's their kingdom; a kingdom organised not from the top-down but the bottom-up. In the Beatitudes, Jesus offers a description of the community of goodwill His teachings will build in this world if we follow them.

*Blessed are the poor in spirit, for theirs is the kingdom of heaven.* The poor in spirit are those who, no matter how much money they may have, realise they are relatively powerless without God's power and empowerment that gives them security in the face of all loss and disaster.

*Blessed are they who mourn, for they will be comforted.* It is God's prerogative to bring good out of evil, light out of darkness, order out of chaos, and even life out of death. Mourning turns us back to God and calls down His love and compassion upon us, a love that empowers us to transcend our losses and rise again to meet new challenges.

*Blessed are the meek, for they will inherit the land.* Being meek does not mean being a wimp. It does not mean being a doormat upon which aggressors wipe their feet.

*Blessed are they who hunger and thirst for righteousness, for they will be satisfied.* Integrity and righteousness are the foundation stones upon which peace and progress are built. Righteousness exalts a nation.

*Blessed are the merciful, for they will be shown mercy.* We would think we are merciful, but often that is merely wishful thinking. While thinking we are compassionate, we cling to our grudges, won't let go of our resentments while remembering in detail all that others have done to hurt us.

*Blessed are the clean of heart, for they will see God.* Purity isn't solely concerned with sexual sins. Having a pure heart involves a whole lot more, such as having a heart that is uncluttered, lucid, and focused.

*Blessed are the peacemakers, for they will be called children of God.* We can become overwhelmed when we consider how we will ever bring peace in our world, a world hopelessly mired in hateful revenge. But let's consider that we can all be peacemakers in our spheres of influence.

*Blessed are they who are persecuted for the sake of righteousness, for theirs is the kingdom of heaven.* The consummation of our lives is an inheritance in heaven above. This should be our utmost desire. Thus we should not lose focus even when the world is turning down on us. For God is our strength and our Saviour.

*Blessed are you when they insult you and persecute you and utter every kind of evil against you falsely because of me. Rejoice and be glad for your reward will be great in heaven.*

# THEME 42
# CALLED TO BE HOLY

*Isaiah 58:7-10; 1 Corinthians 2:1-5; Matthew 5:13-16*

Jesus came from Isaiah's people. Isaiah had commanded them to share their bread with the hungry, shelter the oppressed and the homeless, and to clothe the naked.

"If you remove from your midst oppression, false accusation and malicious speech; if you bestow your bread on the hungry and satisfy the afflicted, if you do justice, then shall you be justified. Then shall your light break forth like the dawn and the glory of the Lord shall shine about you."

In His inaugural address when He began His public ministry after He had returned from being in the desert for forty days and forty nights and was subsequently baptised in the River Jordan by John the Baptiser, Jesus announced to the people of His hometown, the people of Nazareth:

"The Spirit of the Lord is on me because He has anointed me to preach good news to the poor. He has sent me to proclaim freedom for the prisoners and recovery of sight for the blind, to release the oppressed, to proclaim the year of the Lord's favour."

To be holy is to be one with the Holy One, not merely to think nice thoughts about Him. Goodness and holiness are the results of love. Goodness and holiness consist of actively loving others, with deeds, as God loves us. One is holy because one lives with and acts with the One who is holy, Christ Jesus --- God made flesh for us. This is summed up nicely at the end of the Eucharist Prayer of the Mass immediately before we pray the Lord's Prayer. I was to also point out that in the Lord's

Prayer, we pray: "Thy kingdom come, thy will be done on earth as it is in heaven." To be joined in love with Jesus Christ consists of actively living as He lived, in being salt and light for others. Thus Jesus tells us: "You are the salt of the earth, You are the light of the world." These words are God's words calling us to live in concern for others. Salt is active, and light is active, not passive. Being salt and light for others is part and parcel of being a disciple of Christ, of being a Christian. Every Christian has to strive for personal sanctification, but what we need to remember is that to be holy we must be about the task of bringing others to be a part of the One who is holy. Jesus teaches us this; in fact, He commands it. Sharing our personal experience of the presence of God is the substance of being salt and light for others.

St. Therese of Lisieux once wrote:

"I see now that true charity consists in bearing with the faults of those about us, never being surprised at their weaknesses, but edified at the least sign of virtue. I see above all that charity must not remain hidden in the bottom of our hearts: nor do men light a lamp and put it under a bushel, but on a stand, and it gives light to all in the house."

Your love, she wrote, must be seen - not so that people may give you honour and glory but so that they may see your good works and give praise to your Father in heaven. But what if your salt goes flat? How can you restore its flavour? And what if your light is hidden under a bushel? Jesus knows how much we may be tempted to be timid; how often we are motivated and controlled by concern about what others may think of us, how often we are controlled by fear. We so often keep our faith and our religious values hidden. Indeed there are many voices around us telling us to keep our faith private and away from the public square. They do not want us to "impose our values" on them even by expressing them in public. Faith, they say, is a private matter and isn't supposed to make a difference in our society, isn't supposed to be seen in our secularised and multicultural society.

Living for others and unselfishly caring for others like Christ is the most explicit expression of love. The Second Vatican Council emphasised the Christian's duty to be apostolic. Baptism and Confirmation confer this duty upon us (which is also a right) because in Baptism and Confirmation we are anointed to be a part of the Body of Christ here on earth. All of us have countless opportunities to be salt and light for others. The very nature of the Christian life consists in doing good things for others not simply to be nice but in a supernatural spirit, in the life and motivation of Jesus Christ. This is why He told us: "Let your light so shine before men that they may see your good works and give glory to your Father who is in heaven."

You have been baptised and confirmed. The Spirit of the Lord has come upon you; He has anointed you to bring good news to the poor. He has sent you "to proclaim freedom for the prisoners and recovery of sight for the blind, to release the oppressed..." You are to follow Isaiah's command and bestow your bread on the hungry and satisfy those afflicted by oppression and injustice. Then shall you be justified. Then shall your light break forth like the dawn and your salt shall never be flat and good for nothing. And the glory of the Lord shall shine about you, not just for your sake, but for the sake of those around you.

# THEME 43
# A TREE IS KNOWN FOR ITS FRUITS

*Sirach 15:15-20; 1 Corinthians 2:6-10; Matthew 5:17-37*

All of us know people of good character, people who have a reputation of being decent, respectful of others, law-abiders who lead good lives, or so they appear. We also know of some who, even though they enjoy a good reputation, turn out to be a whole lot less than we thought, some of them going on to bring terrible hurt to others and inflict real damage upon them. As the old saying goes, appearances are deceiving. Looking good does not mean that our hearts are filled with goodness.

The Scribes and Pharisees had a certain kind of goodness, even holiness. Jesus did not condemn them for the goodness they sought. Rather, He condemned them for what they did not have in their hearts. They had no depth. They governed their thoughts and actions by their external observance of the Jewish laws and how they appeared in the eyes of others. The love of God and the love of others that flows from our love of God never filled their inner selves, never filled their hearts where they lived. Sure, they did not murder others, but they allowed themselves to hate. Sure, they did not commit adultery, but they allowed themselves to regard women merely as objects for the pleasure of males. Wives were merely useful. That attitude adulterates genuine love and demeans women.

Lest we haughtily consider ourselves to be so much better than they were, we should look at ourselves. Do we govern our actions based on what others will think of us? That's superficial; it governs us based on appearances. That motivation is external, not internal. It's shallow and doesn't come from deep down within us --- where we really live.

Jesus wants His Holy Spirit to dwell deep within us, in our hearts and souls. It's from there that our actions should begin. It's from there that our motives are formed, motives formed in generosity and the unlimited love and care of God for ourselves and others.

To be sure, most of us do not commit physical adultery, but who among us has not had lust in their hearts and looked with lust on others? Isn't that a sort of divorce? Doesn't it divorce us from loving only our wives or husbands? Who among us has not had envy and jealousy over what others have? Lust isn't something that is limited to sex, but it can lead to a divided heart. Merely observing the Commandments only externally allow our hearts to go into wildness and wantonness.

Few among us have committed perjury while under oath in a court of law. But how many of us have said "yes" when we didn't mean it and "no" when we didn't mean it? It used to be the case that when a man gave his word, or a woman gave her word, then everyone who knew them could rely on them. Living up to one's word was a bond, a contract that everyone could take to be faithful and true. Is that true in our day? The Scribes and the Pharisees are among us, here today. They did simply walk the face of the earth over 2,000 years ago.

Few among us will commit murder, but how many times have we murdered the good name and reputation of others with our idle gossiping and chatter? How many times have we murdered our relationship with others by hateful thoughts of resentment and revenge in our hearts, or with abusive language and contempt of others? Oh, to be sure, our external actions may be nice and even polite, but that's not what Jesus wants from us. He expects more than simple minimums and legal observance of the norms, rules, and laws of living in a social order with others.

On one occasion, in another context, Jesus was talking with His disciples about this. He said to them:

> "But what comes out of a person that is what defiles. From within people, from their hearts, come evil thoughts, unchastity, theft, murder, adultery, greed, malice, deceit, licentiousness, envy, blasphemy, arrogance, folly. All these evils come from within, and they defile." (Mark 7: 20-23)

I am not suggesting that laws, rules, and regulations are of no value. They are precious. Many people observe laws because they fear the consequences of violating them. If a person thinks about committing a crime, he may think he can get away with it for a few moments, but the thought of the punishment he will face if he breaks the law causes him to refrain. Breaking a contract has legal consequences even for those who, lacking self-respect, regard giving one's word as of no consequence. Because many lack respect for God and likewise lack self-respect, we as a society must have laws. Laws have a good purpose and serve us well.

Jesus, however, is looking for something far more profound than legal observances. He wants us to be motivated by love, to live loving lives, to care and to unselfishly give of ourselves to others and to our Father in Heaven. This is a way of living that no law can motivate or impose on us. This way of living puts greater demands on us.

Suppose we lived in a society where everyone strictly observed all of its laws. Everyone would behave well, but would such a world be filled with happiness? Jesus wants more from us. Living in strict observance of laws would be good, but would we be living in a world of love? Would it be a loving and caring world, or would it be simply a world in which nobody broke any laws? Jesus wants the best from us, not just our minimum performances.

God gave us a tremendous gift, the gift of free agency. This is because love doesn't truly love unless it is freely given – and freely received. After all, a gift isn't a gift unless and until it is received. God has paid us a tremendous compliment in that He respects our decisions. That is why He never forces our decisions. He offers, and then He waits for our response. His love for us is unconditional. His only law is love, a love within us that governs our choices and the actions that flow from our choices.

This is not something new. It is found in God's Word given to us many centuries before Christ and is expressed in the first reading of today's Mass, a reading taken from the Old Testament's Book of Wisdom: *If you choose, you can keep the commandments; it is loyalty to do His will. And before you is fire and water set; to whichever you choose, stretch forth your hand. Before mankind is life and death, whichever he chooses shall be given him. Immense is the wisdom of the Lord; He is mighty in power and all-seeing. The eyes of God see all He has made; He understands man's every deed.*

We all know full well what we do or don't do. And we all know what others do or don't do. God, however, is more interested in what He finds in our hearts. Do we simply obey rules, or do we choose to live in love and concern for others? That's a question the answer to which can only be found deep down in your heart – where you really live.

# THEME 44
# THE NEW COMMANDMENT

*Leviticus 19:1-2, 17-18; 1 Corinthians 3:16-23; Matthew 5:38-48*

When Jesus declared, "*You have heard it said, you shall love your neighbour and hate your enemy,*" He was not quoting any of the Jewish prophets from any of the writings found in the Old Testament, He was quoting something from outside of the Jewish religion. The command to hate your enemy is found nowhere in the Bible. That bears repeating: The command to hate your enemy is found nowhere in the Bible.

Ancient legal systems had formulas applied to specific crimes, laws that prescribed punishments equal to the offences. A common expression was: "an eye for an eye, a tooth for a tooth." We find another one of those formulas expressed in the Book of Genesis wherein Chapter 9 we read: "*If anyone sheds the blood of man, by man shall his blood be shed...*" *(*Genesis 9:6)

Jesus instructs His disciples to go beyond, to follow a higher law, a law not based on retaliation and retribution but based instead on a more powerful force to govern our human relationships – the Law of Love. However, we must be careful to note that Jesus is not instructing His followers to let evildoers do whatever they please. To do nothing to confront evil is not the response Jesus wants from us. Injustice, Christians must resist this evil when it is encountered. The resistance is to nonviolently break the cycle of violence, which the ancient laws of retribution only reinforced. In those systems, violence was to be countered by the violence of equal proportion. Jesus confronts evil with a power that transcends violence. Let me give you an example from an account I once heard when I was a young man.

Two brothers, one of whom told me this true story, were having a terrible fight, a violent fight during which they were slamming each other bloody with their fists. During their fight, one of them simply dropped his fists and by looking into his brother's eyes, declared: "You can't hurt me because I love you!" Well, at that point, the fight was over; the astonished other brother had been stripped of his weapons. Not only would further bashing be useless, but he was also covered with shame.

In Jesus' teaching, He went on to give His disciples the example of the debtor who, while standing before the judge, stripped off his cloak and his tunic and stood naked before this creditor who had dragged him into court demanding full repayment.

There are times, of course, when the use of deadly force is necessary in self-defence, but that is rarely the case in our individual lives. The question of justifiable war is separate and distinct from what I am speaking about here. Self-defence is undoubtedly justifiable in limited situations. Similarly, the Just War arguments have elements linked to self-defence; these considerations are another topic that we cannot consider here in this short sermon.

God's love has no bounds. His love extends to all of His creation, particularly to human beings. He has made every human being in His image and likeness. God hates evil, and He hates sinful human deeds. Jesus' formula for overcoming evil does not include using evil to overcome evil. After all, using evil to overcome evil only multiplies evil by two; it does not divide it in half or reduce it to zero. Echoing God's boundless love Jesus, dying on His Cross cries out: "Father, forgive them for they know not what they do." With His dying breath, Jesus extends His loving forgiveness to those who have inflicted terrible evil upon Him.

Non-violent love undermines hatred; it breaks the cycle of violence and tears down boundaries that wall us up in hatred. If there is to be retribution, let God mete it out on His terms. We are to be agents of God's love, not God's wrath. We are to be agents of God's boundless love, a love that brings light out of darkness, order out of chaos, meaning out of absurdity, and life out of death. God is the only one who can overcome evil, and His ways are not our ways unless, of course, we walk in the footsteps of Jesus.

This reminds me of a prayer attributed to Native North Americans: *O Great Spirit grant that I do not judge my brother until I have walked a mile in his moccasins.* I am also reminded of a popular bumper sticker from a few years ago: *Perform random acts of kindness and senseless acts of beauty.* What better senseless acts of beauty than overcoming your enemies with your love in turning your other cheek?

Therefore, in family feuds and conflicted relationships, take the initiative and be the first to offer reconciliation. Your offer may be rejected, but how many of God's offers have we rejected? Yet He keeps on loving us enough to continue to offer His love despite our hateful sins.

St. Paul was no namby-pamby. He was nobody's fool, and anyone would be crazy to claim he was weak. Allow me, then, to leave you while repeating his words to his fellow Christians suffering persecution in Rome: *Rejoice in your hope, be patient in tribulation, be constant in prayer. Contribute to the needs of the saints, practice hospitality. Bless those who persecute you; bless and do not curse them. Rejoice with those who rejoice, weep with those who weep. Live in harmony with one another; do not be haughty, but associate with the lowly; never be conceited. Repay no one evil for evil, but take thought for what is noble in the sight of all. If possible, so far as it depends upon you, live peaceably with all. Beloved, never avenge yourselves, but leave it to the wrath of God; for it is written, 'Vengeance is mine, I will repay,' says the Lord. No, if your enemy is hungry, feed him; if he is thirsty, give him drink; for by doing so, you will heap burning coals upon his head.*

*Do not be overcome by evil, but overcome evil with good.* (Romans 12:12-21).

# THEME 45
# WHAT KIND OF GOD IS GOD?

*Isaiah 49:14-15; 1Corinthians 4: 1-5; Matthew 6:24-34*

Today's scripture readings provoke the question: What kind of God is God? Who among us has not pondered the answer to that question? What do we expect God to do for us? As revealing as the answer may be, a further question arises: What does God expect of us? More often than not, we don't want to begin to answer that one. Nevertheless, in moments when we do take time to reflect on life's bigger questions, we ought to face it. Where do we place our trust --- in God or in material comforts and success? To what or to whom do I give my heart? Jesus, who well knows the human heart, clearly warns us that where our treasure is, there we will know what is in our hearts.

The danger to our hearts and our eternal life with God in heaven lies in our ensnarement in the values of this world –power, wealth, fame, and the glitter of this world's treasures, treasures that are by no means safe and secure in our hands. Setting our hearts on them means that we are not putting our hearts to what is truly lasting and of great value. Setting our hearts on them means that we give scant attention to God's love for us, a love that God expresses in today's first reading: *Can a mother forget her infant, be without tenderness for the child of her womb? Even if she should forget, I will always remember you.*

I am frequently puzzled by preachers who project God as vengeful, full of anger, wrath, and ever ready to punish us at any opportunity. I have come to recognise that we can find whatever version of God we want to find in the Bible. Moreover, I recognised that much of the vengeance found in those preachings is the result of human manipulation for political and selfish purposes. Look around you, watch the news, read the newspapers, pay attention to advertising - you need little more confirmation of my observation than this. The result is that all kinds of people use God as an excuse for doing the very things that Jesus taught us we should *not* do. But the sad fact remains that the average person is more motivated by fear than by love. Ask yourself this question: "How many bad decisions have I made because they were grounded in fear and not in love?"

God is a God of justice, and justice requires a certain restoration in which we suffer the consequences of our actions. Crimes ought not to go unpunished. However, restorative justice is not vengeful. Usually, sins bring with them their own punishment. But vengeance? I am reminded of one occasion when Jesus, on His way to Jerusalem was rejected by the citizens of a Samaritan town. St. Luke reports it as follows:

> "When the days drew near for Him to be received up, He set His face to go to Jerusalem. And He sent messengers ahead of Him, who went and entered a village of the Samaritans, to make ready for Him; but the people would not receive him, because His face was set toward Jerusalem. And when His disciples James and John saw it, they said, "Lord, do you want us to bid fire come down from heaven and consume them?" But He turned and rebuked them". (Luke 9: 51-55)

When you stop and consider it, the punishment of those Samaritans was that they denied themselves of the healing and loving presence of God in Christ. While His disciples wanted to call down fire from heaven upon them, Jesus would have none of it. Their punishment did not have vengeance on the top of it. Our Blessed Lord did not come down from heaven to reveal a vengeful God.

We need to see that God's chastisements are designed to bring us to repentance and a return to union with Him. An eye for an eye and tooth for a tooth is an expression found in cultures surrounding the Jews.

Retribution is not in God's thinking. An eye for an eye and a tooth for a tooth is not found in the heart of Jesus. He is interested, very interested, in finding that we treasure His love in our hearts and that we are willing to forego the attractions of this world to secure that "pearl of great price." Repentance and reconciliation are many times necessary for us in order to return to union with God in our hearts and souls. When it comes to repenting, we need not fear. His heart calls to our heart. *Can a mother forget her infant, be without tenderness for the child of her womb? Even should she forget, I,* God declares, *will never forget you.*

"For where your treasure is, there will your heart be also," Jesus tells us. This teaching ought to make us pause and prompt us to do some serious reflecting. If our hearts are filled with worldly visions and values, we put our souls, our inner selves, into mortal danger, the danger of ignoring what God offers us, namely eternal life with Him in heaven. God brought us into being, into a life that has a purpose. We are purpose-made to live in happiness with God forever in heaven. Whether or not we will live in heaven with God in eternal happiness depends on our choices in this life. It is of the most significant importance, then, to see that God is not a wrathful and vengeful God; instead, we need to see and understand that God is friendly and wants us to be happy. He did not make us for His wrath; He made us for His love.

We have choices to make, choices that bring with them enormous and everlasting consequences. Satan is busily at work trying to convince us that we are unworthy and that in our unworthiness, a God of vengeance is going to strike us down, so why bother with God at all? We face problems, sometimes problems that seem to be unbearable. Satan busily tries to convince us that God simply doesn't care, that He's not a friendly God, that He's a punishing God, and that religion is, therefore, useless and nonsense.

I do not believe that God intended for us to live in fear. Jesus taught us over and over to allow love and compassion to guide our every move.

This beauty reinforces this fundamental message from the Bible in the world and in the universe around us. I believe that God intends for us to live hope-filled lives of joy, and to share that hope and joy with as many people as possible.

There are moments when we all experience God's goodness in His creation, in the heavens above, in the great and majestic mountains, in beautiful lakes, on rivers, and in forests. There are moments when we experience the glories of nature, crying out and pointing to the glorious and beautiful goodness of God. Jesus calls us to see that when He cries out:

> "Behold the lilies of the field, how they grow without doing any work, and without running around in circles, yet I tell you that even King Solomon in all of his glory was never dressed as beautifully as these flowers."

In a few weeks from now, we will be surrounded by Easter Lilies in celebrating Christ's resurrection from the dead. How appropriate that we should remember to stop worrying! These beautiful flowers, along with all of the budding, blooming creation of spring, are evidence that God is friendly and He wants us to be happy. So be happy. Repent, convert, turn away from the miseries of sin, and set yourself on the path to real happiness.

There are treasures in heaven, treasures beyond anything we can imagine or value. How foolish to live life here without ensuring that we will die in God's good graces and in His loving embrace. The attraction of things here below ought not to capture the souls that we give no attention or thought but to what awaits us in the next life. The worldly are wrong because all their decisions are based on what pleases us only in this life. They are wrong because they sell short the reason we have lived in the first place and the goal we have in living as God would have us live. Their visions are focused on the things here below, things that are quickly passing. Their vision blinds us to the things that await us if we respond to God's invitation to live in love with Him now so that we can be happy forever living with Him in heaven.

No man can devote himself to two masters. We must not love the things of this world to the exclusion of the love of God. St. Augustine observed that each of us is filled with longings, yearnings, and a deep-seated hunger. Said he: "O God, you have made us for yourself, and our hearts are restless till they find their rest in you."

So, then, in your heart of hearts, what are you seeking?

# THEME 46
# BUILT LIKE A ROCK

*Deuteronomy 11:18, 26-28, 32; Romans 3:21-25, 28; Matthew 7:21-27*

When it comes to an understanding the meaning of any scripture passage, it's always a good idea to put that passage in context, to see if it fits with other passages that precede it and follow it. This being so, we need to see that today's gospel account is a part of the teachings Jesus gave in His famous Sermon on the Mount, teachings that included the Beatitudes and other familiar passages. It was there that St. Matthew reports Jesus taught His disciples the Lord's Prayer. It was there He taught us about how God cares for the lilies of the field and the birds of the air and how much more our Heavenly Father cares for us. The Golden Rule was also among those teachings on the Mount.

Immediately before today's passage, Jesus told His disciples: "Beware of false prophets who come to you disguised as sheep but underneath are ravenous wolves." He went on to tell us:

Not everyone who says to me, 'Lord, Lord,' will enter the kingdom of heaven, but only the one who does the will of my Father in heaven. Many will say to me on that day, 'Lord, Lord, did we not prophesy in your name? Did we not drive out demons in your name? Did we not do mighty deeds in your name?' Then I will declare to them solemnly, 'I never knew you. Depart from me, you evildoers.'

Our newspapers and television news programs have given us reports of people who have presented themselves as God's prophets while duping and then abusing those who were their followers. The world around us is filled with the voices of those who claim to speak for God and then in God's name do monstrous things to human beings, even blowing up and killing innocent people in the name of God.

Beware of false prophets, Jesus said, who come to you in sheep's clothing but underneath are ravenous wolves. By their fruits, you will know them. Do people pick grapes from thornbushes or figs from thistles? Just so, every good tree bears good fruit, and a rotten tree bears bad fruit. A good tree cannot bear bad fruit, nor can a rotten tree bear good fruit. Every tree that does not bear good fruit will be cut down and thrown into the fire. So by their fruits, you will know them. (Matthew 7:15-20).

When we stand with Jesus, we stand on solid ground; we stand on a rock. We know this because He proved who He was by His miracles, by raising people from the dead, and above all by His own rising from the dead. Jesus proved who He was and where He came from. He came from His Father in heaven to speak His Father's words, to give us God's love, and to establish the kingdom of God here on earth. This is something that for us is wonderful.

We live in an unstable world, to say the least! We find ourselves surrounded by a chorus of voices that would lead us down many other paths, many of them being paths that lead us into self-destructive behaviours that bring with them disease, misery, and even death. The only voice that is steady and reliable is the voice of Jesus Christ.

Allow me to point out something in today's gospel passage that can be easily overlooked and missed. It's where Jesus said, *many will say to me on that day, 'Lord, Lord, did we not prophesy in your name?'* Well, what day? What day is our Blessed Lord talking about? That day is none other than the day we die and stand before God. It is likewise the great Judgment Day at the end of time.

Christ is telling us that He will be the Judge. Christ is telling us that we will one day find ourselves standing in front of Him face to face while answering to Him for what we have said and done as well as what we have not said and not done. Christ is claiming divinity for Himself; He's telling us that on Judgment Day, He will be exercising the prerogatives of God! Whether we have led exemplary lives or bad lives, the judgment of our lives will be His judgment, not ours. We so easily fool, and excuse ourselves and so I repeat: The judgment of our lives, whether we have led good lives or bad lives, will be His judgment, not ours.

Bible passages cannot be read quickly. It's so easy to gloss over their words and phrases. Today's gospel passage is a good example of that. Also, we should be looking for interconnectivity among the passages. Today's gospel account is an excellent example of both of these points. It is directly connected with today's first reading taken from the Old Testament Book of Deuteronomy. Moses told the people,

> Take these words of mine into your heart and soul. Bind them at your wrist as a sign, and let them be a pendant on your forehead. I set before you here, this day, a blessing and a curse: a blessing for obeying the commandments of the LORD, your God, which I enjoin on you today; a curse if you do not obey the commandments of the LORD, your God, but turn aside from the way I ordain for you today, to follow other gods, whom you have not known.

In today's gospel account, we heard Jesus speak of building our lives on solid rock. In what other scripture passage do we find Jesus speaking of rock? Of course, we all know. The word "rock" takes us immediately to Jesus' words to St. Peter: '*And so I say to you, you are Peter, and upon this rock, I will build my church, and the gates of the netherworld shall not prevail against it.'* Even though our Church is a Church of sinners and the lives of some of its clergy have been infected with this world's sinful ways, even horrible ways, the abiding and stable presence of God's Spirit is found within it. Despite the human failure, the Church has the stability of God's presence within it.

Our world is unstable, and our lives are anything but stable. But troubled times have always been a major part of human history, the history of our Church, as well as a part of our individual lives. False prophets abound. Promised hopes have failed to materialise. Many of us find out, often too late, that we've built our lives on sand, listened to the wrong advice, or followed faithless leaders. To whom do we turn, or to what do we turn, when we face such instability and turbulence in our lives?

Listening to God's voice, listening to the words of God that come to us from faith-full people, people who live good and Godly lives is not something that is merely "nice." It is essential. Failing to heed God's Wisdom and ignoring God's presence is an invitation to disaster, failure, and misery no matter how vainly we attempt to cover it all up with tinsel, glitter, and in lives filled with empty noise.

Our hearts were made for God's love. We need, truly need, to hear His word for us and to experience His presence in our souls, particularly in the world in which we presently find ourselves. We need to seek and know the mind of God and the love of God. If we do, He will recognise us on Judgment day, and we will dwell in His presence in heaven forever.

Thank God for the season of Lent. May we all use the days of this Lent to see what God wants us to see, hear the things He wants us to hear, and reform the way we live because we have listened to His voice.

# THEME 47
# DELIVER US FROM EVIL

*Genesis 2:7-9,3:1-7; Romans 5:12-19; Matthew 4:1-11*

We've heard much about the economic meltdown, bankruptcies, downsizing, reorganising our corporate businesses, eliminating governmental waste, and determining our true and necessary priorities. What is wasteful and what is essential, and how do we measure them? We simply cannot go on as we have in the past. "These are times that try men's souls," wrote Thomas Paine.

As we begin Lent of 2011, shouldn't we deal with similar questions in our spiritual lives? Isn't it necessary for us to take a hard look at the fundamental questions dealing with how we live measured against the reasons why God has put us here on earth? Asking how the world came to the crisis in which we now find ourselves is important. However, of greater importance is to ask how we as individual Catholics have come to where we're at in our spiritual lives today. Lent is a time of asking questions and taking the necessary steps to change our behaviour and our patterns of living.

Whenever we pray the Lord's Prayer and come upon the words "And deliver us from evil" we are praying something that deserves our considered thought. Throughout the centuries, there have been many translations of the original Hebrew words that Jesus used when He taught the Lord's Prayer. For instance, most of the original translations did not say "And forgive us our trespasses as we forgive those who trespass against us." Those words were originally translated as "And forgive us our sins as we forgive those who sin against us." Just why or where the word "trespass" was substituted for the word "sin" is unknown. Sinning is much more consequential than trespassing.

So also translating the phrase "And deliver us from evil." Other ancient translations render it "And deliver us from the time of trial"; still others render it "deliver us from the time of testing". That being so, I want to pay some attention here to the time of trial or testing Jesus endured out in the desert when Satan, our Ancient Enemy, put Jesus to test with those three great temptations we just heard about in today's gospel account. Satan was taking the measure of Christ's inner convictions and character.

God came to Moses on top of Mt. Sinai. Christ, our Saviour, taught His Beatitudes from the top of a mountain. Later, He was transfigured on top of Mt. Tabor. In his arrogance, Satan leads Jesus to the top of a high mountain, shows Him all of the kingdoms of this world and then takes the measure of Him, tempting Him to be a Messiah other than what God our Father sent Him to be for us.

We should note that it was not God our Father, who was testing Jesus. No, it was Lucifer. Why would God the Father want to "test" His Only-begotten Son? He knew all along what was in His Son's heart and soul. The Devil, of course, did not.

We see that Satan claimed that the world and all that's in it belonged to him and is in his power. "I will give them to you," he haughtily informs our Blessed Lord, "if you worship me and acknowledge my power." Satan was setting himself up as God's equal. This echoes the serpent's original seductive temptation offered to Adam and Eve, "Eat of this fruit, and you will be as God!"

In His complete freedom, God could certainly "test" us. Lots of people think of God that way. Many times, when we face trials, troubles, and suffering, we immediately tell ourselves that "God is testing me," or we tell others in their misfortune that "God is testing you." While we may think that way, it's usually a quick and superficial response that short-circuits a more insightful awareness.

Many trials and troubles beset us, not only throughout our lifetimes but daily. What or who causes these trials? Every day, people "test our limits." How often is your patience tested? And who is testing the boundaries of your patience and your love? You find yourself tested, tempted to anger and wrath, by members of your own family in your own home. Your children test your limits. Your loyalty and patience are tried and tested in your place of work. We easily see that while events and chance occurrences may test you and me, there is no greater testing than that which comes to us from other people. In all of these, we should not forget that the measure of love is to love without measure.

Many such moments of trial and testing come to each one of us every day, which is why Jesus teaches us to pray for our daily bread, to ask God our Father for that heavenly sustenance that gives strength to our souls as we face the trials and challenges of each day in our lives.

Good people face suffering from others and are tested by others. In all such moments, we are given opportunities, opportunities that are gifts hidden within those trials. The highest and best opportunity in every such trial is to enter into the heart of Jesus. St. Paul, in his Epistle to the Hebrews, wrote of Christ, "…because He was tested through what He suffered, He can help those who are being tested."

The Lord's Prayer is composed in the plural, not in the singular. It addresses our Father. It asks God to give us our daily bread. In all of this, we need to realise that we are also collectively tested, tried, and tempted. We are tested as a nation of people.

Both individually and collectively, our character and our limits are being tested. Our resources, our civil liberties, our commitments to freedom, our adherence to the rule of law, and our faith in God are all being tested and put on trial. Do we respond to evil in the way that Jesus responded to Satan? Upon what are our responses based? Satan offered

Jesus a spectacular, superficial, and dazzling way of life, one that did not require faith. In response, Jesus turned to His Father in heaven. You and I should do no less.

Satan is also known as the Great Seducer, the one who seeks to remain in power and control by capitalising on our human weakness. He hides his real agenda, his lust for power over us by lurking and hiding behind our human weakness. "Oh, everybody's doing it, so I can do it" is the sentiment that Satan whispers deep within us. But, we should ask ourselves, what is right no matter how many people don't care about what is right? The kingdom, the power and the glory belong to God. Jesus knew that and remained faithful to that. In Christ's humility, Satan's pride was overcome. In taking the measure of Christ, Satan was exposed for who and what he is. Trials take the measure of our faith.

Christ is very aware of what's running deep within the human heart. He knows how readily we can be swayed and how powerfully the "easy way" tempts us. When, therefore, we are beset by trials and sufferings, when we are tempted to try anyway but God's way, we need to stay focused and to turn to our Higher Power and rely on the powerful love of God.

May this holy season of Lent be an opportunity for you and me to take stock of what's in our souls, to see what we're really made of, to get in touch once again with God's powerful Holy Spirit who abides within us, and then face life with all of its trials, temptations and tests, nourished as we are by the Living Bread God puts here on our table each and every day.

"Deliver us from evil," O Lord. And most of all, deliver us from ourselves, for we do not belong to this world, or to the Great Seducer who roams through this world, or even to ourselves. We are Christ's, and Christ's is yours, O Father in Heaven.

These are times that try men's souls. During this Lent, let you and I see what we're made of.

# THEME 48
# DO NOT BE AFRAID

*Genesis 12:1-4; 2 Timothy 1:8-10; Matthew 17:1-9*

When I was a child, I lived in my own "Garden of Paradise." Everything I wanted or needed was given to me by my parents. I am sure each one of you here knows the feeling – the security and protection of a home, the unquestioned love of our parents, the freedom from want, and so forth. It is something most of us have experienced as little children.

But then came the time, and we've all shared it when we have experienced life outside of our home, our "Garden of Eden," when we knew fear and even came to know evil for the first time. The story of Adam and Eve in Paradise and they are leaving it, the story we heard last week in the Old Testament reading for the First Sunday of Lent, has been recapitulated in our own lives.

Let me share with you here some of the fears we probably experienced:

- The day mom or dad dropped us off at school for the first time.
- The day another child did something or said something mean and hurtful to us, perhaps when we were laughed at or ridiculed.
- The time when we were caught doing something naughty, or caught telling a lie, or caught doing something else that was sinful.
- The moment when we made our first confession of sins.
- The time we first watched our mother or father weeping over the death of someone in our family, perhaps when a grandparent died.

- Our teenage fear of not being chosen, not being liked, or not being popular.
- Our fears when facing exams.

We all have memories of our first fears or our first encounters with the fact that life is not fair.

Let me suggest to you today that life upon leaving our Gardens of Paradise is a journey. It's not a flight from bad things. They are inevitable. Life is more appropriately a journey toward good things, ultimately a journey toward God. Your life should be seen like that, and so should mine. Our spiritual lives, indeed, the spiritual life of all God's people, are like that. The life of Jesus was a journey beginning in His forty days in the desert and ending in Jerusalem --- His journey through rejection and abandonment to the Cross, and from thence to the Resurrection, Ascension and Pentecost.

Last week Holy Mother Church put in front of us those magnificent readings dealing with Adam and Eve in the Garden at the beginning of human history, and Jesus Christ in the desert at the beginning of His public ministry. This week Holy Mother Church puts in front of us the journey of Abraham, the Father of all believers, who is another beginning of God's work after Adam's fall. And she likewise puts in front of us Christ on top of Mount Tabor, a mountain that reminds us of Mt. Sinai. Godlike, Christ is bathed in incandescent light, transfigured in glory as He is about to begin His final journey to Jerusalem and His passion and death.

The response God expected from Abraham is the response God expects from us all, namely trust, a fulsome trust that encompasses faith, hope, obedience, and love of God as our caring and provident Father. God's call to Abraham and Abraham's response signals a reversal of our human rejection of God's ways. Where Adam and Eve said "No" in disobedience, and out of fear that they might be missing out on something that life might offer them, Abraham said "Yes" to God in a tremendous act of obedience and trust, the very opposite of fear. In their grief over not having a child, Abraham and Sarah find they are, in the sterility of their old age, going to have a child. And not only one child, but descendants without measure that will be born out of their faith and trust in God's love for them.

Because they cast aside their fears, along with the doubts that are born of fear, God's blessing is poured out not only on them but on the whole universe. A world caught up in the sterility of sin becomes fecund and pregnant, fruitful in the light and life of love, God's love.

We, each one of us, are not unacquainted with fear. We fear what might happen to our children. We fear the possibility of divorce or AIDS. We fear that our company may downsize and cast us off in the process. We fear that our lives may not be of any significance to anyone in particular and that our time here on earth will go unnoticed and unheeded because we are not needed for anything at all. Many fears beset us.

We have all been driven out of our own personal Gardens of Paradise, and consequently, we are all acquainted with fear. Into all of who we are and what we are God utters His unambiguous command: FEAR NOT! "Do not be afraid" is the constant and specific message of Jesus to each one of us. Do not be afraid, for underneath all that your humanity may cover and hide there is an incandescent lightness of being, an immortal soul that shines within us like sparkling crystal in the Light of the world. We should not hide our light under a bushel or basket of fear, timidity, or embarrassment. We should let it shine before others so that they might see the glory of God.

Our mission, then, is to peel away all that disfigures and disguises who we really are and what we are really made to be. Our mission is to discover, to uncover, and to reveal the transcendent selves within us that God made us to be. Our goal is to transfigure not only ourselves but to transfigure all of humanity and reveal, in the bright luminous cloud of

God's love, that of which human beings are made. In other words, in a surrounding culture that seeks to deny that men and women have souls, our task is to reveal and then set loose into our world the bright, shining souls of the "cloud of witnesses" who give testimony to the Christ of God, to God's anointed one, who reveals to each and all just what it means to be human.

"Fear not," God says to you as He says to me. "Be not afraid, for I am with you." And in Christ, He is not only with us, but He is also within us. His body has become one with ours. His Blood mingles with ours. He is with us no matter what, even when we are abandoned, even when we are in our own Gardens of Gethsemane.

# THEME 49
# THE WATER OF LIFE

*Exodus 17:3-7; Romans 5:1-2, 5-8; John 4:5-42*

Among us at today's liturgy are those about to be baptised or confirmed and become Catholics, those we now know as the Elect. They are undergoing their final scrutinies and so are taking a good look at what they are doing and why they are making this journey into the Catholic Church. Every year at this event, we listen to this gospel passage.

It's interesting to note that while these Elect are experiencing special scrutiny, and putting their faith under scrutiny, the account in this gospel presents Jesus being put under scrutiny by the Samaritan woman.

On the surface, the story appears to be a typical man meets woman story. A man, the hero -- a shepherd, a teacher and an extraordinary leader --- arrives at a famous well and meets a woman who has come to fetch water. The caring hand of a woman and the helping hand of a man are repeatedly found in bible accounts, particularly in those dealing with Jesus.

This particular account recalls the story of Abraham, who was in search of a woman for his son Isaac. His most trusted servant, whom he sent out to search for a wife for his son Isaac arrives at a well where he knew that the local girls would come to draw water in the evening. He prayed to God, saying: "God of Abraham, here I stand at this well, where the women will come to fetch water. God of Abraham, I will ask those women to give me a drink, and the one who cares, she will be the one." Rebecca responds to his request for a drink, and Abraham's servant immediately brings out golden earrings along with golden rings, and the marriage of Abraham's son is thereupon arranged.

Also, there is the biblical story of Jacob meeting Rachel at this very same well, which was at that time covered with a tremendously heavy stone lid. When Jacob's eyes fall upon Rachel, he becomes filled with such manly strength that he is transformed into a power-filled champion who then all by himself lifts the enormous stone lid off of the well.

In the gospel account we just read, the well is the same well. This time, however, the man is Jesus. The woman is a non-Jew foreigner, one who is "unclean" according to Jewish ritual laws.

Jesus shocks everyone by deliberately speaking to her. Rabbis, we recall, did not converse with women in public. Not only was she a woman, but she was also an outcast. Not only was she an outcast, but she had been sleeping around with at least five men. And not only did the dialogue just reported take place between them, but Jesus took her cup and put it to his lips, thereby making her "uncleanness" His own. This encounter blasted all Jewish customs, laws, and religious barriers to smithereens. Also notice that it was the Samaritan woman who was scrutinising Jesus. THAT should excite our attention.

At first, she recognises Him as a Jew. "You are a Jew," she declares. "How can you ask me, a Samaritan and a woman, for a drink?" Jesus responds by asking her to see more than mere appearances, to recognise more than their ethnic and gender differences. "If only you recognised God's gift...," He tells her, suggesting that she could receive living water.

For the people in that region of the world, "living water" was flowing water, not well water. So the Samaritan woman asks Jesus where He expects to get some flowing water. "Besides," she says, "Just who do you think you are? Surely you don't pretend to be greater than Jacob?"

In response, Jesus ups the ante by speaking about water that, if received, will end all thirst, and at the same time, will give eternal life in place of the kind of life we're now living. Additionally, Jesus discloses just what kind of a life she's living by pointing out that she's been sleeping around.

The conversion of the Samaritan woman was instantaneous. She leaves her cup and her water jar on the spot, presumably for Him to drink from, and goes off to evangelise the inhabitants of her village. Does one wonder if Christ drank from that cup? If He did, did He see in it the eventual Cup of Suffering from which He would drink – His passion and death?

At the beginning of this account, Our Blessed Lord arrived at Jacob's well thirsty and the Samaritan woman gave Christ that which He was seeking. Later on, as He hung upon the Cross, we will hear Christ cry out: "I thirst!" Who, we must ask ourselves, has satisfied His thirst?

All of this leads me to point out to you, my friends, that here before us we have those seeking union with us at Easter, those thirsting for the love of God which we will share with them in Holy Communion at Easter. They are being scrutinised, and they are scrutinising their faith. More importantly, they are the Samaritan woman at Jacob's well, scrutinising Christ, the Bridegroom that is God searching for an everlasting marriage with us, His beloved Bride.

In all of these scrutinises, do you recognise your thirst? Do you see just who it is that is here seeking you, and what it is that He offers you? For, you see, you and I, as well as these catechumens and candidates, are the Samaritan woman whom Christ, in His tender mercies, loves so much.

It is we who should be scrutinising our faith. What will God see in us? Will we satisfy His thirst? Only you can answer that question.

# THEME 50
# THE POWER OF THE EYES

*1 Samuel 16:1b, 6-7, 10-13a; Ephesians 5:8-24; John 9:1-41*

Consider with me now the power of the human eye. It is through the eye that we receive most of our impressions and most of the data assimilated by the brain. It is through the eye that much of our non-verbal communication is received. Even within our intellect, our capacity for "insight" is connected deeply with the ability to see and understand with our physical eyes.

Watch the eyes of those who speak with you. Do their eyes look steadily and peacefully into your eyes? You can read much about a person's soul by merely looking into their eyes. When you are engaged in a conversation, the eyes of others can tell you a lot. Do they look directly into yours, or do their eyes flit around the room, looking over your shoulders while searching out other people in the room, roving and cruising while the person with whom you are conversing is talking at you rather than with you?

Our eyes can see others, and be friendly with others, or they can hurt others, or look scornfully down on others, or can scare others. Our eyes can be used to lust after others or to only see others on the surface. Our eyes have the power to penetrate deep into the hearts and souls of others. Our eyes are powerful. God has given us a tremendous power --- the power to see with our eyes and the power to communicate with them.

The sad truth is that we can see everything and yet be blind. We can devour with our eyes, and we can take in the whole heart of another and yet remain empty. We can consume so much and yet remain hungry and empty with our hearts aching for more. Our rapacious self has eyes that are agitated continuously in a hungry search for acquisition, yet the more we devour, the emptier we get, and ever more blind.

God gave us incredible power when He gave us sight. We should use it to its depth and not settle for mere surface examinations. We can use our sight simply to measure and describe the properties of things. We can use our sight like scientists and describe and delineate the boundaries and the physical properties of things and make mathematical predictions about their relational behaviour in our universe. God, however, wants us to see at deeper levels.

When a scientist sees things, or a businessman, or any practical person for that matter --- he sees things so that it doesn't matter who sees them. As a matter of fact, he sees them best when he sees them in the way any man or woman can see them.

We should, however, see things spiritually, as a theologian sees them. For us, it makes a difference to know who is seeking and the purpose of having a vision in the first place. It is the reason for the existence of things, not just their description that is in the vision of a theologian. It is in the meaning of a thing that its value is discerned, not just its usefulness. If our vision is arrested only at the level of usefulness, then persons can be substituted for things. Then we will be living in the blindness of the Pharisees we heard about in today's gospel account.

God did not create us to be blind; He created us to have sight, the higher sight called insight -- that sort of sight that flows from imagination and vision. These faculties are conditioned as they are by data received from our eyes that allow us to see the inner world that is God's world and have eyes to see God's kingdom. To see that, however, we must have eyes that are released from fixation solely on the outer world, a world that is only immediately visible.

Contemplation is a deeper way of seeing things in their reality. Contemplating a great mountain range fills our souls with wonder.

Contemplating the dawn of a new day while watching the sunrise fills our souls with anticipation and hope. Admiring a beautiful picture, spending time drinking it in, fills our souls with beauty. Seeing is something far more profound than merely looking. Seeing, really seeing, takes us into the spiritual world and allows us to wonder, question, and ask the question: Why did God give us what we are looking at?

We need to see with more than just our physical eyesight – we need to see with the eyes of our soul. This allows us to see things in God's Light and to acquire more wisdom and understanding, realities that are far deeper than just facts, information, and data. When we do, we are in-spirited, inspired, and the Holy Spirit gives us His gifts.

When, therefore, we pray, we should pray as the blind man prayed. When we pray, the first words of our prayer ought to be, "Lord, that I may see." For it is upon our vision that everything depends. Our faith depends upon our vision. Our hope depends upon the vision contained in the word "expectation." "Expectation" and "spectacle" are words rooted in the same concept. Hope is directly related to vision and expectations. And so is the virtue of charity, love. Thus we walk by faith, not by sight. Our hearts can see what our eyes cannot see.

God gave us the vision to describe others, see their surface and bodily characteristics, and see who they are and see their meaning and purpose in being whom and what they are. The Pharisees were the men who in today's gospel account were blind. The man born blind had much more vision and could see the reality of Christ, even though his eyes were not sighted. Can we have the vision and insight of the man born blind? We ought to consider just what it is that we see, both see with our eyes and see with eyes of faith, see with insight.

On the day we die we shall take with us into the next life the total of the impressions, the decisions, and the insight that we have acquired in this life. We shall be, for all eternity, what we have seen ourselves to be. We shall be all that we have chosen to be, hopefully, chosen in the vision of faith, in real hope, and in real love. It all hangs in the crucial balance of our vision. It is the soul that is seeing that thus becomes all-important, even more important than what our physical eyes have seen.

"Lord Jesus, that I may see!" should be the opening words in all of our prayers so that we might see ourselves and the world that God has made for us, the self and the world that God created for you in His vision of what we and our world can be. For in the life that is to come, our gift to God will be the self we bring with us when we die, a self that will in large measure be the total of the insights and vision that we have acquired. And if we have seen the gifts God has given us in this life, then in the next life, in eternal life, we shall see the Giver of those gifts.

*LORD THAT I MAY SEE!*

# THEME 51
# JESUS WEPT

*Ezekiel 37:12-14; Roman 8:8-11; John 11:1-45*

The football game is over, and the sportscaster is interviewing the coach of the winning team. They talk knowledgeably about the players and critical plays, and then the sportscaster asks the coach the big question: "What was the turning point in the game?"

Two friends are sharing a whole lot about their lives. The conversation is warm and deep. One of them had just learned the heartbreaking news that his wife was going to divorce him. There were tears as the entire saga of the marriage was reviewed, and then his friend asked; "What was the critical moment, the beginning of the end?"

Or it could be that a retired general is being interviewed on television about a war in which he was involved. The planning, the execution, and the lost and won battles were discussed, along with the personalities of the critical officers and men involved. Finally, the interview focuses on the hinge point, the defining moment, when victory was assured.

In the four gospels of Matthew, Mark, Luke and John, the centrepiece in each one of them is the passion and death of Jesus Christ. All aspects of the four gospels point to that one defining event, not only in our lives but also in the world's history. The defining event for them all is the final week of Christ's life.

For the three Sundays leading up to Palm Sunday, the Church presents us with gospel accounts taken from St. John's gospel. St. John's gospel is not arranged according to chronological events but rather according to themes. From all of the miracles performed by Jesus, John selected seven. He presents them as the Seven Great Signs, signs that are miracles revealing Christ as the divine Son of God, God's Word made flesh, signs revealing God's divinity made present to us in the humanity of Jesus Christ. The Seven Signs are the wedding feast at Cana where Jesus turns water into wine. He can change one substance into another. The healing of the nobleman's son is next, where, in response to faith, Jesus can give life to someone who has died. The healing of the paralysed man then follows. Jesus can restore full life to those who are spiritually paralysed. Next is the feeding of the five thousand, revealing that God's caring and nurturing love is limitless. That miracle is followed by Jesus walking on water, revealing that nothing can keep Our Blessed Lord from those who are in peril and in great need. The healing of the man born blind confounds the Pharisees and those who are spiritually blind while at the same time Jesus gives light and sight to those who, in faith, want to see, who want to see our world in God's Light. The last is the raising of Lazarus from the dead, a powerful miracle that reveals the power of God in a way that none can deny.

That was the critical moment in Christ's life, the tipping point that brought about the inevitable conclusion. As you recall, in Christ's life, there was a gradual build-up of resentment, fear, hatred, and rejection of Jesus Christ. Many events culminated in this one great miracle, the raising of Lazarus from the dead.

The political and religious leadership were now totally threatened. This miracle could not be ignored. Christ's popularity with the crowds was now so great that the leaders faced the complete loss of their privileged positions and power.

It needs to be pointed out that it was not the Jewish people who were threatened by Jesus and wanted to put Him to death. No, the Roman and Jewish authorities were the people holding power and privilege who wanted to do away with Him. After all, we must remember that the first Christians were, for the most part, Jews. St. Luke was Greek. He was not one of the twelve apostles, and they were all Jews. So, too, were

Mary and Joseph. It is a great injustice to claim that the Jewish people were responsible for Our Blessed Lord's crucifixion and death.

We all know full well that people on top of our political and economic systems will commit great evil to protect their power. Some use their privileged positions to commit terrible acts of abuse. The headlines of our newspapers are filled with more than enough examples of that. History and many other events in human history, point to what the human heart is capable of doing in terms of evil. This is particularly true with dictators.

The Old Testament provides many examples of God's holy prophets being rejected and put to death. The fact that they were holy people did not guarantee them safety or protection. They performed miracles, astonishing miracles that could only come about by the power of God, and yet these prophets were put out of the way by influential people who were threatened by them.

So here in today's gospel account, we find the Jews clamouring for Jesus, seeking Him out, and coming to the realisation that His teachings were far more authoritative than the Pharisees, the Sadducees, and the members of the Jewish elite. When Jesus raised Lazarus from the dead, His popularity ratings soared through the roof. From the perspective of those in power and control of the people, something had to be done, and it had to be done NOW!

So they made the critical decision -- they had to kill Jesus of Nazareth. This, of course, was something Jesus knew would happen. He had seen it coming for quite some time. He knew that by bringing Lazarus out of the tomb, He would be entering a tomb. Yes, someone has to die that others may live.

The shortest passage in the New Testament is one you just read. *Jesus wept.* It is also one of the most profound. Well, why did He weep? Obviously, it was not for Lazarus, for Jesus knew the happiness Lazarus and his family were about to receive. Were not those tears the tears of one who knows He has been rejected? The agony in the Garden of Gethsemane begins here. We find Jesus on the Mt. of Olives weeping. Lazarus was buried in a new tomb, Jesus is about to be buried in a new tomb. Both had great stones rolled in front of their entrances. Both bodies were wrapped in linens. How can we miss the parallels?

Jesus knew He was to see the tomb from the inside. The Lazarus event reported here was an event lasting three days. It foreshadowed Christ's own three days in the tomb. Now we see that the raising of Lazarus was the most critical event in Christ's entire ministry. It was the defining moment, the turning point, the beginning of the end.

"Unbind him and let him go free" was Christ's command to the onlookers. Freedom, our freedom, our freedom to do good, to freely choose to do beautiful things for God, is the reason for it all. Christ emptied Lazarus' tomb so He could change places with him. Divinity took on our humanity so that our humanity could take on his divinity. Because of Christ, we are no longer entombed in sin. We are freed of Satan's grip and are no longer destined to end up in hell. Because of Jesus Christ, we are able now, as St. Paul declares, to "walk in the glorious freedom of the children of God."

Because of God's grace, we are Lazarus.

# THEME 52
# THE WORKING OF THE HOLY SPIRIT

*Acts 2:42-47; 1 Peter 1:3-9; John 20, 19-31*

At the Last Supper, shortly before He suffered and died on the Cross, Jesus gave us the stupendous gift of His Body and Blood, now really and truly present to us in the Eucharist. He gave us this gift at the very core of His redemptive sacrifice for us. Then, when He rose from the dead, His very first act was when He breathed out the Holy Spirit upon His apostles and into His Church. *"Peace be with you,"* He said to them. *"As the Father has sent me, so I send you."* And when He had said this, He breathed on them and said to them: *"Receive the Holy Spirit."* What does that mean for us?

Our Church leads us now into what we might call "The time of the handing over of the Spirit." To examine the significance of that time let us return to God's first breathing forth His Holy Spirit, that life-giving creative act of God that we find in the first verses in the Bible, in the Book of Genesis. There we find God's Spirit "brooding over the waters" bringing light out of darkness, order out of chaos, and life to all of God's creatures. God's Holy Spirit brought about creation. "Veni Creator Spiritus" we sing in the words of that famous hymn we all know.

In the fullness of time, Christ Jesus was conceived in the womb of the Virgin "by the power of the Holy Spirit." When Jesus was baptised by John the Baptist in the Jordan River the Holy Spirit, like a dove, descended upon Jesus, signifying that Jesus of Nazareth was the Christ, the Anointed One, the One anointed by God's Holy Spirit. At the beginning of His public ministry, He was led out into the desert by the Spirit, tempted by and to defeat the Devil. When He died on the Cross

St. John tells us that Christ handed over His Spirit. Each one of us is now destined to be a temple of God's Holy Spirit.

It can be fairly said that the reason why Jesus was born among us and the reason why He died on the Cross was to give us God's Holy Spirit, God's holy presence, a presence that was lost when Adam and Eve separated themselves from God in the Garden of Eden. In going to His apostles immediately after He rose from the dead, Christ Jesus was restoring God's presence to us once again, God's personal, life-giving, and loving presence ---God's special presence given to us now as His forgiven prodigal children. What was lost in the Garden of Eden is now restored in the Garden of the Resurrection.

What are the elements within that presence? What is the nature of that presence? Well, certainly, it is not a passive presence. On the contrary, it is a dynamic, creating, moving, and energising presence. Above all, it is a sanctifying presence – we are made whole again, made whole with God. We are once again made holy, holier even than Adam and Eve, holier because, through Christ, God's Holy Spirit is not simply present next to us or around us but lives now *within* us.

Who among us has never asked for a second chance? Who among us has never said: "Give me a break, give me another chance?" Who has never asked God for another chance? That is what the Sacrament of Reconciliation is all about. That is why God in Christ has given us a chance at starting over again, a chance given to us when God restores us into the innocence we had when we were baptised.

Theologians tell us that Jesus Christ was sent to us with the ministry of reconciliation. God comes to us again, this time not in the Garden of Eden but in the Garden of the Resurrection. Risen from the dead, God the Son goes to His apostles and confers upon us the power to start over again. Moments ago in the gospel account, we heard:

> "The disciples rejoiced when they saw the Lord. Jesus said to
> them again, "Peace be with you. As the Father has sent me, so I

send you." And when He had said this, He breathed on them and said to them, "Receive the Holy Spirit. Whose sins you forgive are forgiven of them..."

In his Second Letter to the Corinthians, Paul tells us: *So whoever is in Christ is a new creation: the old things have passed away; behold, new things have come. And all this is from God, who has reconciled us to Himself through Christ and given us the ministry of reconciliation, namely, God was reconciling the world to himself in Christ, not counting their trespasses against them and entrusting to us the message of reconciliation.* (2Cor 5:17-19)

The passion, death, and resurrection of Jesus Christ give us the account of God starting all over again, putting the Garden of Eden behind us and giving us a second chance and new life in the Garden of the Resurrection.

All of this is accomplished because God sent His only begotten Son to us in Christ Jesus to give us His life-giving and creating Holy Spirit, fashioning us as a new creation, making us over anew, answering all of our prayers for another chance.

The time of the handing over of the Spirit culminates in Pentecost. Dying on the Cross, Jesus "handed over His Spirit," St. John tells us. The first act of Jesus after He rose from the dead was to give His Spirit to His apostles. At Pentecost, they were confirmed in the power and strength of the Holy Spirit so they might put their fears behind them and go out into the world, into our world, and share God's recreating, life-giving, reconciling, forgiving, and healing Holy Spirit with you and with me.

It is sometimes said that one religion is as good as another, that it doesn't matter what religion one belongs to. I think it does matter. It matters because I don't find what Jesus did for us -- giving us the power of forgiveness -- present in any other religion. The handing over of the Spirit is for the forgiveness of our sins. It restores us to God's life again.

It is found uniquely in our wonderful Sacrament of Reconciliation. That matters, that really matters. In what other religion can you find that?

One final note. Since God has been so infinitely generous in giving us this gift, a gift that comes to us through the terrible suffering and death of His Christ, ought we not to be generous in sharing our forgiveness with those around us who have sinned against us?

If we feel we don't have the strength and power to do so, we should remember that God has given us the strength and power to forgive. For the gift we have been given is not ours to keep, it is a gift God has given to us so that we might share it with others. We have the power of the Holy Spirit within us to do so. May we offer the world around us the hope and the joy that, because of Jesus Christ, is found in the power to forgive. It is one of the greatest and most necessary gifts we have to share with all those in our world around us.

# THEME 53
# THE POWER OF HIS WORD

*Acts 2:14, 22-33; 1 Peter 1:17-21; Luke 24:13-35*

Last Sunday's gospel account was about the disciples who were huddled in the Upper Room behind locked doors out of fear, and Jesus' appearance among them. Today's gospel account is about another appearance of Jesus, this time with other disciples, dejectedly and walking from Jerusalem to a nearby hamlet called Emmaus.

St. Augustine, along with other Fathers of the Church, suggests that Jesus did not want His disciples to recognise Him right away, that He wanted them to recognise Him in "the breaking of the bread." Moreover, they believed that Jesus wanted the disciples to see and understand what the Jewish prophets had foretold in scripture about how the Messiah was to be recognised. Hence Jesus spent some significant time opening up the scriptures so they might see them in a new light, His light, and then recognise Him.

We can easily overlook the importance Jesus placed on scripture. He repeatedly spoke of it and quoted from it. We should recall that He was discussing it with the Jewish teachers and leaders when Joseph and Mary found Him as a boy in the Temple. Again and again, He taught that He did not want to do away with the Jewish scriptures but rather wanted to fulfil all that was found in the prophets' teachings.

In today's gospel account, we find Jesus again fulfilling what was written in the Old Testament about the Messiah. It must have been quite enlightening because, at the end of today's episode, we hear the disciples exclaim: "Were not our hearts burning within us while He spoke to us on the way and opened the scriptures to us?" [Luke 24:32]

As an aside, I want to point out here that the Catholic Church is often accused of not relying on scripture. Catholics are told that their Church doesn't feed them and nourish them with the Bible. However, we should note, that every celebration of the Mass is divided into two principal parts, the Liturgy of the Word and the Liturgy of the Eucharist. The Liturgy of the Word always begins with a passage from the Old Testament, followed by a reading from one of the Epistles and then a gospel reading. How can it be said that the Catholic Church doesn't nourish you with God's Word from Scripture? Note, too, that there is always a thematic connection, a connection of ideas, between the Old Testament reading and the gospel reading.

To me, the thing that is the most important point in today's account revolves around how the disciples came to recognise Jesus. We find this group of disciples at first failing to recognise Jesus and then, in the end, coming to recognise Him. What happened? Why did they at first think He was a stranger and later come to realise who He was?

You and I have had the experience of hearing what someone is telling us but not really listening to what they are saying. Similarly, we have had the experience of seeing someone, looking at them, but not recognising them for who they are. This can be due to our own inattentiveness, or it can be because the one we are looking at doesn't want to be recognised in the way we expect.

What we're talking about here is God's way of revealing Himself to us. This is not merely a matter of blindness vs sight; it's about revelation and understanding.

You and I are much like those disciples on the road to Emmaus talking as they were about all of the terrible events they had experienced during the previous days in Jerusalem, about the betrayal of Judas, the hatred the religious authorities held against Jesus, and perhaps even about Pilate's question: "Truth? What is the truth?"

As needed, we need to pay attention to whether we are hearing what people tell us vs really listening to what they are saying. Additionally, we need to ask whether we see those around us without recognising who they are.

We are much like those disciples walking along on the road to Emmaus, concerned over the events in our lives. What brought them to recognise Jesus was "the breaking of the bread." Their minds were immediately taken back to the Upper Room and the Last Supper, connecting that with the broken and bloody body of Jesus hanging on His cross.

Can we learn to recognise Jesus in human brokenness? That's the key; that's what opens our eyes to His presence among us. When we encounter people with broken hearts, Jesus is there. When we try to offer comfort to someone with a broken spirit, Jesus is there. When we encounter someone who is experiencing loss, pain, and suffering, Jesus is there. Isn't that what Jesus was telling us when He taught us about the judgment we will receive when we die? He will ask us if we recognised Him in human brokenness: "For I was hungry, and you gave me food, I was thirsty, and you gave me a drink, a stranger, and you welcomed me, naked, and you clothed me, ill, and you cared for me, in prison, and you visited me." (Matthew 25:35-36)

The mystery of Christ's suffering, death, and resurrection isn't something that simply took place long ago. No. It is on-going; it is going on in our days. True, we live in times when men and women have sinned, and our sins have obscured the face of Christ. At times He is not recognised in our world and at times, even when He is recognised there are many who seek to get rid of Him. Nailing Him to the cross is something that is still happening.

But it is there that He reveals Himself. It is in suffering and broken humanity that He is present. It is there that He is to be revered. And it is from there that we receive the promise of Easter – resurrection and new life.

We are walking our own roads through life. Can we --- will we --- like the disciples, recognise that Jesus is walking with us? Will we recognise Him in "the breaking of the bread"?

# THEME 54
# THE GOOD SHEPHERD

*Acts 2:14, 36-41; 1 Peter 2:20-25; John 10:1-10*

Back in Jesus' time, everyone knew about shepherds, their sheep, and how they interacted with each other. The dynamics between them were well known. Not so today. Few of us have watched shepherds tending their sheep. So to understand the full impact of the imagery that Jesus used, we need to take a look at a few points.

During nights back then, shepherds kept their sheep in sheepfolds that were large circles of stones that both penned in the sheep while at the same time protecting them from predatory animals such as wolves. There was a narrow opening to let the sheep in and out. At night the shepherd would spread his bedroll across the base of those openings and sleep there. A predatory animal could enter the sheepfold only by crossing over the body of the shepherd and so, of course, they would not.

Additionally, there were times when the sheep belonging to differing shepherds would get mixed in with each other. But that didn't pose much of a problem because the sheep of each shepherd recognised their own shepherd's voice and would follow only him. No need for painting coloured dyes on the sheep --- voice recognition was enough.

Shepherds knew of verdant grazing fields, and so they would walk ahead of their sheep and lead them to pastures where the sheep would find good food. However, in the movement, sometimes a sheep or two would go off on their own and become lost. Being out on their own they would be easy kills for wolves and other predatory animals. So long as they stayed in the flock, however, they were safe. So the shepherd would leave the flock for a while and go in search of the sheep that strayed and were lost.

Now let me repeat the teaching Jesus was giving to His disciples. Jesus said:

"Amen, amen, I say to you, whoever does not enter a sheepfold through the gate but climbs over elsewhere is a thief and a robber. But whoever enters through the gate is the shepherd of the sheep. The gatekeeper opens it for him, and the sheep hear his voice, as the shepherd calls his own sheep by name and leads them out. When he has driven out all his own, he walks ahead of them, and the sheep follow him because they recognise his voice. But they will not follow a stranger; they will run away from him because they do not recognise the voice of strangers." Although Jesus used this figure of speech, the Pharisees did not realise what He was telling them. So Jesus said again, "Amen, amen, I say to you, I am the gate for the sheep. All who came before me are thieves and robbers, but the sheep did not listen to them. I am the gate. Whoever enters through me will be saved, and will come in and go out and find pasture. A thief comes only to steal and slaughter and destroy; I came so that they might have life and have it more abundantly."

We should ask ourselves: "Whose voice am I following?" Some of us listen to only our own inner voice. Nobody, we tell ourselves, can tell me what to do or what to believe. Others of us listen to the seductive whispers of the world. Still, others pay little attention to any call other than their urges, drives, or desires. We all know that many voices call us, and we need to be aware of them, where they are coming from, and where they will lead us.

Today I want to give some attention to how we can discern and listen to the voice of our Good Shepherd. How does God speak to us?

First of all, you need to expect that God can reach you. Many don't. But how can God communicate with you if you don't think He can? Nevertheless, He is trying to!

Think of the good things that have come to you, the good things that you have experienced. Aren't they from God? On the opposite side, if you have experienced remorse, have you ever considered that it may be God whose voice is reaching you in your remorse? Conscience, after all, literally means "to know with." Remorse knows that you have done something that displeases God and that He is telling you that you can do better. Can God not inspire the voice of penance and regret deep within us?

Prayer is essential. Prayer places your soul at the disposal of God. Prayer can bring us to be reflective, to contemplate, to see and hear the actions and whisperings of the Holy Spirit in our lives. When we are reflective, we gain insights – we see things, and we see people as God wants us to see them. Is that not God calling us, God speaking to us?

The Holy Spirit is quite capable of inspiring our imaginations and inner thoughts. If we don't accept the Holy Spirit's power and ability to inspire our inner thoughts and dispositions, then we are saying that God cannot or will not reach us. In our silent attentiveness, the gentle whisperings of the Holy Spirit can be heard deep within us.

God also speaks to us in the beauty and majesty of creation. Moments, when we are filled with awe and wonder over nature's beauty, are moments when God is speaking to us. We ought not to be deaf to what God is sharing with us.

Then there is an example of good people and their words, attitudes, and disposition. These, too, are ways in which God speaks to us.

Much depends upon your disposition toward God. Do you believe that God is angry with you, that He wants to inflict punishing pain and suffering upon you, or do you believe that God loves you, knows you can do better and wants to free you from guilt and lead you to do better, even extraordinary things? Your disposition controls what you hear and what you do not hear. Is God silent, or are you deaf to His voice?

To be sure, each one of us has been like wandering and lost sheep. If we're fixated on that and feel totally lost, then we will not see our Good Shepherd coming after us to carry us on His shoulders back into the fold from which we have wandered.

Do you think God cares for you? Do you think that God can reach you? If so, then you will understand what today's gospel is telling you. But understanding is only the beginning. What is necessary is for you to let God find you, tell you of His love for you, and then let Him carry you back to where you belong.

# THEME 55
# THE SIN IN SIN



*Acts 6:1-7; 1 Peter 2:4-9; John 14:1-12*

Many people believe that living the gospel message is unrealistic. Numerous times people have begun a conversation with me using the phrase: "Father, out there in the real world ..." Their unspoken assumption is, of course, that because I am a priest, I am somehow not in the real world.

History has given us several philosophers and thinkers who have told us that Jesus was a beautiful man, possessing tenderness of heart, infinite sweetness, and universal charm. In other words, they are saying that Jesus was an idealist who saw and lived life in an idealistic dream world, not as it really is. They like to talk about Jesus, admiring His ethical code and His moral standards while at the same time, they are locating Jesus out of this world, out of touch with reality.

I suspect there are some here in the church who are here just now for a few moments of relief to get out of this world and enter a dream world of sweetness, vague poetry, and universal charm, a place of refuge from the world that is cold, hard, greedy and overly competitive. But the truth is that we are here in order to enter into the world. The truth is that God has sent His Son into the world with the purpose and mission of transforming it and redeeming it from within it and that in Christ, God is sending us to do the same. How else do we understand the prayer: "Thy will be done on earth as it is in heaven?"

Just before He died, we heard Our Blessed Lord tell His disciples: "I am the way, and the truth and the life." This phrase was based on Christ's understanding that He is utterly a realist. For Him, religion wasn't a quiet side street, a sort of lovely garden or park in the middle of our metropolitan world. Oh, no! Christ was asserting that His way, His truth, and His understanding of life is the main road.

In fact, it is the only road in this world that's going anywhere. All other roads lead us into blind alleys and dead-ends. Christ's declaration was not vague poetry, a beautiful novelty to be applauded and admired from a distance. It was the real thing, the only kind of living that ultimately works and has a true destination, one beyond even death itself.

As a matter of fact, Jesus believed His way was the cornerstone for all living. A cornerstone, we must remember, locates the site upon which a building will be constructed. It orients the direction toward which the building will face. It sets the characteristics of all the other stones surrounding it, along with their texture and quality. All other stones are measured against the cornerstone. It is the essential stone that grounds the entire structure.

The worst thing about sin is not what it does to God, even though it put God's Christ, God's Anointed One, on the Cross and into the tomb. No, the worst thing about sin is what it does to the sinner. It brings pain, suffering and ruination to the sinner. Jesus told us a story about the young man who, in total prodigality, threw all restraint and responsibility to the winds, went out on his own willful way, and ended up in the pigpen of life. Jesus then gave us the only thing to do with sin: to face it, acknowledge its existence, see it for what it is, repent of it, and then accept healing forgiveness.

Anyone recovering from addiction, anyone who has found the only realistic way out of the hellish jail of compulsive addiction or alcoholism, will tell you about it only in the utter realism of recovery. There is no hope of recovery without realism, without ruthless and courageous honesty, without a total grasp of reality. Ask yourself this question: Are people living in successful recovery living in the real world or a dream world?

The twelve steps for recovery are all radically grounded on the way, the truth and the life of Jesus. So are the fourth and fifth steps, which require that we make a searching and fearless moral inventory of ourselves and then admit to God, to ourselves, and to another human being the exact nature of our wrongs. As a matter of fact, when you take a look at the fundamental process of psychiatric therapy, you will recognise right away the fact that the road to recovery involves the taking of responsibility for one's actions and then seeking a healthy resolution for what we've done. And where do we find that resolution? We find it in taking ownership of our decisions and in seeking forgiveness.

In this fragmented, hostile, and broken world of ours, a world filled with broken hearts, broken promises, broken trusts, and broken families, in this world that is more and more littered with damaged human hearts and souls, in a world with an ever-increasing culture of destruction and death, what is more realistic, to live as Hollywood TV producers depict us in their so-called "reality" shows, or to live in the family in which Jesus Christ invites us to share life?

When anyone declares to you that Jesus was an idealistic dreamer, a man of "infinite sweetness, vague poetry, and universal charm," when anyone talks to you about religion as if its purpose is only to mould us to live politely and to have good manners, then realise that such a person is only fooling you. He is himself "utterly unrealistic about life." God expects much more from us than that.

Jesus told it like it is: "I am the way, and the truth and the life; no one comes to the Father but through me." Living in truth and living in love makes demands on us, demands that require the courage of faith and the sacrifices of love.

# THEME 56
# THE POWER OF HUMAN WORDS

*Acts 8:5-8, 14-17; 1 Peter 3:15-18; John 14:15-21*

The readings of this Mass impel me to reflect with you upon two things which are interior within us, two things that are mysterious and can be known only in their expression. One is love, and the other is the Holy Spirit. Both cannot be really known in themselves; both are made real for us in their activity, in their expression, in their external manifestations that we bring into our lives in our responses to God's love for us.

As we all know so very well, talk is cheap, and words are without meaning unless expressed in deeds. Love is not simply a nice feeling, a sentiment, or merely a warm emotion. Love becomes real in the decisions we make and in what we do. It is in its actions, actions that result from our choices, that love is realised.

Don't get me wrong; the words of love are of extreme importance. There's nothing wrong with saying, "I love you." In fact, those three little words can be the most beautiful and powerful of all the words in a person's life. Husbands need to tell their wives that they love them, and wives need to tell their husbands that they love them. Children need to hear words of love from their moms and dads. But while the words are important, the deeds are even more important, even of the essence.

And for friends, too. Friends should not be ashamed to openly declare their love for one another. When you're told that you are loved, a redemptive force is let loose inside you --- a powerful force lifts you up out of feelings of depression, loneliness, and feelings of being unappreciated and used. More lives have likely been changed by those three little words than by all of the sermons ever preached.

Jesus did not discount the value of the verbal communication of love. He went beyond it. He knew that love is much more than mere words. In fact, He knew of love's power to change the whole world, telling us even to love our enemies, and that if we truly did, the world would be radically changed. And then Jesus went on to prove it in the way He died for us, in the way He died to redeem our world, to buy it back from this world's loveless miseries.

What a realist this Jesus is! We, however, are the ones who tend to make love unrealistic. We tend to make love into something soft, dreamy, and cheap, merely a feeling. If you think we don't, then just take a look at what television does with love, and how Hollywood treats it. On the other hand, Jesus defines love in terms that are strong, concrete, self-sacrificial, and very real. Love is action; love is a way of living; love is an attitude toward others that expresses God's attitude toward others. And then Jesus went on to cry out: "The one who hears my words and keeps them is the one who loves me." That's how we know that we live and have our being in love.

The Holy Spirit, the Third Person of the Holy Trinity, who is love personified, acts internally within each one of us. The Holy Spirit is present within our hearts and souls, animating, vivifying, and inspiring us. We can never see the Holy Spirit as separate and apart --- standing alone. The Holy Spirit lives and breathes within our souls. We see the Holy Spirit in our actions and in the actions of others.

The Bible assigns several different names to the Holy Spirit, identifying Him as the Consoler, the Advocate, the Sanctifier, and the Paraclete. As the Bible presents Him, the Holy Spirit protects and defends us against our Ancient Enemy. He is our Advocate, the One who stands with us, particularly when we feel worthless, useless, and of no value in God's eyes. His consolations strengthen us when we feel weak, inadequate, and powerless.

Love and the Holy Spirit --- both cannot be known in and of themselves. Both are made present to us, made real for us. Both are realised in acts, in deeds, in things that are done. Both animate and vivify us, filling us with their special life. Both are expressions of God. God makes Himself real for us, expresses Himself, and becomes present to us in both love and His Holy Spirit.

Jesus told it like it is: "I am the way, and the truth and the life; no one comes to the Father but through me." Living in truth and living in love makes demands on us, demands that require the courage of faith and the sacrifices of love.

And so as we approach the Ascension of our Lord and the great Solemnity of Pentecost, we should look to God with expectant faith while seeking for His great gift to us --- the sending of His Holy Spirit into us, that same Spirit who raised humanity of Jesus Christ from the dead and who can, if we respond to God, raise up ours also and the world around us.

# THEME 57
# TAKEN UP INTO HEAVEN

*Acts 1:1-11; Ephesians 1:17-23; Matthew 28:16-20*

God the Father inaugurated His presence among us when Abraham responded to Him in faith. The Nativity of Our Lord inaugurated God the Son's presence among us when God's self-expression became flesh and was born among us as one of us. This Solemnity of the Ascension of Our Lord into heaven inaugurates the time of God the Holy Spirit's presence among us. Jesus Christ's Ascension into heaven opens the door to the Holy Spirit's dwelling within those who have been baptised into the Body of Christ.

Our Blessed Lord's Ascension into heaven challenges us to see God in a new way. Christ's Ascension is not an ending, but it's a beginning. On the surface, it appears that Christ's Ascension is a departure, but actually, it is not. Spirit-filled in His resurrection, Christ now comes to us in a new way --- in His Holy Spirit. It is a new beginning. Christ in His humanity is now taken to a new status, the highest of all states of being. Now at the right hand of the Father in the fullness of divinity, Christ comes to us in the power of the Holy Spirit --- particularly in His Sacraments. He will always be with us; He will never leave us. The infallible sign of His Presence among us is love. We can love even in a world such as ours. We do, in fact, love in a world such as ours. The power of God's love is being made manifest among us. You are making that powerful presence felt in your lives and in the lives of those whom you cherish. You are making the presence of the resurrected and ascended Christ real in the lives of those around you.

If there is one sentence I want you to take home with you today, it is this: Everything and everyone you love is being redeemed. Those whom you love are being redeemed not just by your love, but by Christ's love within you that reaches them. Jesus Christ, risen from the dead and ascended into heaven is at work through you, with you, and in you. He has not left us orphans - He is here. Because of His Ascension, He is here!

As we celebrate the feast of the Ascension, we remember the "exaltation" of Jesus, as He is raised up to share the glory of His Father. Before His departure, He introduces His disciples to their mission. Jesus, who confined Himself to the people of Israel, now tells them to continue His work worldwide. They will be able to do what Jesus Himself did not do, namely, to proclaim the word to all. He tells them that those who believe in Him will also do the works that He has been doing. He promises them that more wondrous works than these He will do for them because He is going to the Father. They now have the mission to preach the gospel to the whole world. This mission involves the call to evangelise people, continue the healing work of Jesus, and preach the good news after being enriched by the power of the Holy Spirit. At this juncture, Jesus introduces the Holy Spirit to them. The reception of the Holy Spirit was critical because He had been chosen and sent by the Father and the Son to sustain Christianity in a new era of sacred history, the era of the Church and its mission. He tells them that the Christian community is never alone. They will have the Trinitarian presence of the Father, the Son Jesus and the Holy Spirit. This presence will give new life to the Church. Hence the feast of Ascension reminds us that Jesus is present with us in the Church. He is present in His apostolic Church, in the Holy Eucharist, in the word of God and in the Christian community. As mysterious as it appears, while He has ascended, our faith affirms that He is still here with us.

The feast of Ascension is part of what we call the Paschal Mystery. There are four inter-related parts: suffering and death; resurrection;

Ascension; and the sending of the Spirit. They are closely interlocked as one reality. If the resurrection says that the crucified Jesus is alive, the Ascension says that the living Jesus has entered into glory, sharing on an equal level the glory of His Father. Simultaneously, the feast affirms that Jesus is the Messiah. Luke emphasised that the proclaiming of repentance and the forgiveness of sins was to be proclaimed in His Name, which is the messianic task. This emphasis, in "His Name," shifts the faith of the believers from Yahweh, the God of the Old Testament, to the Person of Jesus. Therefore, St Paul tells us that in Him, all the fullness of God was pleased to dwell bodily. At the same time, the Ascension opened the door for the beginning of the Divine ministry of the Holy Spirit. The gospel tells us that Jesus raised His hands and blessed His disciples. The blessing of Jesus was not just an ordinary blessing but the blessing of the True High Priest, who is returning to His Father. This same Jesus, who has gone to His Father, will come again to gather together and save those eagerly waiting for Him.

The Ascension of our Lord took place a long time ago, but His parting words are still vibrant to us and must be carried out courageously to be His witnesses in the world of today like the first Apostles. Hence the feast of the Ascension is not to commemorate a departure but the celebration of the living and lasting presence of Jesus in the Church. He is the Lord, the living head of His Body, the Church, always remains with us as He promised, but now in a new way. He is spiritually present. In fact, by this celebration, we proclaim that the risen Jesus enters into the fullness of the glory given Him by His Father. For the followers of Jesus, His presence with them can make this earth, the daily life, real heaven. In order to continue to be present with His disciples, and make them truly experience Him, Jesus had to leave them. His "old" presence in one human body, in one small corner of the world, was able to reach only a small number of people, in one tiny period of history. But now this gives way to a new presence that will reach the whole world in every age. From now on wherever there is love, joy, peace, patience, kindness, faithfulness, gentleness, wherever there is truth, compassion, justice, freedom, beauty, the Spirit of Jesus is there. Further, He gives the Church His own Spirit to guide it into His mission. As we live this Ascension of our Lord, let us look forward to experiencing Him in our lives and be His messengers in the world of today.

The days of Pentecost and all of the days thereafter are at hand. We have a Saviour who loves us, a glorious Redeemer who at the right hand of the Father intercedes for us, and the Spirit of God at work in us. By your faith, in your hope, and because of your love, all the gifts of God are at work in you, and our world has the promise of being made into a much better place. Because of the Ascension of Christ, we are given the task of revealing God's kingdom here on earth. Christ has established the kingdom. Ours is now, by the power of the Holy Spirit, the task of revealing God's kingdom in all that we say and do.

*"Behold," declares God, "I make all things new."*

# THEME 58
# THE COMING OF THE HOLY SPIRIT

*Acts 2:1-11; 1 Corinthians 12:3-7, 12-13; John 20:19-23*

In speaking with you about Pentecost, I must speak of what cannot be fully explained. All we can do is reverently gaze into the mystery of God's final movement toward us, the alienated and distant men and women who, with Adam and Eve, have broken off relations with God. Words cannot capture the enormity of God's merciful love for us; they buckle under the weight of it. So scripture and the Church employ symbols to try to carry Pentecost's meaning to us. Sometimes symbols are more effective than words in conveying the truth of spectacular events.

Essentially, Pentecost is the final movement of God's journey toward us. The initial movement begins in Genesis with God in the Garden of Eden. Note that it is God who makes a move. It is God who initiates; God who offers; God who loves us first. He chooses us. We do not choose Him. He chooses us first because He is superior. If it was otherwise, and indeed when people think they first choose God, then men and women in their pride would fancy that they are in control.

The Tower of Babel is the story of the prideful people who thought they could build a tower to God. But in doing that they were usurping God's role. They were the initiators, they were trying to be in control, they were setting the specifications, they were going to discover God, and then they would determine His existence. What they forgot is that it is God who discovers man; it is God who determines our existence; God speaks first. It is only when God speaks that things come into existence.

And so the story of the Tower of Babel is a recapitulation of the story of Adam and Eve. Once again, man is filled with pride. Once again, man tries to be God. And once again, the reality is fractured, nations are shattered, destruction, disunion, misunderstanding, and a total breakdown in communications occurs. Mankind now speaks in different languages, and even people who speak the same language are no longer able to understand each other.

But despite human arrogance, God continues to move toward us. God pursues us in His everlasting search for those who have strayed from the sheepfold of fundamental truth and reality. He sends us prophets, kings, and priests. The message of His love and truth flashes across the pages of human history and human religions. Finally, by the power of the Holy Spirit, Christ is born in the womb of humanity; a child is born to us, a Son is given us. He is named Mighty Counselor, Prince of Peace, and the Anointed One who can heal those who are alienated, shattered, and miserable. God utters and sends His Word in a language that everyone can understand.

In the Incarnation, God's Word becomes flesh, and God lives and moves even closer to us. On the Cross God's Word hands over His Spirit and thus inaugurates God's final movement toward us. Actually, in the context of the cosmic vision that we see here, death, resurrection, Ascension, and Pentecost are events forming one unitary whole. In that context, Pentecost becomes the completion of the Annunciation. The Word of God becomes human flesh and blood. Thus, God enters our history, not only into our temples and holy places but into human hearts and souls and all that it means to be human.

It is all so marvellous, all so universal and huge, all so beyond our comprehension, that mere words buckle and only symbols can hope to carry the precious freight. So we speak of the Dove, of the Wind-Breath of God, of the Paraclete, and the tongues of fire. We are into the most profound part of the mystery, namely that God created us not just to follow the rules and regulations but in order that He might be intimate with us deep within us, in the deepest meanings of the word love so that we can now live our ordinary lives in extraordinary ways. We are empowered now to fill all that is ordinary with the extraordinary love of God.

The work of Christ in giving us His Holy Spirit is the work of bringing us into a language that we can all understand. It is the work of religion, of re-ligamenting, bringing our bare-bones, dried up because of lack of love, back into one body filled with the Blood of Christ and the life of God. The work of Christ in sending us His Holy Spirit is that of making us His blood brothers and sisters. The work of Christ and the Spirit is that of reconciling and forgiving, the work of loosening that which holds us in isolation and our sterile self-centredness. The work of Christ, now raised in power by the Holy Spirit, is the work of bringing a holistic communion to a people that are alienated, fractured, shattered, and divided in the desert of not loving when they could have loved. The work of Christ and the Holy Spirit is overcoming sin. Sin is the name of all that has caused us to ignore our chances to be better persons. Sin is the name we put on all that hurts, divides, and separates us from each other and God. But Christ has given us the power of the Holy Spirit to forgive and overcome sin.

The Church speaks in the tongues of all men and women of every race, culture, and nationality. She speaks with a common language because she utters God's only and unitary Word. Of all the diversities in humanity, the Church makes one inter-dependent unity. She is the opposite of the Tower of Babel because she is built by God, not by men and women. We call Pentecost "the birthday of the Church" because she is animated on this day to speak and utter the Word of God and bring common understanding and common union in every language in a way everyone can understand.

Our task, therefore, is to be that source of healing for others. Ours is the mission of speaking God's language where we work, among our colleagues, associates, friends and neighbours.

Ours is the ministry of healing which is divided, of inspiring those who have become jaded and cynical, of animating those who have lost hope, and of telling all who have missed their chances of being better persons that there is a second chance because there is the Second Coming of Jesus Christ. The Holy Spirit is at work in the mysteries of life --- in death, love, suffering, and beauty. Because of Pentecost, God is to be found in the mystery of insight, those insights that turn truth into wisdom. He is present in the mystery of ourselves and in the mysteries of those around us. Anytime we struggle with these mysteries, the Spirit of Pentecost is moving in us, crying out: "Abba, Father", and our struggle becomes the question or questing of God's meaning and purpose in our lives.

May the Holy Spirit become the Person whom you quest and the Spirit of your lives. And may you find moments in His presence, moments snatched away from the ordinary busy-ness of our daily lives, moments when you receive Wisdom, Understanding, Counsel, Knowledge, Strength, Sanctification and Reverence plus the twelve fruits of the Holy Spirit, they are Charity, Joy, Peace, Patience, Benignity, Goodness, Longanimity, Mildness, Faith, Modesty, Continence and Chastity for God's mysterious presence and purpose in your life and in our shared lives.

# THEME 59
# ONE GOD IN THREE PERSONS

*Exodus 34:4-6, 8-9; 2 Corinthians 13:11-13; John 3:16-18*

You may wonder why the Church gives so much attention to our human experience of the community. In a nation built on rugged individualism, why is our worship experience focused so much on our shared prayers at Mass, the Kiss of Peace, processing together to receive Holy Communion, communal penance services, and so forth? Well, the answer has a great deal to do with the very nature of God in whose image and likeness we are made.

Today we rejoice in the revelation of the Holy Trinity. It is upon this reality that Christianity is built. One of the most radical revelations of Jesus is that God is in Himself community that we are made in God's image and likeness, and that in Christ, we are to become like God. God is Three Persons, a community of Persons that exists in love. That is God's inner nature, that is the life of heaven, and that is what we are called to live here on earth.

It is interesting to note that in the Book of Genesis, we find God saying: "Let us make man in our image…" We are called into existence, to be in and to live in a relational existence. We discover ourselves, find the meaning of life, and know who we are when we see and understand ourselves in the eyes of those who know us, love us, and who relate to us. Do you have really good friends who deeply know you? Have you experienced the joy of loving and being loved by a number of people? If you have, you've begun to taste heaven and to experience the ultimate community of God, the communion of the Three who are One. Not only that, but also when you live in communion with others, you become more than just yourself. Who you are is expanded, broadened, and deepened in loving others and in being loved by others.

It is for this that we praise and thank God in the Preface of today's Mass. We give Him thanks always and everywhere because He is more than solitary. We praise God because He is a union of persons who are absolutely in love and in total union with each other. What a blessing that is for you, a blessing because if you lived just with yourself and for yourself, life would be horrible.

Some are troubled with the Christian doctrine of the Holy Trinity. It appears to them to be so unreasonable, so incredible, and so impossible. From where we might ask, does this teaching come? Well, it comes from Jesus. It is uniquely His revelation to us. No other religion in history has anything like it. No philosopher ever reasoned to it. It is original to Christ, while at the same time, we find hints of it in the Jewish Testament, the Old Testament.

This belief in the Holy Trinity rests upon Christ's life and is found in His continual references to His Father in Heaven and the Spirit of God. Belief in the Holy Trinity does not come to us from the thoughts of men, nor is it a construct produced from deep within the psychological recesses of our human subconscious mind. It is not a doctrine found in any other great religions in human history, nor did any philosopher ever teach it. It is beyond human speculation about who God really is. It's beyond any human thought about what God might be like. Yet, it is central and vital to the message of the gospels, the faith of the Apostles, and consequently to our faith.

A man like St. Paul, trained as a Jewish leader and acknowledging only the one God when brought into the Christian world by Jesus, completely changed his ideas about God. We have so very often at Mass heard the result of Paul's newfound faith, a Trinitarian faith. He went on to frequently speak of the Holy Spirit, calling us to let the Spirit lead us, the Spirit of adoption which leads us says St. Paul, to cry out: "Abba,

Father." The Spirit himself, St. Paul writes, gives witness with our own spirits that we are children of God. "And," says St. Paul, "we are heirs as well; heirs of God, heirs with Christ..."

Another and much more important aspect is that Jesus' teachings about the Holy Trinity allow us to participate in the life of God. This is what the Catholic Church teaches us in its concept of sanctifying grace, that gift from God that sanctifies us and makes us holy. When we become more like God in the way we live with others --- God's presence, power, and love make all that much more real for those who live around us. The more we live in a caring communion of love with those around us, the more we become filled with God's holiness, not only for our own sake but for the sake of others who know us and love us.

Loving others, you see, isn't something that's simply nice, it is essential; it is of the essence of being one with Christ. It is only in love and in deep relationships with others that we can understand what St. John is talking about when he says that God is love and he who loves has found God, and God lives in Him.

Finally, the Trinity's doctrine is the foundation of Christian ethics, social justice, and morality. Upon it rests the two great commandments: Love God and love your neighbour as yourself. Upon it also rests the Ten Commandments and the teachings of our great saints. They all call us into the right relationships with others. What is good and evil depends on how we relate to others, and the quality of love we share with them. Community life depends upon those commandments, commandments having their foundation on the Triune God who is a community of persons in union and in love.

So rather than being puzzled by Christ's teaching about the Holy Trinity, and rather than trying to question it from the distance of detached examination, let you and I throw ourselves into life and love, and so experience the life of the Trinity in our own relationships with others. Let us share a life in which we can be so much more of our true selves. It is there that we can know God. It is in loving others deeply, closely, and consistently that we can begin to feel the wonder of life and the joy of knowing who God is and what His life is like.

Jesus told us that heaven begins here on earth. The kingdom of heaven is here, among you, He told us. We are not far from it. The life of God begins to be experienced here. Heaven is not a carrot dangled in front of us. Heaven isn't the reward at the end of a road of pain, trial, and suffering. Heaven begins when we discover ourselves, when we discover each other, when we begin to live a Trinitarian life with others, and when we begin to live in that communion with others that is God's.

# THEME 60
# THE BODY OF CHRIST

*Deuteronomy 8:2-3, 14-16; 1 Corinthians 10:16-17; John 6:51-18*

In your imagination, I would like to take you with me back to an Upper Room somewhere in Jerusalem. It's nighttime, and there is a tense, ominous silence in the dark streets. Covering it all is the looming shadow of the Roman Emperor, the overwhelming presence of the military force of Rome's legions, the dark despotism of Rome's enforced peace, along with Rome's worship of brute force and dominative power. Violence could erupt anywhere at any time. Trapped men might lash-out in frustration and bitterness at any moment. The grinding intersection between dominative power and man's legitimate desire for freedom was wearing thin. In this context, Jesus Christ at the Last Supper met with His twelve disciples to freely hand over to them His very self in the form of His Body and Blood, both of which were about to be sacrificed to the Roman gods of dominative power.

How many would claim that what Jesus was doing was relevant to the situation that was surrounding Him? Moreover, how many would say that what we are doing here in this hour on this Sunday is relevant to the situation in the world outside that surrounds us? The questions are connected. By being here, we are re-entering that same Upper Room to share in that same Lord's Supper in contexts that are 2,000 years apart but very much the same.

Outside is a world of political corruption, of lies and deceit, of military and civil violence, a world wherein trapped men and women can lash-out anywhere at any time in order to try to be free of the dominative powers that hover over us. It is a world in which a powerful few control the lives and destinies of the many, a world in which a wealthy few live at the expense of the many who have relatively little wealth. The frustration flashes out at us in accounts of gang-roving youngsters trying to control their neighbourhoods, in instances where the elderly are mugged, beaten nearly to death, and robbed of a few pitiable nairas. In that same world, many government officials seem more interested in acquiring greater personal power and little interested in giving citizens protection from the violence that surrounds and traps them. In other words, the parallels between what is pursued in our own culture and what was pursued in the Roman culture of Christ's time are uncomfortably similar.

Thus, it is that the greatest need of the twelve disciples and our greatest need, to find the strength to out-live, out-love, and thereby transform the world that surrounds us. And this is precisely what Jesus is doing in both contexts back then and now.

There is great power in a person who does God's will, who lives in God's love and follows a divine logic different from this world's logic. There is great power in one who lives in honesty and truth, who lives in the innocence of a clean conscience, and who gives himself over in the strength of self-sacrificial love for others. The broken body of Christ and His poured-out blood become the sources of that sort of power, a strength that can transcend the world, a power that drains the use of dominative power rendering it weak and impotent. That is the relevance of being here today, during this hour each Sunday. We are here, as were the twelve apostles, to receive a power that integrates us into God's power and that allows us to go through a door that frees us from the prison of this world's lust for power that only manipulates, dominates, crush, devours, and destroys. Love, however, is irresistible.

Secondly, we are here to judge the world. Jesus Christ God has judged the world. He has shown us the relative value of things. His judgment shows us what things are better than others. And when we find

Jesus kneeling with a towel around His waist, washing the feet of His disciples, and when we encounter Jesus coming to us in mere bread and a few drops of common wine, handing Himself over to us in utter simplicity and humility in His quiet invitation of love rather than in the domination of brute power, then we see that we and our world are judged. Pride is judged. Acquisitiveness is judged. Dominative and manipulative power is judged. Control of others is judged. Domineering selfishness is judged. Lying conniving officials in government, in business, and in labour unions are all judged.

When we participate in the Lord's Supper, we are acting as witnesses. Over and against the standards of this world, we proclaim something by our sharing in this hour. St. Paul tells us: "As often as you eat this bread and drink this cup, you proclaim the Lord's death until He comes again in glory." The celebration of Holy Mass set amid the course of ordinary human events stands as a judgment. It is a measuring ruler whereby we judge the relative value of things, whereby this world's values are measured against God's, and whereby we declare that the cross is planted in the centre of our universe and that it penetrates down through all of the levels of our political, social, and economic lives to the very core of what it means to be a human being who is endowed by our Creator with certain rights that cannot even be given away, namely freedom, the pursuit of truth, and pursuit of God. In such a light, many things that men and women do each week, particularly those who have and use dominative power, are revealed to be shabby, pitifully mean, and even demonic. To say it in another summary way, our participation in the Holy Sacrifice of the Mass is a very relevant act because it is a judgment that saves us even as it searches and condemns the hearts and the consciences of all men and women.

Finally, this hour is very relevant to all of the hours of each week because it frees us from the prison of time and allows us to walk through a time door that leads us to eternity. All around us people (and many of us along with them) are in pursuit of what is merely passing. We do everything we can to save time, only to be able to waste it. This leads many into a pervading sort of cynicism and frustration that makes people question whether there is anything at all that can be called eternity.

The Roman culture that surrounded Christ, with its crushing power, corrupt values, and lust for what is merely temporal, produced cynical citizens. On many of the gravestones of Romans back then was found the following inscription: NON FUI, FUI, NON SUM, NON CURO. "I was not, I was, I am not, and I do not care." What could be a more hopeless, more cynical, and emptier way to bury your wife, child, or husband? What could be a better inscription over the graves of trapped and victimised people than to say: "I was not, I was, I am not, and I do not care!" Would anyone claim this is an expression of strength or power? No, of course not. It is the expression of surrender to despair, the expression of a soul that has been seduced and abused by the values of a culture that views religion and Christ as irrelevant.

This is the Feast of Corpus Christi, and each celebration of the Eucharistic Liturgy is another moment that allows us to enter the Upper Room and share once again in our everlasting Lord's Supper and His one sacrifice that is the Last Supper because it is still going on and there will not be another. Each Mass is a highly relevant hour in all of the hours of each week. Each Mass is an event in which we receive power, in which we find judgment, and in which we touch the eternal. What could be more relevant than that? Corpus Christi is food indeed and His blood is drink indeed.

The Upper Room, the Lord's Supper, Holy Mass, is a place in which we unlock the secrets of spiritual power, human dignity and freedom, of values, of eternal hope, and the secret of walking through life with our heads held high, filled with strength, with a purpose for living and reason for dying. May the Body and Blood of our Lord Jesus Christ bring you, and bring me with you, into His kingdom and everlasting life.

# THEME 61
# FREEDOM OF THE CHILDREN OF GOD

*Zechariah 9:9-10; Romans 8:9, 11-13; Matthew 11:25-30*

To properly understand what St. Paul is teaching us in today's second reading; we need to know the meaning of the words he uses. That is why I want to take a look at the word "flesh" and begin this reflection by asking you not to equate "flesh" with "body." St. Paul uses the word flesh to speak of human frailty, a concept that goes far beyond that which is merely sensual. St. Paul isn't limiting himself to sins of human sensuality. He is instead pointing to human weaknesses, particularly sins that include idolatry, materialism, hatred and racism, rivalry and competitiveness, jealousy, envy, elitism, arrogance, acts of violence, and all such like. When we contrast the concept of flesh (as St. Paul understands it) with its opposite, we find him speaking about the dominion of the Spirit. In another epistle, he tells us that what the Spirit produces in us is love, joy, peace, patience, kindness, generosity, faithfulness and self-control.

Christ, Paul writes, frees us from the dominion of the flesh and, by the power of the Holy Spirit, establishes us in God's new creation, making us His new children, His new sons and daughters in the resurrected life of His Spirit-filled Christ. The world of the flesh, the world that is separated from God, wears us down and exhausts us with its heavy burdens. Sins of sensuality bring us disease and addictions. Hatred, envy, arrogance, and elitism tear nations apart in wars. Prejudice and racism tear nations asunder internally and bring exhausting tensions between us as we attempt to live together as one nation. Competitiveness, envy, and self-centeredness cause us to be held captive in our business and professional careers at the cost of taking us away from our spouses, children, and families.

Our misdeeds heavily burden us. The weight of their consequences is a heavy load indeed. Christ in His merciful compassion knows that our hearts are heavy. Sent by His Father to give us God's forgiveness and reconciliation, Christ takes on Himself our sins, suffers and dies under their weight, and then gives us His power to lift their yoke from our shoulders. To have those loads lifted, we must be humble. Taking them away is something we cannot do by ourselves. As a matter of fact, we cannot do it by ourselves. In the simplicity of children, we must trust and hope in what Christ can do for us. We must take His yoke upon us and let Him join us in pulling our loads through life. God offers, we respond. If we respond in humble acceptance of what He wants to give us, no load will be too heavy. Why? Because the Son of God partners Himself with us. Yoked together, like oxen are yoked, we can, with Christ at our side, pull any load. No load that life imposes on us can be too heavy if we are joined with Christ. Every heavy load will become light. Most astoundingly and astonishingly, God has offered His power to us in the life, death, and resurrection of His Son, Jesus Christ.

The shocking thing is that so few have accepted God's offer. That is a great mystery to me; God's ways are indeed mysterious. But what is really mysterious to me is the rebellion that lurks in our hearts. One of life's greatest mysteries is our rejection of the presence, power, and love of God that comes to us in Jesus Christ. Have you known rejection? Jesus has. Betrayal? Jesus has. Loneliness? Jesus has. Pain? Jesus has. Have you been victimised? Jesus has. The butt of jokes? Jesus has. Abused? Jesus has. Used and then thrown away? Jesus has.

Why not let Him give you His promise of rest? All of us are looking for rest and relief from what burdens down our hearts and souls. None of us can escape life's burdens, but all of us can find Christ's loving care and concern. What keeps us from experiencing the rest and relief He can give us? What keeps us distant and apart from His love and His power to help us? You just heard His invitation to you: "I give praise to you, Father, Lord of Heaven and Earth, for although you have hidden these things from the wise and the learned, you have revealed them to the childlike.... Come to me, all you who labour and are burdened, and I will give you rest. Take my yoke upon you and learn from me, for I am meek and humble of heart; and you will find rest for yourselves. For my yoke is easy, and my burden light." You and I should take His promise seriously and accept His offer.

# THEME 62
# ORIGIN OF EVIL

*Wisdom 12:13, 16-19, Rom 8:26-27, Matthew 13: 24-43*

One of the great questions found in literature, philosophy, and the history of ideas is that we are a mixture of good and evil, both in our personal lives and in our culture with its array of institutions. The fundamental question is this: Why is there evil? Why are there weeds in the garden of our world and all that it produces? Many thinkers give us many answers, the best to my way of thinking deal with another question: Why are we free to choose? Why didn't God create a world in which we would always choose what is decent, right, and good?

Freedom of choice – that's the problem, isn't it? Love is not love unless it is the result of choices, choices that are open to a Yes answer and a No answer. Love has value because it is a positive decision, not a negative one.

Thus, we live in a strange world, don't we? So many people begin things with good intentions, beautiful visions and really want to make things better, both in their own lives and in the lives of others. But, as in so many great efforts, things can eventually go wrong.

The same is true in our personal lives. People fall in love and get married with nothing but the best intentions, with high hopes, hearts filled with love, and wonderful visions. Then, somewhere along the line, things turn sour.

Life is a mixture of good and evil. We are imperfect people living in an imperfect world. There is much in our nation that is both good and bad. Our governmental officials are both good and bad. There is much in our Church that is good, and there are some bad things too. If we're honest, we see both good and bad in us individually and collectively. Everywhere we look, we find this strange mixture of what's right and what's wrong.

The worlds of great literature and great art try to help us deal with this mixture of good and evil. The famous Star Wars movie series presents good people who, for some mysterious reason, go over to the Dark Side. The authors and producers of Star Wars don't explain why this happens; they give us only the epic struggle of good overcoming evil. The world's great writers, novelists and poets give us no ultimate answer to the problem of evil's origins; the only thing they can do is help us deal with the problem of evil, not solve it.

The Bible tells us that Lucifer was one of the greatest of all God's angels. His name, Lucifer, means "Light Bearer." He was one of the highest of God's creatures; he bore God's own light. And yet, for some reason, he became the Prince of Darkness. The reason? Lucifer put his will before God's will. He refused to obey God. He opted to go his own way. He defied God. The mystery is: Why did he do that?

As followers of Jesus Christ, what do we do with the problem of evil? That's the question raised in today's readings. Answering the question is a big problem for all of us. Just what do we do when it comes to ridding ourselves and our world of evil? In today's first reading and today's gospel account, the scripture passages suggest that we deal with evil as God deals with it, with patience and forbearance. Evil will eventually reveal itself, and evil will eventually suffer the consequences it brings down upon itself. Sin brings with it suffering and punishment. God, however, is not quick to render final judgments upon us. In His infinite patience and loving mercy, God gives us plenty of time to make multiple decisions to choose what is decent, right, and good. In a very real sense, God doesn't have to condemn us; we do a good job in condemning ourselves. That is perhaps why God is both just and merciful at the same time.

There are a couple of interesting points about the parable of Jesus that we just read that I want to point out to you. One is that when He was asked where the weeds came from, Jesus replied: "An enemy has done this." He doesn't tell us why God has enemies; He simply states it as a fact. He is a realist, not a dreamy-eyed idealist. To take a realistic view of life, we simply must begin with the facts – evil exists, and it comes from people who have chosen to defy God. It may not make any sense to us, but we simply must take it as a fact of life. Of their own free will, people choose to defy God and do things quite apart from Him. In the world of human choices, things are not as they ought to be; things are quite apart from what God intended them to be. The price of human freedom of choice is costly, not only to us, but to God. Jesus Christ, the Son of God, had to pay that price.

Why, we ask, doesn't God simply pull up all of evil's weeds? Why doesn't God, with fire and brimstone, simply blast evil off the face of the earth? Well, that's a lot easier said than done. Suppose God did, what would happen? What would happen to each one of us? Aren't we all a mixture of good and evil? Wouldn't we get caught up on their firestorm of evil's destruction?

This brings me to the second point, namely that so very often, what is evil appears to be good, and what is good appears to be evil. We can't do the sorting; only God can.

# THEME 63
# COUNTING THE PRICE

*1 Kings 3:5, 7-12; Romans 8:28-30; Matthew 13:44-52*

In today's gospel, we find Jesus addressing two questions: "How much does it cost? And "Is it worth the price I'll have to pay?"

Today's parable tells us of a man who stumbled upon a buried treasure, a pearl of great price. Was he a day labourer? Was he a hired hand with few resources?  No, he was a merchant, a savvy businessman who knows the value of things. He was a risk-taker who sold everything and made a risk-capital investment to secure that hidden treasure. Pearl merchants back then were men of means. This merchant's career was buying and selling fine jewels; he was well acquainted with the worth of things. He converted all of his assets to cash to buy this one very precious and costly pearl.

The point to note is not the fact that we come upon God's treasures in our lives. They are hidden in the ordinary days and events in our lives. Often, we stumble upon them or else something happens that causes us to realise that God's gifts have been with us all along; we simply failed to notice them. This is true for all of us, me included. But that's not the point I'm raising with you today. What I want us to examine today is what we do when we discover them. What actions do we take? It seems to me that this is the point of Jesus' parable. God offers – He's always offering us His love and care. The big question deals with how we respond if we respond at all.

To follow Jesus is costly – or so we tell ourselves. But how costly? Is it really costly to follow in the way of Jesus? To be sure, it will place demands on our hearts, our minds, and our souls, but the big question is not how much it will cost us. It's rather the worth of what we will get. What Jesus offers us is worth any price. All the really valuable things in life need to be judged not in terms of how much they cost but what they are worth.

Some things in life simply cost too much, and foolishly acting without wisdom, we buy into them. Take, for instance, a middle-aged man who is enchanted by a younger woman. She makes him feel young again. Losing his self-respect and violating his marriage vows, he trashes his relationship with his family and God and gives himself over to her. He also loses the confidence and trust of his children, his friends, and crushes the heart of a good woman, his wife.

Is it a bargain? Some things simply cost too much. For instance, what is the cost of the loss of our self-respect? What is it worth to have self-respect? What's the cost of our loss of the respect of others? What's it worth to have the respect of others? What's the cost of the loss of the love of others? The loss of our honour? The loss of a clean and peaceful conscience? What is it worth to have all of those virtues in our character? What's it worth to be known as a man or a woman who has those qualities, to be known as a person of honesty, integrity, loyalty, and possessed of the highest of character?

Some things are worth whatever they cost. Some things are worth every sacrifice and price we have to pay for them. For example, the respect we receive from others. The freedom of knowing that God sees you and respects you; what would it be like to be in the presence of God without any shame? Imagine living so that you never have to apologise to anyone for anything you think, say, or do? What value would you put on living with yourself like that?

Let's not fool ourselves. The greatness of character comes at a price. A great life is expensive and costly. Oh, not in terms of money, but rather in terms of paying the price of giving up being lazy, giving up our comfortable ease, giving up self-centredness and some concern. Being a great human being demands a lot from us. It requires discipline and self-sacrifice; it requires self-denial, hard work, and care in our relationships with others. Conversely, selfish living in the smallness of heart can be expensive; it can cost us some of the things that we hold most dear in life.

Wisdom leads us and invites us to discern our greatest treasures. Wisdom is a gift from God, and we need to pray for it. We need to ask God to give us the wisdom to take a good, hard, honest look at ourselves and our lives in the light of these two big questions: How much does it cost, and is it worth the price we must pay for it?

Jesus has some answers to these two questions. Are our answers any better than His?

God's wisdom is available if we want it, but we have to seek it, to learn to pray for it and then pay attention to God's voice in our hearts. Wise persons learn and listen, have a teachable heart and do not pretend to know it all. Wise persons take time each day to reflect and think things over in the presence of God. Humbly "ask, and you will receive," Jesus tells us. And when asking, "...seek first the kingdom and all will be given to you as well," He told us.

Again, let me emphasise that it is we who must do the seeking. God has already been busy seeking us out. Everything depends upon our responses.

# THEME 64
# DIVINE INVITATION

*Isaiah 55:1-3, Romans 8:35, 37-39; Matthew 14:13-21*

We just heard these words from the prophet Isaiah: Thus says the LORD: All you thirsty come to the water! You who have no money, come, receive grain and eat; come, without paying and without cost, drink wine and milk! Why spend your money for what is not bread; your wages for what fails to satisfy? Heed me, and you shall eat well, you shall delight in rich fare.

What we are hearing is God's divine invitation to feed not our stomachs but our souls. A walk in any market will show you that we are well fed when it comes to stomachs. How many flat bellies will you see in any "joint"? Not very many! But what we don't see are the starved and malnourished souls within those bodies. What you won't see are those who have hidden desires, hunger dealing with self-acceptance and respect, hunger for love, and for lives that matter. The same would be true if you observed people in a bar or a lounge. They thirst. They thirst for love, for a life of meaning, and not finding it. Many drown their sorrowful loneliness in booze, small talk, and superficial distractions.

Thousands of years ago, the author of the Old Testament Book of Ecclesiastes wrote the following, words that echo in the hearts of many today: I surrounded myself with every possible pleasure. I did not withhold my heart and my very self from any joy or any pleasure. One day, I drew a line under the total of it all and came up with a sum that amounted to nothing.

Years ago, a famous English poet (T.S. Eliot) wrote a magnificent poem titled "The Wasteland." It was a devastating look into, and commentary upon, our present-day culture. He showed us how we are spiritually living in a modern desert, a wasteland, a deserted place. Eliot was echoing the cry of Isaiah: Why spend your money for what is not bread; your wages for what fails to satisfy?

Jesus took His disciples out into a deserted place, a place of human loneliness, hunger, and thirst. Hungry and thirsty people followed Him out there. When the day was getting long, His disciples told Him the obvious. "They are hungry." Jesus' response was:

"Feed them yourselves." We, His modern-day disciples, need to recognise what He is telling us. Do we feed the malnourished spirits of those around us? We are likely to reply, as did His disciples back then, "All we've got are five measly barely loves and only two fish. What good is that in the face of all that has to be done?"

You and I live amongst the shattered dreams of the last two centuries. We have had material progress beyond anything that people living before us ever imagined. But spiritually, we hunger and thirst. Many have turned to gurus, psychics, crystals, New Age offerings, and even witchcraft. Pop-psych religions abound, and in the spirit of it all, many lead lives of quiet desperation.

What should we do? The first thing we need to do is to seek the Lord in quiet times of prayer. We should take God's invitation seriously to be fed by Him. He will never withdraw His invitation. He offers Himself to us, especially here in Holy Communion. God offers, we respond. But nothing will happen unless and until we respond. How have we responded to His invitation to us?

Our first response should be to turn off our cell phones, our iPads, our laptops, and all of the electronic gizmos that fill us up with nothing but noise. Are we afraid of silence? Are we afraid that we will have nothing to say to God in our moments of prayer? Are we afraid that God will have nothing to say to us? Just why don't we pray? Are we simply too busy or, on a deeper level, do we fear the silence of prayer? Perhaps our prayers are filled with too much self-accusation, and so, in our shame, we avoid being close to God. However, we need to remember that God offers Himself to us amid our failures and sins.

Apart from prayer, what about some quiet moments of thoughtful self-reflection? Moments of reflection provide us with opportunities to see mountains, rivers, and lakes, all of them opportunities to contemplate the beauties of nature. But, wonderful as all that may be, all of them are outside of us. If we are to nourish our hearts and souls, we need to take a look at what's inside ourselves instead of focusing on all that's outside and around us. If we don't have time for self-reflection, then we will hunger and thirst.

Are we willing to admit that we have needs, hunger, and thirst? Are we willing to admit that we are dependent on others to nourish our hearts and souls? It's wonderful and it's good to be self-sufficient and self-sustaining, but too much of self will leave us with nothing else, and then we will truly hunger and thirst.

Finally, we need to ask ourselves: "What really sustains us? What is our true sustenance? Just what sort of food is feeding us? Junk food? Food that doesn't nourish us? Are our bodies bloated and fat while our souls are lean and hungry? Why should we go on living in spiritual starvation?

Do not leave this Mass, thinking you have nothing to give others. Do not think you have nothing to give them so that they might overcome their hunger and thirst. Jesus is here to give you the Bread of Life, not so that you can keep it all to yourself but so that you can feed countless numbers of those around you who are looking for the same thing you are – a life lived in the closeness of God, a life of meaning and purpose. After all, He is the one who will do the feeding. All we have to do is share His food, His tender loving mercies, His presence, and His love. If you don't, those in the world around you will continue to starve.

Thus says the LORD: All you who are thirsty come to the water! You who have no money, come, receive grain and eat; come, without paying and drink wine and milk! Why spend your money for what is not bread; your wages for what fails to satisfy? Heed me, and you shall eat well, you shall delight in rich fare.

# THEME 65
# THE STAYING POWER

*1 Kings 19:9, 11-13; Romans 9:1-5; Matthew 14:22-33*

I want to share some thoughts with you today about the basic movements we find in today's first reading and the gospel reading. What I'm looking at is God's movements toward us and our responses to Him.

The divine presence is something that comes to meet us as just as God came to meet Adam and Eve in the Garden of Paradise. That is likewise, what happened to the disciples in their storm-tossed boat. Christ came to meet them, summoning them to have faith, trust, and believe in Him. To see Him with the eyes of faith, we must leave behind our ordinary ways of seeing reality. As seems to be the case with God, we must do this to see things in God's dimension, in a fourth dimension, so to speak. We must expect and accept the unexpected and then perceive with eyes and ears unaccustomed to a new light, God's light that Jesus Christ illumines for us. Seeing the world through the eyes of love makes a difference, a huge difference.

How does God speak to us, in big events or in life's storms? Do we call on Him only when we're hit by the storms and rough seas of life? We need to be open to God at all times. We all know what it's like to make a phone call only to be put on hold. Do we put God on hold when He's trying to reach us? How long of a hold? How patient are we when we're put on hold? How patient is God with us when we put Him on hold?

When Peter was filled with fright, he took his attention away from Christ. The consequence was that fear controlled him and so he began to sink. When he reconnected with Jesus, he was able to get back on board again.

The important point we should not forget is that our Saviour remained open to Peter's prayer and cry for help. Sometimes, when distress and calamity beset us, we think that God is absent. But the truth is that God never abandons us to our fate; He remains steadfastly available to us. He is always present to us. Peter is a good model for us.

Being overcome with fear, we sometimes sink into despair and, in doing so, abandon our faith in God, telling ourselves that God doesn't care or that He's not there for us. But the opposite is true. It is we who abandon God's caring love for us; God never abandons us. We have to have enough faith to continue being open to God and to recognise Him in His quiet whisperings to us in our hearts just as Elijah did at the entrance to his cave where he had taken refuge from life's earthquakes and storms.

We all have our life-shaking events – our personal earthquakes. We all have our own storms to ride out, our own terrible tornados and hurricanes that threaten to blow us away. Faith is not just for quiet times; faith is for moments of stampeding desperation; faith is for all of life's events.

We should not neglect to pay attention to the boat we heard about in today's gospel account. The boat is a symbol; it's a symbol of the Church. Jesus and His disciples were all back in that boat together. When that happened, they were no longer fearful, and the storms and heavy seas of life no longer had their control over them. The same should be true for us. We should see the Church and the presence of Christ in His sacraments as our refuge and our strength. We should get on board with Peter and the apostles.

Coming to Church and receiving Christ isn't simply nice; it's essential for our salvation and peace of mind. It is essential for our own reaching out for Christ's helping hand. How do we deal with what life throws at us? Do all of these fears and worries turn our eyes away from the presence of God so that we focus only on our fears? Our Blessed Lord always presents Himself to us; what attention do we give Him? All of us are a lot like Peter. With Peter, we need to call out to our Lord and allow Him to be with us in our fears and distress. We also need to give thanks to God in our moments of happiness, victory, and success.

Yes, many things assault our hearts and souls. However, I would fail you if I did not point out that much of what causes us distress comes from forces outside of ourselves. However formidable they may be, there is another distress about which we should be mindful, namely the struggle we all have to maintain our faith in God. This is why we must develop and maintain a strong spirituality, a life of prayer, and the times we spend becoming aware of God's presence within us and His love for us. Storm tossed as our lives may be, there is a deep sense of calmness and peace that can be God's gift to us if we turn our eyes, as Peter did, to the Lord who comes to us walking over the stormy waters of chaos. Should we neglect to do that, we will be robbed of inner peace, sink into spiritual and emotional depths and be overwhelmed. Jesus continually told His followers, and He tells us also: "Fear not. I am with you. Have courage and be not afraid."

With all of this in mind, here is a morning prayer you may find helpful to pray at the beginning of each of your days: Lord of Light, creator of the sun and our world, I thank you for the gifts you will give me today. I want to use them to accomplish your purposes and to reveal your kingdom here on earth as it is in heaven. I place myself into your hands, my Divine Friend and my Companion, who watches over me as I move throughout this day. Join the problems and pains I face into the sufferings of your Christ, as in Him, I surrender myself into your will. Bless this day all people and let me find you in those whom I serve in your special ways. Lord of light and life, I join myself into your Son to bring your love into the world you have given me. Amen.

# THEME 66
# CONVERSION THROUGH CONVERSATION

*Isaiah 56:1, 6-7; Romans 11:13-15, 29-32; Matthew 15:21-28*

Today's gospel account contains one of the most memorable and at the same time, quite disturbing verbal duels recorded in the four gospels, and one of the most important. We need to draw some golden nuggets out of this significant passag

First of all, it is important to note that Jesus is speaking here to a woman, something rabbis in those days did not do in public. Not only that, but she was a foreigner, a Canaanite woman from what we now call Lebanon. The Jews and their neighbours did not get along well with each other at all, and the same is true even today.

Like the Magi, those wise men from the East that we find at Christ's birth, this non-Jew presents herself to Jesus and addresses Him as "Son of David" as she begs His help for her daughter who is possessed by some mysterious inner demonic force. The title "Son of David" was revered by the Jews as their expected Messiah's title. The fact that this Canaanite woman uses it is quite significant.

In this account, there are three movements. The first involves the Canaanite woman's journey of faith. Leaving her religion behind, she turns to a Jewish rabbi, Jesus, and places her faith in Him. She looks to Him for a miraculous cure for her daughter. There is nothing that makes a woman's audacity more pronounced than concern for her child's health and safety.

For her trouble, she received silence from Jesus. She was rebuffed, humiliated, and given the cold shoulder from Him. Never was it known, before or since, that Jesus would rebuff a plea for His compassionate help. Furthermore, Jesus' disciples, annoyed by the fact that she was bothering Him with her loud crying, seek to get rid of her. They want Jesus to send her away. So Jesus says to her, "I was sent only to the lost sheep of the house of Israel," another rebuff.

Then comes the second movement. The woman presses in on Jesus, and falling on her knees in front of Him, she cries out, "Lord, help me." She is blocking Him and thereby saying: "You're not going to get rid of me!"

For her second effort, Jesus tells her, "It is not right to take the food of the children and throw it to the dogs." How utterly humiliating that was. In effect, He was calling her a dog! Her humility was turned into what appeared to be a terrible humiliation. People in the Middle East are very sensitive about things that we are very aware of in our dealings with them in our time. But this woman didn't give up.

Then comes the final movement. In abject humility with her face in the dirt, stripped of her dignity, having abandoned her own religious background, she has nothing left, not even her pride. "Please, Lord," she softly insists, "even the dogs eat the scraps that fall from the table of their masters." The hidden implication is that she is making herself a part of His household, one of the children of God, His Father. Was not Christ's mission for all people, not just the Israelites?

Additionally, what the Canaanite woman was saying is that she doesn't deserve anything. "But," she asks, "how about giving me scraps that accidentally fall from your abundance?" With that, the heart of Jesus is vanquished. The scene would be repeated at the end of His life. His own humiliation and abandonment would be connected as it was with the Last Supper, plays out in a way strikingly similar to this account. Like the woman here, He wouldn't give up.

The key that unlocks the mystery contained in this verbal duel is to recognise that Jesus saw in this Canaanite woman a reality that she didn't even see herself. He saw in her a faith that could withstand any assault; a divine love; a hope that could not be shaken. He tested her mettle, and she found something within herself that she didn't know even existed. Joined into the humiliation that Christ would later suffer, she transcended ordinary humanity and came into a level of life and love that was God's. Her three-step journey in faith mirrored Christ's.

The critical point of it all is that Jesus sees the same thing in you and me. He has an unrealised dream about who you really are and what you're really made of. In Christ's life, passion, and death, we find the stuff of our real humanity, particularly so when we share in His suffering, passion, and death.

Had Jesus granted her request right away, this woman would never have ascended to the heights of glory that she did. We must see that the more we lose in the divine scheme of things, the more we win. The more we give away, the more we gain. The more we go down, the higher we ascend. In that, we pass from what is human into what is divine. It's the path of Jesus.

Should Jesus grant our prayer requests right away, we would never ascend to the heights of glory that are hidden within our destinies That is why when in the Garden of Gethsemane, Jesus prayed that His Father rescues Him; His Father did not. The answer to Jesus' prayer was not the rescue --- it was the resurrection. We should expect that our prayers will be answered in the same way.

St. Paul presents this journey in three parts in his Letter to the Philippians. In Chapter Two, we find that threefold movement in Christ's own life when Paul writes: His state was divine, yet he did not cling to His equality with God but emptied Himself to assume the condition of a slave and became as men are; and being as all men are, He was humbler yet, even to accepting death, death on a cross. But God raised Him on high and gave Him a name which is above all other names so that all beings in the heavens, on earth and in the underworld, should bend the knee at the name of Jesus and that every tongue should acclaim Jesus Christ as Lord, to the glory of God the Father.

The first movement is the abandonment of His proper place, His native place at the right hand of His Father in heaven. He moves from His Father's side into a place of alienation and separation, into total immersion with us where we are at, more importantly, into who we are.

The second movement is downward into our sinful humanity, and not only that but to a level below that which we are usually willing to accept. He is spat upon, humiliated, and stripped naked of all His dignity. His face is rubbed in the dirt, as was the Canaanite woman's face.

The third movement is upward. He rises from the dead into a new Spirit-filled, resurrected life and then ascends into glory back to His Father's side. Victorious over all that is demonic within our humanity, He heals far more than the Canaanite woman's daughter. He gives His healing power to all of us, His Mystical Body, the Church.

In the divine scheme of things, the more we lose, the more we win. The more we give, the more we receive. The more we give away, the more we gain. The more we go down, the higher we ascend.

God came among us with healing power, and He is looking for our faith. The Canaanite woman came to God in faith and in search of healing and found it. Your task and mine as well are to live a life-story just like hers.

Can you? Can I? Yes, we can, because Jesus lived it first and then gave us the power and the capacity to live lives like that. The question is not: Can we? The real question is: Will we? Will we find what God sees in us?

# THEME 67
# THE KEY OF PETER



*Isaiah 22:19-23; Romans 11:33-36; Matthew 16:13-20*

In the first reading, we heard of God, speaking through Isaiah the prophet, electing Eliakim to exercise headship over Israel. The word of God was: "And I will place on his shoulders the key to the house of David; he shall open, and none shall shut, and he shall shut, and none shall open."

In the gospel reading for today, we heard God in Christ speaking about St. Peter: "And I tell you, you are Peter, and on this rock, I will build my church, and the powers of death shall not prevail against it. I will give you the keys of the kingdom of heaven, and whatever you bind on earth shall be bound in heaven, and whatever you loose on earth shall be loosed in heaven."

To these two readings which we have just heard, I would like to add another. This one is from another gospel passage found in the 18th chapter of St. Matthew's gospel in which Christ is addressing all His apostles, not just Peter. "Truly, I say to you," He declares, "whatever you bind on earth shall be bound in heaven, and whatever is loosed on earth shall be loosed in heaven."

Today, my first point is to note the symbolism of the keys, both in the Old and New Testaments. In the Old Testament, we know that the person who was given the keys by the king was the highest official in the king's court; he was the king's chief executive officer. That was always clearly and unmistakably understood by all the Israelites. In the New Testament, Christ used this well-known Jewish symbol to constitute Peter as His chief executive officer among the apostles. The symbolism of the keys could not escape them or admit of any other meaning.

My second point concerns the granting of the keys. In both the Jewish Testament and in the Christian Testament, the granting of keys comes from God. It comes from no one else. The conferral of this office did not come from popular elections. The people did not grant the office; it was granted only by God. Authority was not granted to any individual by any sort of a popular choice; it was conferred by God, who alone has the authority to give it. Authority in both Old and New Testaments comes only from God. He and He alone granted and conferred it on individuals of His own selection.

The third factor that I would like to bring to bear is in St. Matthew's gospel, the 18th chapter. Here we find God in Christ speaking not just to St. Peter but rather to all of His apostles. He gives them, along with Peter, the power to bind and loose, telling them that what is bound on earth will be bound in heaven, and what is loosed on earth will be loosed in heaven.

What we have here is a break from the Old Testament tradition. We have a special granting of authority to one individual, Peter, and to one individual, Peter, and a college of leaders with whom He must work with and with whom He must share the power of the keys. This is a remarkable and innovative departure from the Old Testament custom and tradition of the Jews. It places authority in a new form of corporate leadership with one of their numbers being their leader in holding them together in unity and charity. It places authority squarely in the Church. It is a conferral and exercise. Its authentication and recognition are now placed by Christ in His Church and subject to conferral and authentication processes that are to be developed by His Church. This is truly a remarkable shift.

The practical consequences in our own lives ought to be examined in the context of these understandings.

The first and most apparent ramification is one that we witness when, in Rome, a new Bishop of Rome is elected by the College of Cardinals. The selection process is an extraordinary one. There is a form of so-called politics involved, but it is not political in the usual sense of the word. The discernment process is filled with prayer, invocations of the Holy Spirit, and the absence of the usual form of political factions and power blocs commonly understood by using the word "politics." The inspiration of the divine and the election by God is clearly present. If we put all of our cynicism aside and mute our prejudices, I think that we all must admit that God's election is in evidence. The cardinals make a clear statement that authority does not reside in them, it resides in God, and they make a good faith attempt not only to recognise that fact but to act upon it.

The second ramification is to note that in the pope's selection process and the selection and ordination of deacons, priests, and bishops, the power of the keys operates through twenty centuries of the Church's life. God calls one to be a deacon, a priest, or a bishop. One does not take authority in the Church upon himself by his own choice. Nor is there a popular election in the usual sense present in these instances. If one feels one has a vocation, a calling from God, one submits to a centuries-long developed process for these offices' authentication conferral. In plain and direct language, headship over Christians, at least in the Catholic Church, is conferred by the Church's processes in which the power of the keys resides, and not through anyone else's process. One does not by himself choose to be a priest – the Church, relying on the power of the keys, chooses who is to be a priest, deacon, or bishop.

This brings me now to God's gift to us of confidence, a gift we should hold dear in these times of loss of confidence, loss of confidence in our government, in our economy, and, yes, loss of confidence in some of our Church authorities and leaders. We should not lose hope. We should turn again to the promise of Christ: "Thou art Peter, and upon this rock, I will build my Church, and the gates of Hell shall not prevail against it." Along with this promise came Christ's promise of the Holy Spirit who would protect His Church despite its failures.

"Thou art Peter, and upon this rock, I will build my Church, and the gates of Hell shall not prevail against it." That promise does not come to us from a politician; it comes to us from Our Blessed Lord Himself. Upon Him, our confidence and hope for our future rest.

# THEME 68
# DEALING WITH SUFFERING

*Jeremiah 20:7-9; Romans 12:1-2; Matthew 16:21-27*

A litany of pain and woes beset us all. The news media, movies, television, and the Internet are filled with tales of human suffering, pain, and loss. How do we deal with it? Over the centuries of human history, philosophers and thinkers have given us ways that attempt to deal with it. Mental suffering is worse than physical suffering because mental suffering buries our souls in an agony that is far more profound than physical suffering. In the midst of all this, we hear Jesus declare: "Whoever wishes to come after me must deny himself, take up his cross, and follow me."

Let me put before you now that we are Christians and therefore, all suffering should be seen in Christ's suffering. Others may deal with suffering differently. But for us, we see that Jesus Christ, God's incarnate and personal presence among us as one of us, accepted suffering purposefully. He did not passively submit to it. That would be useless. Christ's suffering was infinitely meaningful, so much so that in His suffering, He negated the power of evil and defeated all of the forces of evil. Rising from the dead, Christ drained the power of evil to hold us in bondage and opened for us the way to heaven.

Whenever we enter into a Catholic church, we are immediately confronted with the crucifix; that visualisation presents us with the truth that it is not only Christ who suffers but also all of humanity that writhes crucified in pain. It is horrible; it depicts our reality. It tells us that our humanity is nailed to crosses of pain.

Various forms of escapism lead many to seek pleasure to compensate for their pain, but such compensatory escapism never works; it often leads only to greater suffering. For the Christian, however, we see that Easter can follow our Good Fridays.

Suffering doesn't work like we think it should. Often it strikes down the righteous and spares the wicked. Nevertheless, regardless of our age, I.Q., religion, or wealth, most of us cannot avoid its sting.

Here I want to point out for you the spiritual wisdom of our modern world's most beloved pope, John Paul II, and the rich theology of suffering he articulated in his writings about the most pressing challenge to faith -- the problem of suffering.

To put it into summary words, Jesus Christ did not accept suffering passively. He accepted suffering purposefully. If St. Paul taught us anything, he taught us that. Not only did St. Paul preach that, but he also lived it out, suffering as he did great sufferings in multiple ways. Declared St. Paul: "Now I rejoice in my sufferings for your sake, and in my flesh, I complete what is lacking in Christ's afflictions for the sake of His body, that is, the church." (Colossians 1:24)

What's lacking is our personal presentation of Christ's sufferings to the people for whom He died, all of us. Christ's afflictions are lacking because they are not seen and known among the nations of people worldwide. Those sufferings must be carried by us, by you and I who are ministers of the gospel. Thus, in living out Christ's life, we fill up what is lacking in the afflictions of Christ by extending them to others in our own sufferings that share in Christ's.

In another passage, St. Paul writes; "Grace to you and peace from God our Father and the Lord Jesus Christ. Blessed be the God and Father of our Lord Jesus Christ, the Father of mercies and God of all comfort, who comforts us in all our affliction, so that we may be able to comfort those who are in any affliction, with the comfort with which we ourselves are comforted by God. For as we share abundantly in Christ's sufferings, so through Christ, we share abundantly in comfort too." (2 Corinthians 1:2-5)

What does that mean for us? It means that taking up one's cross and following Christ does not indicate that we should passively submit to oppression, discrimination, and abuses in their varied forms. That was the constant message of John Paul II, a message that he lived out. We can be comforted in the knowledge that our personal sufferings can be given meaning, infinite meaning and purpose because we can make them a part of Christ's redemptive sacrifice. Therein lay the power of non-violent revolution led and lived by Mahatma Gandhi and Dr. Martin Luther King. Both understood the power and meaning of what Jesus Christ was holding up for us to see, understand, and accept. Those who cause others to suffer abuse their Creator.

We are precious and loveable in God's eyes, and we should identify ourselves as such. Those who abuse us and force us into submission abuse and degrade God's love. Suffering, oppression, and abuse are to be actively resisted and overcome. We need to hold before our eyes, the strategies and tactics of Mahatma Gandhi and Martin Luther King.

Denying one's self isn't Christ's call for us to passively submit to injustices; that would be useless. Denying one's self calls us to unselfishly live in Christ, to share in His identity and purposes. It means to follow in His intentions not, in our own strategies. It means employing strategies that cut the ground out from those who seek to hold others down by powers of domination and submission.

Those who exercise dominating power and control over others, the principalities and powers of this world want us to see ourselves as powerless and victims. On the other hand, Jesus wants us to identify ourselves in Him in precisely the opposite ways the power brokers want us to see ourselves. Jesus was tried, condemned, and crucified by the power elite, by the political and religious authorities who realised He was a tremendous threat to them because He was draining them of their power to dominate and control.

One does not overcome violence with greater violence because that only multiplies violence by two. One does not overcome evil by further evil because that only multiplies evil by two. Jesus lived life differently. He stood silently in front of Pilate because He wanted Truth to speak for itself. Actually, it did because Pilate allowed Him to be crucified only to please the mob, not because justice required Jesus to be condemned and executed. We need to see Pilate's motives clearly, and we need to see the motives of the religious authorities who wanted to do away with Jesus. Pilate was afraid of the crowd; the powerful religious establishment was afraid because they saw clearly the inner power and strength of Jesus and its origins. They were enforcers of dominating power, not enablers. For them, law trumped love. Theirs was a religion of punishments, punishments in the name of an angry God. Jesus, on the other hand, was a caring healer. With Him, the crippled could stand up and walk. With love and forgiveness, He freed those shackled by guilt and set them free to walk in the glorious freedom of the sons and daughters of God. No worldly power and control system can stand up against that, particularly if people really believe in it. Truly, the kingdom of God is nothing at all like the kingdoms of this world.

So when it comes to dealing with suffering, do we face it with passive acceptance, or do we accept it with a purpose? That question is always before us. But we are one with Christ, and His victory is ours to claim. Our participation in the Holy Sacrifice of the Mass places us through Christ's Body and Blood into the reality of who He is and into His resurrection from the dead, the victim no longer and victorious over all that is evil.

# THEME 69
# DEALING WITH CONFLICTS

*Ezekiel 33:7-9; Romans 13:8-10; Matthew 18:15-20*

Harbouring wounds and nursing resentments are like cancers that diminish all of us and eat up our energies. Harbouring them is like closing a wound and leaving all of their consuming diseases inside and untreated. The longer our resentments fester within us, the more energy is sapped away from our living in happier relationships and better lives. All of us have had to deal with them; we know how they can eat away at our hearts.

We can't get along with everyone all of the time. Furthermore, if we hold to certain principles and stand up for certain things, we will offend some people. And they will make it their business not to get along with us.

Today's gospel reading reveals that some early Christian communities had to deal with members who were tearing each other apart. We don't know exactly what those hurtful actions were, but we know that hurtful things were being said and done.

Jesus was a realist. He had to deal with this part of life. He was opposed, even hated. Anyone who lives the values and principles of Jesus Christ will likely not get along with some people. There will be conflict. And perhaps there should be conflict in our lives.

Now it is to be expected that we will not get along with our enemies. But the fact of the matter is that we often find ourselves in conflict with those close to us and whom we want to love us. Husbands and wives can love each other dearly and still have to deal with conflicts. Families face it, and the best of friends can find themselves living in serious conflict and disagreement with each other. Jesus warned His disciples, and us with them, to expect that to be the case, and so He gave them the power to free folks from being bound up by the wounds we cause each other. That is what today's gospel account is all about, the most important part being the commission He gave to the leaders of His Church: "Amen, I say to you, whatever you bind on earth shall be bound in heaven, and whatever is loosed on earth shall be loosed in heaven."

Jesus is speaking as a realist in today's gospel reading. He asked everyone to love as He has loved, knowing that disputes would arise, feelings would be hurt, and resentments would eat away at them like cancers. And He offered His disciples and us with them principles to deal with conflict and resentments.

The first principle is that the offended party should take the initiative. It's the hardest one, too. We should note that even though we offended God by sinning against His love, He took the initiative. He came to us sinners, the ones who had offended His love; He made the first move. Our salvation's biblical history is one wherein God is always taking the initiative to bring about reconciliation, forgiveness, and healing. Jesus points us toward God's ways: "If your brother should commit some wrong against you, go and point out his fault."

But what do we do, and all too often? Well, we gossip behind the backs of those who sinned against us or otherwise have offended us. We go to friends and whine and complain. We throw up walls of protection. We put the offending party into a deep and freezing silence – the so-called "cold shoulder." We slink into the cave of our souls and there nurse and build up our resentments and hurt feelings. We claim victimhood and prepare our public announcements of our victimhood at the hands of these terrible perpetrators.

Supposing, however, that you attempt reconciliation, but the two of you can't work it out. When that happens, it's time, Jesus tells us, to take the matter to a trusted third party. Failure to do so only heaps new layers of resentment, hurt, and victimhood. When you talk the matter out with a trusted third party, the very act of voicing your feelings can have a tremendously therapeutic effect on you. It can also begin the process of objectifying the matter, bringing it out of the swamp of emotional subjectivity. Hurt feelings and age-old resentments distort our vision and make it impossible to see things as they really were or are. And then pride does its evil work in our hearts and souls. Bringing in a third party, a reconciler is all-important.

It takes humility to heal relationships, the sort of humility God has in taking the initiative to come to us and invite us to work with Him in overcoming our estrangement from Him. Our pride often sabotages the healing process at this point. Countless numbers of spouses have come to me alone, with the other spouse absent. Usually, the absent party claims they can solve their problem if they indeed admit that there is a problem. Pride lurks there. "A priest," they ask? What do we need a priest for? A priest can't help us. What does a priest know about marriage?

# THEME 70
# TO FORGIVE IS TRULY DIVINE

*Sirach 27:30-28:7; Romans 14:7-9; Matthew 18:21-35*

The classic format for writing a drama is to present it in three acts. So let us look at today's gospel account in that format.

*Act I – Balancing the Books*

We have here a debtor who owes his master ten thousand talents. Now, a talent was an amount of money equal to one thousand denarii, and a denarius was a Roman silver coin equal to one day's labour. Doing the arithmetic, the amount of debt equalled ten million days' wages.

Responding to the debtor's request, the king, in the act of subtle sensitivity, changes the obligation from a debt to a loan. Did you notice that in the reading? It tells us: "Moved with compassion the master of that servant let him go and *forgave him the loan.*"

What is striking is that the debtor didn't ask for forgiveness. He asked only for time to pay it back. Was he nuts? He must have been! How could he possibly think he could pay back the huge obligation he owed his master?

Setting aside the man's psychiatric condition, let's take a look at his spiritual state, which is, of course, what Jesus is talking about. We should also keep in mind that Jesus is talking about your spiritual condition as well as mine. All of Jesus' parables are not about other people; they are about you and me.

And the point? The debtor was concerned only about observing the dictates of the law. His arrogant self-righteousness remained. His focus was only on himself. There was no change in the debtor's heart, only an attempt to manipulate laws, rules, and regulations.

### Act II – Self-righteousness

Filled with his self-righteousness, the debtor went out and found a fellow servant, one of his equals, who owed him a small amount of money. It amounted to only a hundred days' wages, a minuscule sum compared to ten thousand talents he owed. Instead of treating his fellow servant with a changed heart, he treats his fellow servant to a strict application of the law and, after choking him, has his fellow servant thrown into the debtors' prison.

And the lesson? You can offer forgiveness to someone who has sinned against you, but it won't be effective if he or she has not repented and asked for forgiveness. The parable is pointing out that even God can't forgive someone with a hardened heart. It's called "sinning against the Holy Spirit," the only unforgivable sin. It's unforgivable because the sinner does not allow himself to be influenced by the Holy Spirit and God's tender, loving mercies.

### Act III – The King Acts

The king then acts on behalf of the powerless. He exercises legal judgment and employs the law on behalf of the poor and powerless fellow servant. He applies the full force of the law against the debtor who owed him the ten thousand talents.

We need to see that God comes to us looking for a change in our hearts, not simply a change in our ways of thinking and acting. Changing our ways are "externals," not "internals." It's your heart that God wants.

The old law of "an eye for an eye, and a tooth for a tooth" was designed to control and contain our vengeful attitudes and our lust to "get even." If one was limited to an eye or a tooth, one could not go beyond those boundaries and then kill in the name of justice.

Nevertheless, "getting even" is very much a part of our ways of doing things, even in today's world. All one needs to do is to pay attention to the news headlines that confront us daily. Our world is still held hostage to notions of "getting even," believing that justice will be served in that way or that some sort of balance will be restored.

Jesus wants us to see that forgiveness is liberating, and it is the most liberating for the one doing the forgiving. Forgiveness allows us to walk in the freedom of the sons and daughters of God, not as children of the law.

Living under the law leads us to "an eye for an eye, a tooth for a tooth" approach. Living under the law leads us to attitudes that seek retribution and justice alone without any change in our hearts.

Many of us cling to resentments in horrible prisons of pent-up anger, in the grip of resentments and our lust to "get even." This throws us into victimhood. We feel like we are victims and seek ways to find just compensation, revenge and retribution. We live under the law.

Jesus Christ is risen from the dead, victim no longer. He is free because He is forgiving. He teaches us to ask God to "Forgive us our sins as we forgive those who have sinned against us." *As* is the controlling word – we will be forgiven to the length, height and depth that we measure out forgiveness to others, all the while remembering that the people we forgive are forgiven only if they repent, convert their hearts, and then accept forgiveness. For forgiveness to work, both parties must be involved.

Forgiveness is not "selling out;" it's not saying that what people have done to us is somehow "okay," or that it does not matter. Forgiveness liberates us from the ways of this world; it takes us into the heart of God. To forgive is truly divine, and the presence of God is something we all desperately need in our lives, particularly in the days in which we presently live.

With all of that in mind, I want us to listen again to the wisdom offered us in God's holy word, to the wisdom that is found in today's first reading that came to us from the Old Testament Book of Wisdom:

Wrath and anger are hateful things, yet the sinner hugs them tight. The vengeful will suffer the LORD's vengeance, for He remembers their sins in detail. Forgive your neighbour's injustice; then, when you pray, your sins will be forgiven. Could anyone nourish anger against another and expect healing from the LORD? Could anyone refuse mercy to another like himself? Can he seek pardon for his sins? If one who is but flesh cherishes wrath, who will forgive his sins? Remember your last days, set enmity aside; remember death and decay, and cease from sin! Think of the commandments, hate not your neighbour; remember the Most High's covenant, and overlook faults.

And so let us -- let you and me -- find freedom for ourselves in forgiving others.

# THEME 71
# STANDARDS OF GOD'S JUSTICE

*Isaiah 55:6-9; Philippians 20-24, 27; Matthew 20:1-16*

The big question we are all facing these days is centered on fairness. What is fair when it comes to bringing recovery to our staggering economy? In the minds of many, today's gospel raises questions about God's mercy! Isn't God too generous when He shows His mercy to sinners?

The parable we have just heard raises some critical questions for believers and those who are questioning faith and are trying to find out who God really is. There are other parables along similar lines with this one that is equally as hard to fathom. Take, for example, the parable of the prodigal son. The critical question in today's gospel account is: What do we do with those who went out to work at dawn, the ones who worked so hard, who bore the heavy burdens of the day's work and then received the same wage as the last group who only had an hour's work? Or how do we see the elder son who had to watch the prodigal son get the big feast even though he had stayed at home, remaining in His father's house while following all the rules?

The questions raised are manifold. Why should we observe all the rules of morality if God is going to forgive everybody anyway? Another question that is raised is about justice. Is there no justice in God's ways if everybody, saint and sinner alike, receive the same reward at the end of their lives?

In attempting to answer the questions raised by these parables, the first thing we must do is put behind us all feelings of jealousy, envy, and self-pity, along with any sort of "an eye for an eye and a tooth for a tooth" mindset. Also, we must set aside all standards of human justice. The justice of God is not the justice of man. Our ways are not God's ways. Our God is the God who justifies sinners, people just like us, and He has His ways in doing so. God is not like our symbol of human justice -- the blindfolded woman holding a sword in one hand and a set of scales in the other.

Once we have put aside our feelings of jealousy and envy, once we stop judging God's mercy, and once we have put to rest our propensity to question God's intentions critically, then we can turn to the first part of the answer, the part that deals with justice. I have had many counselling situations, and I've talked with people who are extremely upset with themselves and judge themselves very harshly and critically because others seem to be more favoured by God than they. "Why is it, Father," they ask, "that my friends have greater gifts than I do? Why are they always so close to the Lord, and I am not? Why is God always doing things for them, and I seem to be so distant from the Lord? Why are others more talented and gifted than I and have more friends than I do?" Mind you, these questions are not always couched in jealousy or envy; rather, many times, they are couched in terms of self-condemnation. Self-condemnation is one of the most insidious works of the devil.

The proper response in such situations is to bring them to where they drop the measuring scales of justice held by the blindfolded lady with the sword. They, and we with them, need to think in terms of the God who, because of Jesus Christ, is justifying sinners. We need to pay attention to our justification in God's mercy. Comparison with others is always odious. Who authenticates you? No one but God, and God alone! Who justifies you? God and God alone! Do not judge His love or measure His work within you by comparing yourself with others. Such comparisons can lead to spiritual pride or spiritual despair. Comparisons can likewise lead to gossiping, backbiting, envy, jealously, and destruction of the peace and communion God has in mind for all of our relationships with all of those around us.

Having then put down the measuring scales of human justice, what do we then address the questions raised in the parables? Many resort to the economic approach and devise a system whereby we think we can earn God's favour. This approach counsels us to toil and labour so that if we work hard enough, God will be obliged to give us His love because we have earned it. We think He cannot deny us because we claim we have earned it through a hard-fought life and therefore deserve it. However, God will thwart us and tell us that as high as the heavens are above the earth, so are His ways are above our ways. No one of us can earn God's love, just as no one of us can earn the love of another human being. Love is neither the subject of justice nor of economics. There is no price tag on it. It cannot be bought, just as it cannot be sold. When it comes to the earning theory, we all get the same wage; the one who went to work in the first hour of the day receives the same wage as the one who went to work in the last hour of the day. The prodigal son and the elder son share in equal measure, their father's love and goods.

With what, then, are we left? We are left, my friends, with the glory the beauty of working not to save our skins, not for our justification, but of working hard to love others and working for their salvation. The owner's vineyard is the field of human relationships in which we labour and toil unselfishly for the good of others, not for our rights or our favoured relationship with God. What we are left with is a system of morality, of ethics, and of behaviour that gives us glory and dignity insofar as we love our enemies, do good to those who hurt us, throw aside human justice and economics while simply and humbly living as Christ did, for the sake of others that they might develop and grow. Like the Good Samaritan, we live in a system wherein the strong stop by the wayside and share their strength with the weak. Just as the Samaritan stopped to share his strength with the battered and victimised man lying helpless in the ditch, so we live to do the same, whether it be the sharing of our surplus wealth or the overflowing excesses of God's graces within us, His mercy and forgiveness included.

The workers in God's vineyard ought to be working for the sake of others, not simply for their own gain. The toil described by St. Paul in his letter to the Philippians, which we read in today's second reading, is a labour of love for others' sake. Paul frankly confesses that he would rather be dead, that dying would be for his own gain since he would be with Christ in heaven. But he goes on living in the flesh while toiling in the vineyard for the sake of those whom he loves rather than for the sake of his own comfort and gain. This is the true posture and the genuine attitude of the Christian. Rejoice with me, says God our Father because my Son, who was dead, has come back to life. All of your work and all of your devotion redounds to His risen life. Besides, you haven't lost a thing. Instead, you've gained a brother or a sister. Or are you jealous and envious because you have to share all of these good things with them? Did you stay at home remaining faithful to me and do all of the work you did just to keep it all to yourself?

This, my friends, is the ultimate foundation of morality and any ethical system. We keep our behaviour good, not for our own sake but the sake of others, be they, friend or enemy, be they Catholic or Protestant, be they Jew, or Arab, or Gentile, be they male or female. Isaiah tells us in the first reading: *"Let the scoundrel forsake his way, and the wicked man his thoughts; let him turn to the Lord for mercy, to our God, who is generous in forgiving."* My friends, how are they to know that God is generous and forgiving unless He is manifested to the wicked, manifested by we who are members of the Body of Christ? His temple built of living flesh, our flesh, offers God's presence and God's ways to men and women who need to see and receive His mercy, His generosity, and His forgiveness.

Far from being cheated, far from being denied justice, far from being defrauded of your wages, you, the sons and daughters of God, whether you yourselves are the prodigals, or whether you have been the faithful ones who stayed at home and worked hard in your Father's vineyard, you the little ones, the ones with little fame and no renown, you are the hidden power and glory of Christ. For you are the signs of contradiction, you are the hidden Christ tucked deep down within the guts of all that is human. You are God's salt, God's seed, and God's productive toil for the salvation of those who are lost but destined, just as you are, to share in His limitless and measureless Love. You are infinitely blessed with God's gifts!

# THEME 72
# GOD IS ALL-POWERFUL ABOVE ALL
# IN HIS MERCY AND COMPASSION

*Ezekiel 18:25-28; Philippians 2:1-11; Matthew 21:28-32*

We just heard about the man with the two sons, one of whom told his father he would work as his father had requested and then did not, the other having said "no" to his father and then changed his mind and did his father's bidding. What changed that son's mind? Was it a sense of shame? Was it a sense of guilt? I suspect it was the latter, his sense of guilt.

All of us have regrets, memories of unkind or hurtful or downright evil things we've done. All of us have feelings of guilt. We'd all like the chance to do certain things over again, to make things different, to right the wrongs we've done. The Persian writer Omar Khayyam once wrote: "The moving finger writes, and having written it, moves on. Nor all your piety nor wit can lure it back to cancel half a line. Nor all your tears wash out one word of it."

What, then, do we do with our awareness of guilt? The parable of Jesus we just heard gives us a sense of direction. After all, guilt can be a good thing - it can move us in a constructive direction.

Not everyone agrees with that proposition. There are those in the world around us who maintain that guilt is a device used by preachers to manipulate and control you, to get money out of you, to hold you in fear and to threaten you with hell. Still, others say that there's no such thing as sin; it's just a sickness, they say; that it's psychically pathological to even recall sin and guilt. Still, others wallow in guilt and self-pity, using it as an excuse for drinking, using drugs, or other sorts of compensatory behaviours to deaden the sense of guilt.

The truth is that guilt, remorse, and regret can be potent and potentially useful emotions. They can move us away from wasting our gifts, abusing other people, along with powerfully motivating us to make our lives and the lives of those around us much happier and fulfilled.

Responsibility, the ability to respond, is directly related to guilt. While we all have a sense of guilt and regret over things we have done, some of us go one step further and begin to examine what we have not done. I have not shared moments of kindness, tenderness, and compassion with people who have needed those things from me. I have not been as courageous as I could have been. I have shunned valour, missed opportunities to lead, passed by moments of truth, avoided conflicts that would have changed people for the better, and not done what God had allowed me to do. I have been the older son, not the younger one depicted in that famous other parable of Jesus, namely the parable of the Prodigal Son.

Moreover, some of us have blamed others and used the bad example of others as an excuse. I have appealed to the empty phrase: "Everybody's doing it," and even decreed certain things not to be sinful, things that God has clearly told us are truly sinful.

One of the best definitions of insanity I've ever heard goes like this: "To keep on doing the same things in the same way, while expecting a different result each time." Truly, that is a crazy way to live and act. Yet I've done it. The only sensible thing to do with our regrets, our remorse and our guilt is to change the way we act. That's the simple message of Jesus' parable. It is insanity to declare the reality of sin to be something else. To do that is to be out of touch with reality. It is equally insane to regret what we've done or have not done and yet keep on doing what we're doing or not doing. The only sane and sensible thing to do with our regrets, our remorse, and our guilt is to face what we have done or not done and then embark on a positive course of action, to make active, decisive and positive changes in the way we behave.

Because of his sense of guilt, the second son faced reality and then went out to accomplish his father's task. He experienced guilt and then took action. "Regret" was something he felt deep down within his heart and soul. "Went" is something he did with the soles of his feet.

You and I are loved sinners. We are not saints, nor are we condemned to hell. We are "being redeemed sinners," those beloved by God for whom He sent His only-begotten Son, not to condemn but to save. It's only when we admit to God, to ourselves, and to another human being the exact nature of our wrongs that we can begin to get in touch with reality and move out of the insanity of our denial. Once freed from denial, we can live and move and have our being in the freedom of the children of God. And that freedom is precisely the freedom to do what is right, decent, and good.

Doing what is right, decent, and good is the only sanity that gives us the freedom for our hearts' hunger and thirst and fills us with the food and nourishment and strength needed for that freedom. Jesus is about to come down to earth once again right here on this altar to give you and to give me the Bread of Life, that which can make us healthy and whole, that which can bring sanity and the power we need to accomplish His work here on earth as it is in heaven.

The most straightforward interpretation of the teachings of Jesus speaks to my heart, telling me that through God's forgiveness, in His eyes, I am no longer a sinner. In the depths of my conscience, I am no longer guilty. That is what we all want, and Jesus tells us that it is true. God is the Good. He is infinitely free, freedom beyond anything we can conceive. He is utterly free, free of all ties, far beyond what we can conceive as good. God lives in the freedom of love and as such, can proclaim to you and me, "Your sin no longer exists!" But I would never hear those words unless I repent and admit my guilt. This is the great freedom we experience when we receive the Sacrament of Reconciliation.

# THEME 73
# WHEREVER THERE IS GOD,
# THERE IS THE FUTURE

*Pope's Homily at Freiburg Airport in Germany*

Dear Brothers and Sisters, It is moving for me to be here once again to celebrate this Eucharist, this Thanksgiving, with so many people from different parts of Germany and the neighbouring countries. We offer our thanks above all to God, in whom we live and move. But I would also like to thank all of you for your prayers that the Successor of Peter may continue to carry out his ministry with joy and faithful hope, and that he may strengthen his brothers in faith.

"Father, you show your almighty power in your mercy and forgiveness", as we said in today's Collect. In the first reading, we heard how God manifested the power of His mercy in Israel's history. The Babylonian Exile experience caused the people to fall into a crisis of faith: Why did this calamity happen? Perhaps God was not truly powerful?

In the face of all the terrible things that happen in the world today, there are theologians who say that God cannot be all-powerful. In response to this, we profess God, the all-powerful Creator of heaven and earth. We are glad and thankful that God is all-powerful. At the same time, we have to be aware that He exercises His power differently from the way we normally do. He has placed a limit on His power by recognising the freedom of His creatures. We are glad and thankful for the gift of freedom. However, when we see the terrible things that happen as a result of it, we are frightened. Let us put our trust in God, whose power manifests itself above all in mercy and forgiveness. Let us be certain, dear faithful, that God desires the salvation of His people. He desires our salvation. He is always close to us, especially in times of danger and radical change, His heart aches for us, and He reaches out to us. We need to open ourselves to Him so that the power of His mercy can touch our hearts. We have to be ready to abandon evil, to raise ourselves from indifference, and make room for His word. God respects our freedom. He does not constrain us.

In the Gospel, Jesus takes up this fundamental theme of prophetic preaching. He recounts the parable of the two sons invited by their father to work in the vineyard. The first son responded: 'I will not go', but afterward he repented and went. Instead, the other son said to the father: 'I go, sir,' but did not go. When asked by Jesus, which of the two sons did the father's will, those listening respond: "the first" (Mt 21:29-31). The parable message is clear: it is not words that matter, but deeds, deeds of conversion, and faith. Jesus directs this message to the chief priests and elders of the people, that is, to the experts of religion for Israel's people. At first, they say "yes" to God's will, but their piety becomes routine, and God no longer matters to them.

For this reason, they find the message of John the Baptist and the message of Jesus disturbing. The Lord concludes His parable with harsh words: "Truly, the tax collectors and the harlots go into the kingdom of God before you. For John came to you in the way of righteousness, and you did not believe him, but the tax collectors and the harlots believed him, and even when you saw it, you did not afterwards repent and believe him" (Mt 21:32). Translated into the language of our time, this statement might sound something like this: agnostics, who are constantly exercised by the question of God, those who long for a pure heart but suffer on account of our sin, are closer to the kingdom of God than believers whose life of faith is "routine" and who regard the Church merely as an institution, without letting their hearts be touched by faith.

The words of Jesus should make us all pause, and in fact, they should disturb us. However, this is by no means to suggest that everyone who lives in the Church and works for her should be considered far from Jesus and the kingdom of God. Absolutely not! On the contrary, this is a time to offer a word of profound gratitude to the many co-workers, employees and volunteers, without whom life in the parishes and in the entire Church would be hard to imagine. The Church in Germany has many social and charitable institutions through which the love of neighbour is practised in ways that bring social benefits and reach to the ends of the earth. I would like to express my gratitude and appreciation to all those working in Caritas Germany and in other church organisations who give their time and effort generously in voluntary service to the Church. In the first place, such a service requires objective and professional expertise. But in the spirit of Jesus' teaching, something more is needed – an open heart that allows itself to be touched by the love of Christ, and thus gives to our neighbour, who needs us, something more than a technical service: it gives love, in which the other person is able to see Christ, the loving God. So let us ask ourselves, how is my relationship with God: in prayer, in participation at Sunday Mass, in exploring my faith through meditation on sacred scripture and study of the Catechism of the Catholic Church? Dear friends, in the last analysis, the renewal of the Church will only come about through openness to conversion and through renewed faith.

The gospel for this Sunday speaks of two sons, but behind them, mysteriously, there is a third son. The first son says "no," but does the father's will. The second son says, "yes," but does not do what he was asked. The third son both says "yes" and does what he was asked. This third son is the Only-begotten Son of God, Jesus Christ, who has gathered us all here. Jesus, on entering the world, said: "Lo, I have come to do thy will, O God" (Heb 10:7). He not only said "yes," he acted on it. As the Christological hymn from the second reading says: "Though he was in the form of God, [Jesus] did not count equality with God a thing to be grasped, but emptied himself, taking the form of a servant, being born in the likeness of men. And being found in human form, he humbled himself and became obedient unto death, even death on a Cross" (Phil. 2: 6-8). In humility and obedience, Jesus fulfilled the will of the Father, and by dying on the Cross for his brothers and sisters, He saved us from our pride and obstinacy. Let us thank Him for His sacrifice, let us bend our knees before His name and proclaim together with the disciples of the first generation: "Jesus Christ is Lord, to the glory of God the Father" (Phil 2:11).

The Christian life must continually measure itself by Christ: "Have this mind among yourselves, which is yours in Christ Jesus" (Phil 2:5), as Saint Paul says in the introduction to the Christological hymn. A few verses before, he exhorts his readers: "So if there is any encouragement in Christ, any incentive of love, any participation in the Spirit, any affection and sympathy, complete my joy by being of the same mind, having the same love, being in full accord and of one mind" (Phil 2:1-2). Just as Christ was united to the Father and obedient to Him, so too, the disciples must obey God and be of one mind among themselves. Dear friends, I dare to exhort you with Paul: complete my joy by being firmly united in Christ. The Church in Germany will overcome the great challenges of the present and future. It will remain a leaven in society if the priests, consecrated men and women, and the lay faithful, in fidelity to their respective vocations, work together in unity, if the parishes, communities, and movements support and enrich each other, if the baptised and confirmed, in union with their bishop, lift high the torch of untarnished faith and allow it to enlighten their abundant knowledge and skills. The Church in Germany will continue to be a blessing for the entire Catholic world: if she remains faithfully united with the Successors of Saint Peter and the Apostles, if she fosters cooperation in various ways with mission countries and allows herself to be "infected" by the joy that marks the faith of these young Churches.

To his exhortation to unity, Paul adds a call to humility: "Do nothing from selfishness or conceit, but in humility count others better than yourselves. Let each of you look not only to his interests but also to the interests of others" (Phil 2:3-4). The Christian life is a life for others: existing for others, humble service of neighbours, and the common good. Dear friends, humility is a virtue that does not enjoy great esteem today. But the Lord's disciples know that this virtue is, so to speak, the oil that makes the process of dialogue fruitful, cooperation simple and unity sincere. The Latin word for humility, humilitas, is derived from humus and indicates a closeness to the earth. Those who are humble stand with their two feet on the ground, but above all, they listen to Christ, the Word of God, who ceaselessly renews the Church and each of her members.

Let us ask God for the courage and the humility to walk the path of faith, to draw from the riches of His mercy, and to fix our gaze on Christ, the Word, who makes all things new and is for us "the way, the truth, and the life" (Jn 14:6): He is our future.

# THEME 74
# GOD IS THROWING A PARTY

*Isaiah 25:6-10; Philippians 41:11-14; Matthew 22:11-14*

For a moment, I would like you to imagine yourself at a party, maybe a party you have been to, or one you have given for friends and acquaintances. Let's say it's a costume party and people are there with altered ways of seeing each other. Everyone has a fresh start and a new beginning at being different persons. Past histories are forgotten. The guests present themselves and are seen by others, as new persons.

Everyone at the party is having a wonderful time, chatting, laughing, enjoying each other, and sharing the happiness of a really good time. But then you notice someone over in the corner, all alone and sulking, miserable in his isolation and loneliness. You go over and try to talk with him, but all you get for your trouble are a few grunts and a sour look. The more you try to break through his isolation, the more you discover that he is disgusted with people who have a good time and resentful that you have even given a party. It's almost as if everyone else doesn't have a right to have a good time because he is miserable and wants everyone else to be miserable. No amount of coaxing moves him out of his protective and miserable shell. He absolutely refuses to receive the good time you wish to give him. There is nothing that you can do, nothing you can give him that will make him happy.

Let me now point out that God is throwing a party for us. He made the earth a garden of beauty. Even when in the Garden of Eden things didn't turn out right; God started over. And He did so again and again after that. Finally, He sent his Son to throw us a party, a celebration in a new garden, the Garden of the Resurrection.

Listen again now to the prophet Isaiah: *On this mountain, the Lord of hosts will provide for all peoples a feast of rich food and choice wines, juicy, rich food and pure, choice wines. On this mountain, he will destroy the veil that veils all peoples, the web that is woven over all nations; he will destroy death forever.*

In St. Matthew's gospel, we hear: *The servants went out into the byroads and rounded up everyone they met, the bad as well as the good. This filled the wedding hall with banqueters. However, when the king came in to meet the guests, he caught sight of a man not properly dressed for a wedding feast.*

The point of it all is that we come to God's party, His banquet life, not because we have earned a right to be there, not because we can buy an invitation, not because our friends have good political influence with Him, but simply because He gives us entrance out of His free generosity. The enjoyment of life comes to us from God's free choice and totally because of His sheer generosity.

There is a more subtle point. The bad, as well as the good, are at the party. All are predestined to attend. All are there with new faces, as new persons with new beginnings because God's forgiveness has made them new again, new persons with new histories and new beginnings. Our past mistakes and sins are blotted out. We are wearing new visages and new costumes because we are wearing His wedding garments, clothed with His gifts. God's judgment is His mercy. Our predestination allows us to be made over again, the bad as well as the good, in the new creation that is given us by the Son of God, the Word made into one of us and then raised from the death of our sins and our history into a new life, in a new Garden of Eden, in the banquet thrown by God in the Resurrection of His Son.

Now the difficulty comes in our response to God's invitation to His party. After all is said and done, God offers, and we respond. He wants us to have a good time, a joyful time with Him in His world, in the life He has given us. The difficulty is found in those who sit off in the corner, sulking, muttering to themselves, and hating all of those who are enjoying themselves in God's party.

Some people who do not like to receive anything at all, even gifts. We all know of them. Perhaps we may even see them in ourselves. They are the ones who tell us: "I'll pay for everything I get; I can earn my way, and I don't need anybody's charity; I don't need anybody or anything; I can take care of myself."

That attitude is particularly noticeable when it comes to receiving forgiveness. Many people just cannot say that they are sorry or confess their sins. They simply cannot receive the gratuity and the sheer gift of forgiveness. Why? Well, for many reasons, I suppose, but I think a big reason is pride. It's found in the fact that receiving forgiveness means an admission of need, the fear of being dependent upon another's love, and so forth. Many reasons. But they all mean that such persons come to God's party, God's celebration of life, without a wedding garment, the garment that is being clothed with Christ. They cannot rid themselves of their past and be seen in a new light, as new persons. It means they can't join the party and are bitterly resentful of those that do.

Receiving a gift is difficult. One immediately feels an obligation. One feels that one simply has to give in return; feels indebted; feels a sudden loss of independence and self-sufficiency. It happens at Christmas, birthdays. It happens in moments of crisis. It happens when one needs forgiveness. I know of several bad marriages when I could have helped the couples involved but could not because one or both parties would not come to me for help. They could not admit they needed help or admit that they could not take care of their problem all by themselves.

God has given us life, and He wants us to enjoy ourselves in this life. He is throwing a banquet for us by giving us life, a feast of the rich food in choice wines, juicy, rich and pure. He knows that we will make mistakes and so He is prepared to reconcile us in the death and resurrection of His only Son. Ultimately, when we are judged by God at the end of our lives, He will see our humanity in the humanity of His Son. He will judge us in that way. But that means that we have to come to God's banquet table of life properly dressed, dressed in the wedding garment offered to us by His Son. It means putting off our old clothes of self-sufficiency, privatism, independence, and grand isolation. It means putting on the wedding garment of acceptance, acceptance of ourselves in the limitations and imperfections we have, acceptance of our need for forgiveness, acceptance of the gift of His Son offered to us by God our Father. Our destiny is there. But the consequence of our life rests in our own decisions. What will be the sum total of our life's decisions when we die? What grand decision will they all add up to? To know the answer to that question, we have only to examine the pattern of our daily living and our willingness to receive God's gifts, the gifts of life and the gifts of others that come to us in this life.

Truly in this instance, it is more blessed to receive than to give.

# THEME 75
# LOVE IS A CHOICE

*Exodus 22:20-26; 1 Thessalonians 1:5-10; Matthew 22:34-40*

There are some people for whom we simply cannot feel any love at all, or so we tell ourselves. Too much resentment, too much distrust, some people are just "too much" for us.

Take, for instance, a relative who is arrogant, self-centred, opinionated, and who is given over to his own pleasure and comfort. He thinks everyone else is stupid. We feel sure that when he dies and meets Jesus Christ face to face, he will manage to tell Christ that he could have redeemed the human race in a much better way. He will likewise point out all of God's faults and failures, particularly how God botched the job of creating human beings. At best, we can only tolerate this sort of person. The greater the distance between us we feel, the better.

What, then, is the meaning of Christ's mandate to us, telling us to love everyone as we love ourselves? How can we possibly love such a person?

First of all, we should take it for what it is - a mandate, a command, something that has nothing to do with feelings. No one can command you to have warm feelings toward another. Not even God commands *that* of us. We cannot even tell ourselves to do so. Even if we could, would it be worth doing? I daresay it wouldn't. Even abusers of women tell us that they have powerful emotional feelings of affection for the women they abuse, along with overpowering lust, envy, jealousy and possessiveness.

No, Jesus is not speaking of emotions and feelings. He knows how fickle and unreliable feelings are. Feelings come, and feelings go as they wish leaving us alone with ourselves after they have vacated our hearts, along with the wreckage they leave behind.

Please don't get me wrong. "Falling in love" is a wonderful thing, even a beautiful thing. Young boys and girls fall in love. Young mothers and young fathers fall in love with their newborn babies. The emotions of affection and the feelings of love are beautiful things, the stuff of novels, movies, love songs, and poems. There's nothing wrong with them. But they shouldn't control us. Love is a choice, not a feeling. Feelings come and go; commitments do not.

In today's gospel account, Jesus is talking about love as something we do, not something we feel. He knew full well that affection is something we feel. He is looking for us to love. Love is a choice, a commitment to do things; that is why Jesus is commanding us to love others. It's what we do for them, not what we feel toward them, that is the point.

I recently heard of a couple who were celebrating their 50th wedding anniversary, their Golden Jubilee. A friend asked them how they did it. "Did you ever think about getting a divorce?" "No," said the bride of fifty years, "I never thought about that. I didn't consider divorce to be an option." Then, with a twinkle in her eye, she added, "But a few times I have thought about murder!"

When two people marry, they promise to act toward each other in ways they will not act toward anyone else. Feelings come, and feelings go --- we have little control over them. Love and commitments, however, are choices. Furthermore, as psychologists tell us, feelings can be shaped by the way we act. This is why Jesus commands us to act toward others lovingly, regardless of how we feel. Love makes commitments; feelings can follow along.

All of us have feelings of fondness toward others. Even pagans feel fondness and affection. So there's no particular Christian virtue in feeling fondness and affection for another. Consequently, there is no sin in feelings of fondness toward another. Virtue and sin are found; however, in what we choose to *do* with other people. This is why Jesus always placed His emphasis, not on how we feel toward others, but how we *act* toward them.

We need to pay attention to the Last Judgment scene depicted in Matthew's gospel account. That last judgment has to do with deeds --- feelings are entirely omitted. God does not say: "I was hungry, and you felt sorry for me. I was naked, and you felt embarrassed. I was sick, and you had feelings of sympathy toward me." All of which would have been simply nice. And many churches preach a gospel of nice feelings --- religion is only a matter of feeling nice toward others. But Christianity is more than being nice or simply having nice feelings.

When did Jesus ever mention being "nice" toward others? The only thing that counted with Him was that the hungry were fed, the naked were clothed, and that the lonely and abandoned were sought out and cared for.

Jesus Christ is the ultimate realist. He commands us. He mandates us to love our neighbours as we love ourselves, even those who are unlovable. Perhaps He even means *particularly* those who are unlovable. He closes our little loopholes and presents us with the most demanding of all gospel messages, allowing us no compromises. It was a call to get extremely serious about what we do, not what we feel.

I don't care how you feel, Jesus says; just love your neighbour, *all* of your neighbours no matter who they are and how you act toward them. All of those complicated feelings of yours will eventually follow along. Religion is a matter of what you do, how you act.

Jesus isn't inventing something new. No, He's giving us the mandate of our Father in heaven, one that was expressed to us long, long ago in the Book of Exodus, the Second Book in the Old Testament. The challenge has always been before us, a challenge as old as the Bible, one that we just heard from the first Book of Exodus:

Thus says the LORD: "You shall not molest or oppress an alien, for you were once aliens yourselves in the land of Egypt. You shall not wrong any widow or orphan. If ever you wrong them, and they cry out to me, I will surely hear their cry. My wrath will flare up, and I will kill you with the sword; then your wives will be widows, and your children orphans. If you lend money to one of your poor neighbours among my people, you shall not act like an extortioner toward him by demanding interest from him. If you take your neighbour's cloak as a pledge, you shall return it to him before sunset; for this cloak of his is the only covering he has for his body. What else has he to sleep in? If he cries out to me, I will hear him, for I am compassionate."

Love, then, is not merely a nice feeling; it is a challenge.

# THEME 76
# TALENTS ARE FOR USE



*Wisdom 6:12-16; Thessalonians 4:13-18; Matthew 25:1-13*

I want to begin today by noting that in Jesus' time among us, a talent was a huge amount of money. The coin denominated as a talent was very valuable indeed. For us today, we think of talents, not as money but as special personal gifts we may have. You may have musical talent; you may be a talented writer, artist, or entertainer; you may have intellectual talent, and so forth. We speak of such a person as "gifted." We are not all equally gifted; obviously, some of us are more gifted than others. Just as in the parable, some may have five, some two, some just one.

Today's gospel parable is one of a three-part series of gospel parables dealing with the use of our God-given talents. Two Sundays ago, we heard of the wily servant who cooked His master's accounting books. Last Sunday, we heard about the wise and foolish bridesmaids. Today we hear about the servant who, out of fear, did nothing with His God-given talent except to bury it. In other parables, we hear about servants who fail to be profitable servants and suffer the consequences.

Today's parable opens by noting that our Father in heaven has given us various talents in varying amounts while expecting that we wisely use whatever He has given us these talents to develop His kingdom here on earth. In the parable, we heard: *While the servants who received the five and the two talents used them wisely and doubled their holdings, the third servant left His talent unused and buried in the ground.*

I want to highlight here the beautiful picture painted in today's first reading, the reading about the good wife who is not only a good wife but also a successful businesswoman, a productive and generous businesswoman who employs her talents well and who reaches out to the poor and extends her hands to the needy. She knows what to do with her profits – she cares for her family while at the same time, she generously cares for the poor and needy.

The challenge that faces you and me in today's parable is where we hear that on His return, the master, a true businessman, questions each servant as to the use he has made of the money given to him and wants to know what profit they had gained. What return was made on their master's investments in them? As in all such cases, and in what we have done with our lives, there is an eventual accounting.

The parable goes on to instruct us that those who acted wisely, like the good wife in today's first reading, were praised and then promised that even more would be coming to them. Furthermore, they would no longer be servants or slaves but would instead have honoured places in their master's household. Then comes the part that ought to concern us the most. The servant who had not used the talent given to him tried to excuse his negligence by saying that he knew how hard and demanding the master was and therefore did not risk investing His money out of fear that he might lose it.

But was it fear? Perhaps. I think, however, it could also be that the master knew that the real reason why this servant did not invest his talent was because of his sinful neglect and sloth. The servant claimed he knew the master was demanding and exacting but likely thought he was safe during His master's absence. Maybe he even convinced himself that his master would never return.

Now his troubles really begin. The master instructs that the talent he had failed to use be taken from him and given to the servant who had five talents and earned five more. Because this unproductive servant refuses to earn anything for a master he called hard and exacting, he is not admitted to the master's household.

Was the master to be feared? Was he hard of heart and exacting, as the unproductive servant claimed? Or was the unproductive servant using that as an excuse? We shouldn't overlook the fact that the master generously allowed the productive servants to keep what had been given to them and keep what they had earned. On top of that, the master brought them into his household and made them a part of his family. He was, in fact, very generous.

God will not be outdone in generosity. If we are faithful and loyal to Him, we will be greatly rewarded, while the disloyal will lose even the original gifts given them because they did not use them as they should. Instead of being received into the household of the master, the unfaithful servants will be cast into the "outer darkness," a metaphor used to describe a lot of those who exclude themselves from heaven by their choices. In hell's darkness, they will weep and gnash their teeth in bitter disgust with themselves, self-inflicted torture for those who have ignored their real purpose in life.

Is God harsh? Is God unfair? Many atheists or agnostics make that claim. But the evidence of God's love and mercy demonstrates that the opposite is true. Moreover, if we end up in the same place as the unproductive servant, we will have no one to blame but ourselves. Why? Because God respects us enough not to control us but rather to honour our choices. He utterly respects our decisions and will not cancel them out.

If you think that your decisions don't matter, then your soul is in peril. If you think that God will overlook your choices in the end, then your soul is in peril. If you think God is a harsh taskmaster, exacting and lacking in generosity, then your soul is in peril. If you think that God has not given you any talents and that you are good for nothing, then your soul is in peril. God is not interested in being a punishing God, the greatest punishment we face is self-punishment, self-punishment expressed in our own weeping and gnashing of teeth over the choices we have made, choices that have rejected the love of God.

God never rejects us. It is we who ignore His love. It is we who have ignored God's gifts of the friends He has given us, the members of our family He has given us, the beauties of the world He has given us, and especially the gift of His Christ present to us in His sacraments.

God will not be outdone in generosity. But while that is true, it is likewise true that a gift is not a gift until it is received and valued. Your talents are God's gift to you. What you do with them is your gift to God, a gift that will result in immeasurable happiness for you in God's very own household.

So live, give, love, and pray. Then when your day of accounting arrives, you will be taken by Christ into the home prepared for you by the God who is love. We came into being by love, and it is to love that we are called and gifted as we make our passage through life back home into the household of God.

# THEME 77
# CHRIST, KING OF KINGS

*Ezekiel 34:11-12, 15-17; 1 Corinthians 15:20-26, 28; Matthew 25:31-46*

If there is no divine being above us, we will be consumed by all that is around us. If Christ in His kingship is removed from our lives, we will be at the mercy of any and all forces in this world that are more powerful than our own powers.

As Christians, we claim Jesus Christ to be our King. We place ourselves under His kingship because we believe that we can establish His justice and peace among us with His power. But to do so, Christ relies on our freely chosen allegiance. He relies on our willing cooperation, and He relies on the gift of our very lives and souls to reveal His kingdom here on earth as it is in heaven. That kingdom is found in the way we relate to the people we find in our lives. It's realised, made real, in our personal relationships.

This is the way it is in Christ's kingdom. If Christ's kingdom is to be revealed here on earth, made real in our world as it is in heaven, we must work to make it so. Do we expect God to be a "Big Daddy" and give it all to us without any effort on our part, despite our indifference, neglect and even our rejection of Him? That would be childish nonsense. That would be a foolish presumption. That would be arrogance on our part, namely the expectation that God will do it all for us anyway, even though we pay scant attention to Him and give Him little, if anything, of our hearts and souls.

My first words to you in this homily were: "If there is no divine being above us, we will be consumed by all that is around us." In other words, if Christ is not our king, then the principalities and powers of this world will rule us. We will have sold out to them, sold our hearts and souls for the cheap glitz and glitter of fool's gold. If God is not our Father and Christ is not our king when we shall have our gods and goddesses -- and they will give us nothing. In the end, we will have betrayed ourselves and lost our citizenship in the everlasting kingdom of God. Who are the gods and goddesses that our culture presents to us? What have they given us in return?

Christ is our King so that the powers of this world cannot hold us in their grip. Our freedom is found in "the glorious freedom of the sons and daughters of God." If Christ is not our king, then we will be consumed by all that is around us.

In a few moments, we will pray the words of the Preface for this Mass. In that Preface, we can find Christ's mission statement. This mission statement of Christ is also our mission statement:

As King, He claims dominion over all creation, that He may present to you, His almighty Father,

- An eternal and universal kingdom,
- A kingdom of truth and life,
- A kingdom of holiness and grace,
- A kingdom of justice, love, and peace.

This means that we must be a people of truth, a people who protect the dignity of life in all of its forms. We must be a people liberated from the seductive lures of this world and who live fully in God's gifts to us. We must be a people of justice, love others without self-interest, and work for peace.

How easy it is to say those lovely words! How hard it is to truly live them! But that's why we're here, isn't it? We know that with men and women living and working independently, it is impossible to live out those ideals. But with God, with Christ as our King, all things are possible. He was crucified, died, and rose from the dead to hand over

His Spirit to us so that, in the power of His Holy Spirit, we might eventually reveal His kingdom here on earth as it is in heaven.

# THEME 78
# GOD SPEAKS HIS WORD TO US

*Isaiah 40:1-5, 9-11; 2 Peter 3:8-14; Mark 1:1-8*

When we find ourselves in spiritual darkness and emotional darkness, what do we do? How do we respond? Some of us respond with fatalistic resignation, others of us with anger, and some in despair that has led them into alcoholism or medicine-cabinet drug addiction. Our psyches and souls can fill up with bitterness causing others to distance themselves from us, driving us into bitter isolation and feelings of abandonment.

We live in a time of economic gloom, an economic depression that has affected not only our pocketbooks but our national spirit as well. Our dysfunctional government is symptomatic of how sick we are. Where do we look for hope? In economic indicators or elsewhere? Where are the first lights of a dawning new day? To what horizon do we look? Has God abandoned us, or is God bidding us to look beyond what imprisons us in darkness?

Last Sunday, we considered the broad sweep of Advent. We reminded ourselves that Advent begins with us looking toward the end of the world. It is right that we should be anxious and concerned about the judgment of God on the Day of Judgment. But we should not be held in the grip of fear. Why? Because God's judgment is that we are worth saving. God's judgment comes to us with His grace and mercy. His grace and mercy are given to us in His Son, Jesus Christ.

That theme continues this weekend. The first words in today's first reading come from the prophet Isaiah. God tells Isaiah to comfort His people. "Speak tenderly to Jerusalem," He tells Isaiah "and proclaim to her that her time of trial is coming to an end. Every valley shall be filled in; every mountain and hill shall be made low; the rugged land shall be made plain, and the rough country made a broad valley. Then the glory of the Lord shall be revealed." Isaiah was speaking God's word to Israel, His people who had been driven from their homeland and living in captivity in Babylon. And Isaiah speaks to us as well, in our time.

Tenderly God speaks to those captive Israelites through His prophet Isaiah. "Comfort, give comfort to my people... Speak tenderly to Jerusalem." Tell them that their trials are about to end and that their guilt is expiated. In the desert, God's power will make things gentle for them. Valleys will be filled, mountains will be levelled, and rough ways will be smoothed. God will care for them like a shepherd, guide and nourish them, gathering them in His arms and speaking tenderly to them. God cares for us also.

The gospel account picks up on that scene. However, we need to note that all this will all not come about unless we do our part, unless we repent, change our ways, and prepare to meet God on His terms, not ours. The comfortable will be afflicted, and the afflicted will be comforted. The way back home to God is not automatic; it is not simply handed to us on a silver platter. The situation of the Israelites differs from the situation in which we presently find ourselves. As challenging as theirs was, ours is more challenging.

To provide for us in our challenge, God sent us His only Son to work with us, not simply for us. We often find ourselves praying to God to do things for us without, at the same time offering God what we will do for Him. Therein is found our challenge. What DO we do for Him? How do we work with Him?

If we think God has afflicted us with various sufferings, ought we not to reflect on the reality that we afflicted His Son, grievously afflicted Him? Once having reflected on that, what have we done to comfort Him with repentant hearts, hearts opened with love so that His love can enter our hearts?

When we have broken away from those who love us, when we have alienated ourselves like the Prodigal Son was alienated from his father and his home, what path do we take to return to them? When we have hurt those whom we love, how do we get back into their hearts? For those, however, who live apart from God's love, the path is difficult, daunting, and perhaps not possible to find. For those who live in God's favour, the valleys will be filled, the mountains levelled, the rough ways will be made smooth, and the trip back will be gentle.

Life is filled with afflictions, many of them severe. The Evil One will use them to drive our hearts further away from God. The devil's tools are doubt, disillusionment, discouragement, depression, defeat, despair, and spiritual death. Living under those clouds can imprison our souls in the devil's captivity.

God has spoken His Word to us. His Word made flesh. Ever present, God speaks to us in the words of the prophet Isaiah: "Comfort, give comfort to my people, says your God. Speak tenderly to Jerusalem, and proclaim to her that her service is at an end, her guilt is expiated..." Our Church, standing now in the shoes of John the Baptist, cries out: In the desert prepare the way of the Lord! Make straight in the wasteland a highway for our God! Every valley shall be filled in, every mountain and hill shall be made low; the rugged land shall be made a plain, the rough country, a broad valley. Here is your God! He comes with power, the Lord God who rules by His strong arm; here is His reward. Like a shepherd, He feeds His flock; in His arms, He gathers His lambs, carrying them next to His heart, leading them with care.

All the more marvellous, then, is the fact that God's only Son entered into our humanity. He became fully and truly human to share in our darkness, to share in our moments of depression and despair. This is so that we, in our darkest moments and in our times of disillusionment and depression, might find there His voice and hear His call to us:

"Behold, I am with you. Fear not; be not afraid; have courage. Walk in my way, in my truth, and in my life, and I will be there with you as your gentle shepherd, holding you in my arms next to my heart, all the while bringing you home, back to the home in which you belong."

Jesus Christ knows suffering. He has not remained above and apart from us. He has entered into our suffering and shared in it. His mother, too, knows suffering. She has shared in it fully and in our suffering loves us with a mother's love. Jesus Christ and His mother offer us power and strength so that we need not remain passive victims. They give us both strength and hope. Their message is empowering. They give us a power this world knows not of. We are not trapped in hopelessness and powerlessness. God's tender loving care is there for us if only we turn from this world's ways and enter into their way, the only way that leads to victory over all that this world can throw at us.

Like a shepherd, God leads us, feeds us, and strengthens us. In His arms, He gathers us, carrying us close to His heart and leading us home to our heavenly home, a journey that is both challenging and comforting.

# THEME 79
# THE COMING OF CHRISTMAS

*Isaiah 61:1-2, 10-11; 1 Thessalonians 5:16-24; John 1:6-8, 19-28*

If you go out into the Internet and search for thoughts from notable people about Christmas, you will find lots of uplifting and heartwarming thoughts about the holidays, thoughts from people of faith, and thoughts from people of no particular faith all rejoicing over the coming of Christmas.

Here are but just a few of them:

Said one: "Christmas is a necessity. There has to be at least one day of the year to remind us that we're here for something else besides ourselves."

Said another:

"I have always thought of Christmas time, when it has come round, as a good time; a kind, forgiving, charitable time; the only time I know of, in the long calendar of the year when men and women seem by one consent to open their shut-up hearts freely and to think of people less fortunate than ourselves whom we should regard as if they were fellow passengers to the grave, and not another race of creatures bound on other journeys."

A third said: "Our hearts grow tender with childhood memories and love of kindred, and we are better throughout the year for having, in spirit, become a child again at Christmas-time."

One of our more famous American authors said: "This is the message of Christmas: We are never alone."

Our Church reminds us that Advent is the time of the coming of God into our humanity, and into our personal lives. It is that mysterious time of the year when we recognise the tension between what already IS and what is yet to be; between what we ARE and what we CAN BE; between what has been accomplished and what remains unfinished in our personal enterprise of life. The birth of Jesus Christ empowers us to move beyond what has been and to move into God's kingdom here on earth. We are, after all is said and done, called by God not only to enter heaven after we die but to usher in His kingdom here on earth as it is in heaven. To say it quite simply, we are to be concerned about what is happening now, not just what we hope will happen in the future.

For us, as Christians, we see that a Child lifts us to heaven, and heaven, in the birth of that Christ, stoops to earth. The message of Christmas is that the visible material world is now, by the birth of God's Son among us, bound to the invisible spiritual world. What humans regard as merely material is now invested with the presence of God. It is God's world, not just ours.

My mother once told me: "Happiness is something to do, someone to love, and something to hope for." If you and I can live lives dedicated to making the lives of others a little bit better than they once were, if we can find ourselves in the reality of what is transcendent in life, giving love to the loveless, and being loved in return, and if we can live each day fully in the Presence of Christ, or rather with His Presence reaching and touching others through us, that is no small thing to have happened to any man or woman.

Here are some personal qualities that should identify who we are and what we are as Catholics who celebrate the Birth of Christ and who receive Him in Holy Communion:

- We are known for attending Mass and receiving Jesus Christ into our souls every Sunday, and perhaps even known to celebrate daily Masses from time to time.

- We are known to be moral persons, respected for having high standards of ethics, morality, and character. There should be plenty of evidence by which others can identify us as persons of principle and goodness in the way we conduct our affairs, our businesses, and in the way we treat others. People should be able to take us at our word without really needing a contract to enforce our agreements and commitments.

- We are known to be prayerful persons. I don't mean that we ostentatiously pray in public so that we will be seen, but rather that being prayerful persons, we have a certain aura about us --- an atmosphere of serenity and peace surrounding us --- a spirit of peace and calmness that people recognise as coming only from being a profoundly prayerful person.

- We have an attitude, a habit of being, that is kind, gentle, respectful, sensitive to others, compassionate, and caring toward others. We have an attitude that can be seen in Mother Theresa of Calcutta's eyes, a face that reveals the presence of the heart of Christ, a smile, and a tone of voice that can only come from being close to Christ.

- We are known as persons who are sensitive to the presence of God in all things, in events, and in the seeming coincidences that occur in our lives and in our world, coincidences that point to the activities of God in our lives and in our world.

Today's readings from sacred scripture have several significant themes within them. One of them has to do with identity, John the Baptist's identity, Christ's identity, as well as your identity and mine. John the Baptist had a firm grasp of who he was not, as well as an inspired grasp of who he was, and what his life was all about.

# THEME 80
# COME AND SEE

*1 Sam. 3-10.19; 1 Cor. 6:13-15. 17-20; Jn. 1:35-42*

Here we are at the beginning of a new year with high hopes that this year will be better than 2011. We have our hopes even though we know that there is much in our world that is wrong. Without going into a long, dismal list of the many wrong things, let me point out just a few of them. The gap between the rich and the poor is widening, not closing. Political corruption and the politics of gridlock darken our perceptions of those we have elected to office. We face much that is sinful, evil, and criminal in our world. All of these things we know quite well are exceptions to the way things ought to be; they are out of the general order of what should be present in our relations with others.

How do we know that? What gives us this perspective and recognition of what is good, what is just, what is fair, and what ought to be? Today's gospel gives us the point of reference. It takes us back to the very beginning of the Christian movement, the movement of God into our humanity in Jesus Christ. The story is so familiar, so simple that we easily lose sight of its overwhelming importance. The jingle bells of Christmas divert our attention to the magnificent truth that God has entered into our humanity and thereby blessed it with His holy presence in all that it means to be human. In Jesus Christ, God brings His Light to what it means to be human and how we should live with each other.

John the Baptist initiates this coming of God to us by introducing two of his own disciples to Jesus, Andrew being the key player. John points Jesus out to them by exclaiming: "Look, there is the Lamb of God!" It's sort of like being at a social function when a very significant person enters the room, and a friend says to you: "Well, look who's here!"

A conversation then develops between Andrew and Jesus; a conversation sprinkled with seeking words like, "What do you want?" "Where do you live?" "Come and see," and "Come with me," all of them filled with the relational words of friendship. Let me emphasise here that these are the inviting words of friendship, not the commanding words of submission and obedience. These are words that invite us to live closely with Jesus.

My point is that our religion in its most distilled form is a friendship between ourselves and God in Jesus Christ. It is the one operative principle throughout Christ's entire life. Even at the end of His life during the Last Supper, Jesus gets down on His knees, washes His disciples' feet, stands up and looking each one in the eye, says: "I no longer call you slaves, I call you friends."

Jesus had no army. He neither needed one nor wanted one. He had the only one power with which to conquer the human spirit, the power of a loving friendship. That is the only thing that can invade and conquer the human heart. Brute force always fails; love always wins.

Our Catholic faith is one of the largest and most influential globally, and its membership is presently over one billion souls. It has built thousands of churches, hospitals, children's homes, nursing homes, schools, and even universities. It has rites, rituals, ceremonies, and the holy Sacraments of Jesus Christ. It has theologies, philosophies, systems of ethics, moral codes and even a Code of Canon Law abound. It is vast; it is intricate, and it is complex. But it is built on one thing and one thing alone, namely a personal, warm, intimate, and loving friendship with Jesus Christ. From that flows all of Christianity's hope, power, and vision of the truth about who we are.

Jesus was tempted to be a military leader, a dazzling magician, a revolutionary who would construct a new social order, and a universal healer and provider for us in all of our hurts, wants, and needs. But He resisted all of those temptations and asked for only one thing from us, which is friendship! He loved us and still does, even when we don't deserve it. He forgives us even when we can't forgive ourselves. He gives us far more than we ask for or even expect. He gives us a loveliness that is not pretty but powerful. He asks us to be more than nice; He asks of us everything. And amid war, famine, despair, and powerlessness, He gives us, in His friendship bringing with it the one gift our humanity needs more than anything else, namely hope.

Whenever we feel lost in a religious life that seems too complicated, or whenever we feel lost in a world that seems to be unmanageable and out of control, and whenever we're tempted to give up on ourselves, remember that our faith in its purest form is the personal friendship we can have with Jesus. That is how it began with Andrew and his brother Peter. And that is the solid rock upon which our relationship with Jesus is grounded.

For no matter what happens in our world, or in our spiritual lives, or in our relationships with others, we can always find our way once again with those seeking and questing words we heard in today's gospel message to you and me. "What do you want?" "Come and see!"

Listening to God's voice is of the essence of religion. It is the nourishment of our spiritual lives. When we celebrate the Mass, the first thing the Church does is offer us God's word. Then having received His word for our hearts and minds, we receive His Word made flesh for our human nature in Holy Communion.

Some defend themselves from intimacy; some are afraid to love. Because of their fear of losing their independent autonomy, they either flee from religion or turn it into something ridiculous. Some seek to turn religion into a series of laws, rules and regulations that must be followed. However, that approach requires only mindless obedience and thus misses the whole point about our relationship with Jesus.

The truth is that God has a word for you, personally. He has something He wants to say to you. The story of Samuel we heard in the first reading today is a story that we should make our own. The story in today's gospel account is a story we should likewise make our own. God is calling you and inviting you to come and stay with Him, to come and be close to Him.

I don't know how you pray your morning prayers, but I would suggest that a good way to start your day is to repeat Samuel's words each morning. When you begin the day with your first morning thoughts about God, say: "Speak, Lord, for your servant is listening." And then, at the close of each day, when you interpret the events of the day and try to make some sense out of them, repeat Samuel's words: "Speak, Lord, for your servant is listening." Each time you pray, after having told God about all that's happening in your life and about all that you need from Him, say: "Speak, Lord, for your servant is listening."

God has a word for you. He has something to say to you in words of friendship and love. For the sake of your own soul, let Him!

# THEME 81
# JESUS SPEAKS IN HIS NAME

*Deuteronomy 18:15-20; Psalm 95:1-2, 6-9; I Corinthians 732-35;*
*Mark 1: 21-28*

Two words in the gospel account you just heard captured my attention... "astonished" and "amazed." St. Mark reports that the people in Capernaum's synagogue were astonished at Jesus' teaching, and all were amazed. So the question arises: Why? Why were they so astonished and amazed? After all, they thought Jesus was a rabbi, someone who speaks God's word, and they were, after all, in a synagogue, a place where one would expect to be hearing about what God had to say. So why were they so astonished and amazed?

First of all, we need to notice that this event occurred at the very beginning of Our Blessed Lord's public ministry. St. Mark reports this event in the first chapter, twenty-first verse of his gospel account. Jesus has just finished gathering His twelve apostles and is now "going public," so to speak. Jesus had not as yet performed His dazzling miracles. He had not as yet cured the blind, healed the lepers, healed the crippled, and raised people from the dead. The most astounding miracle of all --- His resurrection from the dead --- had not yet occurred.

Why then was there astonishment and amazement at His first words here, at the beginning of His public ministry? It was common, we know, for rabbis to have followers and to move from synagogue to synagogue. What was so amazing about Jesus? Wasn't He teaching the way rabbis taught? Wasn't Jesus proclaiming the word of God to His people – something all rabbis did?

What I want to point out is the particular style of speech used by Jesus and to note the way He taught. He did not say, "The Lord's words for you today are…" Nor did He say: "The God who sent me says this…" No. Jesus spoke in His own name, on His own authority. There is, you see, a big difference in Jesus' speech here. He is telling everyone what He, the Christ, is declaring to them. He is not speaking on behalf of God --- He is speaking as God!

In another gospel account, St. Matthew reports Jesus as saying:

"You have heard the commandment imposed on your forefathers, 'You shall not commit murder; every murderer will be liable to judgment.' What I say to you is, everyone who grows angry with his brother shall be liable to judgment. You have heard the commandment, 'You shall not commit adultery.' What I say to you is: anyone who looks lustfully at a woman has already committed adultery with her in his thoughts. You have heard the commandment imposed on your forefathers, 'Do not take a false oath; rather, make good to the Lord all your pledges.' What I tell you is: do not swear at all. Say, 'Yes' when you mean 'Yes' and 'No' when you mean 'No.' Anything beyond that is from the evil one."

The Israelites revered the Ten Commandments. Those commandments and the tablets upon which they were written connected them --- directly connected them --- with God Himself. To alter or tamper with them was, for the Jews, absolutely unthinkable. To hear Jesus expand on those commandments was, to say the very least, astonishing and amazing. What Jesus taught was marvellous. It was luminous, enlightening, and brilliant. But how He taught was mind-boggling because the way Jesus spoke was as God speaking. He didn't speak about God. He didn't begin by saying: Thus says the Lord…" No. He simply and directly spoke as only God would speak. Nothing could be more astonishing than that. Either Jesus is whom He claimed to be and demonstrated Himself to be, or else He was a charlatan, a fraud, and a liar. He is either God the Son in human flesh, or He is not. One has to choose. One cannot escape making that choice.

Have you ever heard it stated that it doesn't matter what religion you belong to since they're all leading us to God? When you hear that said, you should realise that sort of thinking flies in the face of what we just heard about Jesus Christ, both in today's passage as well as in many others. Because if it is true that Our Blessed Lord is God made flesh for us, then it does matter what religion we have. The devils themselves recognised Him. Why do those who claim to be religious people refuse to acknowledge who He is? It wasn't the devils that gave Jesus a bad time. They simply vacated; they simply fled from His presence and went elsewhere to do their dirty work. It was the religious know-it-alls who gave Jesus a hard time. The more they realised that Jesus of Nazareth was really Someone, the more they understood what He was claiming to be, the more they wanted to rid themselves of Him. He spoke with God's authority. He was a terrible threat to the claimed authority of the big know-it-alls.

Now there are many ways people try to rid themselves of Christ. They tried to kill Him, bury Him in a tomb and then post detail of soldiers to guard that tomb. We know, however, how useless that was. Another way is to simply ignore Him. Many have done that, are doing it now, and will do it in the future. The danger of ignoring Him is equivalent to ignoring the instructions on drug prescriptions or ignoring directions on how to fly an aeroplane.

Still, another way is to claim that Jesus is just another interesting religious figure in human history. You simply decide that Buddha or Mohammed, or some guru from the Far East is just as good as Jesus when it comes to journeying to God. But if that's true, then why bother with going to church? Why not simply start your own church? I mean, after all, if you believe that one religion is just as good as another, you can probably do a better job with organising a religion than the ones we've got. But when you do, let's see you cure people with various diseases, make the blind see, restore crippled limbs, and raise people from the dead. Finally, and most importantly, let us see you rise from the dead three days after you've been buried.

So is it true that one religion is just as good as another? Do we take the words and teachings of Jesus with ultimate seriousness, or do we just relativise His life, death, resurrection and teachings? Is His voice just one of many? Or is He the Word of God spoken for us?

Now I'm quite aware that all of you here today do not dismiss Jesus. You wouldn't be here listening to His words and receiving His Body and Blood if your hearts and souls were elsewhere. But I'll bet you have heard members of your families reduce religion to something equal to a cafeteria choice by declaring it doesn't matter what you pick and choose. Will you simply let those statements pass by unchallenged? Will you let your children, your grandchildren and members of your family, as well as your friends who say these things, go on without responding with your own convictions about Jesus Christ? We need to love them enough to call them to take Jesus of Nazareth seriously. After all, He really does speak with authority and not like the others.

We've all heard a lot of talk about evangelising. Evangelising doesn't mean that we have to go around town, knocking on doors and preaching at others about our religion. It can be something far less difficult and far less offensive than that. Evangelising can be as easy as simply and clearly stating the truth about Jesus and telling others, "We have never heard anyone else speak with such authority."

# THEME 82
# DELIVER US, LORD, FROM EVERY EVIL

*Job 7:1-4; 1 Corinthians 9:16-19, 22-23; Mark 1:29-39*

In the Book of Genesis, we learn that God made the world not only good but beautiful, wondrous, and a place of loveliness and happiness. The Garden of Eden was created as a paradise, a garden of delights. It was God's original gift to us. How, then, did our world turn into a place of pain, loss, and suffering?

We can begin to answer that question by asking another: Did God take back His gift or did His creatures --- human beings --- abuse it and reject it? We cannot watch a television news show, check out the news on the Internet, or read a newspaper without being immersed in reports of people suffering in many ways. Some are suffering from starvation, others from violence and structures that make it possible for injustice, untruth, and charity to be lacking.

How appropriate it is for us to hear in today's readings about the terrible losses suffered by the Old Testament figure of Job. Job lost everything to an almost unimaginable extent. Even his wife and friends turned on him. His wife said to him: "Curse God and die." (Job 2:9) At the end of today's first reading, we hear Job exclaim: "I shall not see happiness again," a thought that many have these days.

On top of it all, we know of people who chide us for being people of faith. What kind of a God would allow all of this, they ask? They and others resort to the blame-game, something we hear a lot in Congress's halls, in the newspaper columns of the opinion-makers, or from the chattering classes we watch in television programs. How we might ask, can we retain faith in God in the midst of all of these losses while the voices of others take God to task for it all?

Whenever we celebrate Holy Mass, we pray the Lord's Prayer and immediately following, we hear the words: *Deliver us, Lord, from every evil and grant us peace in our day. In your mercy, keep us free from sin and protect us from all anxiety as we wait in joyful hope for the coming of our Lord and Saviour Jesus Christ.* If we reflect on the Lord's Prayer and on those words that immediately follow it, we will come to the realisation that God does not want us to suffer. He wants to deliver us from suffering. God does not inflict pain on us; He wants to heal us of our infirmities.

Jesus Christ reveals a God who is quite different than what we think He is. Jesus Christ reveals a God who comes to us not to condemn us, but to save us, heal us of our infirmities, and deliver us from evil. He wants to deliver us from evil, not inflict it upon us. Amid our trials, we should turn to Him.

The healing of Simon and Andrew's mother is one of the first of a long series of healings Jesus performed during His public ministry.

Last Sunday, we heard of inner healing, the healing of a man possessed by a demon. The Jews of Christ's day thought that outward physical illnesses were as a result of inner, spiritual illnesses. God punishes people who sinned, they believed, punished them by inflicting physical pain, and suffering on sinners. They were wrong. When asked about such things, and when asked about the existence of evil, Jesus responded by asserting: "An enemy hath done this."

In His humanity, Christ Jesus took on the suffering, pain, and loss that we all endure at the hands of our Ancient Enemy, the Enemy of God, the angelic rebel known as Lucifer, the Light Bearer. With his colossal ego, he defied God and then seduced Adam and Eve into joining him in his rebellion against God, the God of love and goodness who created them to share His love with them.

There is not a complete disconnect between sin and suffering. Ask anyone who has suffered because of alcoholism or drug addiction what it was that empowered them to deal with their lives of drudgery and pain and they will tell you about their spiritual recovery. Ask people who manage to deal with their losses and pain and they will tell you about their faith in God and what God has done for them.

Being born among us, Jesus gave us His Father. Dying among us, He gave us His mother. Teaching among us He taught us how to pray, the prayer we know of as the Lord's Prayer. Because of Jesus, we can dare to call God our Father and dare to pray to Him as our Father, as Jesus' Father and ours because of Him. Not only that, but we can pray in joyful hope even amid our sorrows and losses. *Deliver us Lord, we pray, from every evil, graciously grant peace in our days, that by the help of your mercy we may always be free from sin and from all distress as we await the blessed hope and coming of our Saviour, Jesus Christ.*

In the villages, the people flocked to Jesus wherever He went. Time and time again He was sought out; time and time again, He healed and delivered. He healed and delivered them not only of their physical maladies but healed their wounded hearts and wearied souls. It was the inner healings that interested Him the most. It was in those inner hearts and souls that He accomplished His greatest miracles. The first recovery is our spiritual recovery. All other forms of recovery are built on that.

On Christmas Eve, our children await the coming of Jesus; they await in obvious, outer, and radiant joyful hope. It isn't Father Christmas that we look for. It is the One who can gift our souls with joy, happiness, and peace.

What kind of a God is God, we ask? The answer is fashioned by what we are looking for. Just what are we expecting from God?

Simon and Andrew's mother was completely energised. Once driven away, the fiery fever allowed their mother to resurrect so she could care for her sons and their Guest with renewed energy, freed by Jesus as she was from what had flattened her.

By turning to God amid our trials, we can find renewed energy. With it, we can find renewed faith in ourselves, hope for our futures, and a renewed love for the One who created us for happiness and honoured us with the task of working with Him to push back the boundaries of chaos and darkness and join with Him in bringing His creation to fulfilment and completion.

Deliver us, we pray, as we wait in joyful hope, all the while working with You, O Lord, to overcome all that would tear away our happiness and the happiness of those around us.

# THEME 83
# READING THE GOSPEL IN OUR LIVES

*1 Leviticus 13:1-2, 44-46; 1 Corinthians 10:31-11:1; Mark 1:40-45*

The first reading for today's Mass along with the gospel passage, speak of those who are outcasts, those who are cast out from the communities of Israel. In today's society, we have our own outcasts of a different sort, but nevertheless similar. In our day, we have a few who are quarantined due to disease or illness. However, they remain in our hospitals and so are not literally cast out. The same can perhaps be said for psychotics and others who suffer from mental disorders that threaten others in our society. We also have outcasts in our modern times who are imprisoned for long times because of their crimes.

The first reading of today's Mass and the gospel reading, speak of lepers who have been literally cast out of normal Jewish social contact. But beyond the physical level, the readings speak of sin and the healing of both physical and spiritual leprosy.

The response of Jesus is what is significant for us. The gospel account tells us that Jesus touched the leper. It is the touching of the outcast that brought about his healing. Jesus reached out to him and touched him. It was a touch of gentleness; a touch filled with such fire and power that the sickness was burned away; it was a touch that gave new life, a whole new life to someone condemned to live in the hell of isolation and loneliness.

It needs to be pointed out again and again that we can read the gospels in our daily lives, that the gospels are like newspaper accounts of what is happening in our lives, they are accurate reports of what is happening in our lives and in our times. There are people today who have been driven out from their own families, ostracised by their kin. For one reason or another, some are shunned, shunned where they work, even shunned by their peers. Many kids in our high schools suffer from being shunned and cast out from the "in" crowds.

It needs likewise to be pointed out that in all too many instances, those who do the casting out are themselves victims of sin, suffering from spiritual leprosy, and that all too often those who do the casting out are projecting onto the outcasts the very things that they fear can be found deep within themselves.

We need to ask ourselves some very uncomfortable questions. Do our jails rehabilitate inmates, or do they merely keep inmates out of our clean society? If they do not rehabilitate, is there any unwritten public policy behind the failure to rehabilitate? The most uncomfortable question of all is: To what extent are we honest with ourselves in recognising our own leprosy, our own sinfulness?

The point of it all is that the outcast system, the social ostracism system, is breaking down. It is breaking down because mere outcasting in itself is doomed to failure. It is doomed to failure because it has nothing to do with God, particularly God's methodology for effecting cures of both social and personal evil.

Let me go back now to the beginning of these observations. Jesus, the gospel says, touched the leper. That's the key, reaching out and touching the outcasts around us. Why? Because touch brings healing within it. Human contact, caring human contact, bears within it healing powers.

The outcast system is doomed to failure because it keeps the so-called healthy ones in pride. It prevents them from recognising their own need for a cure. It arrests them in the delusion that they are pure and clean, and holy and without fault or defect. Yet how can they possibly cure anyone else unless they are first cured? No, the social outcast system simply keeps us out of touch, out of communion, and out of the community of faith that God wills for us. Healing and wholesomeness, under such conditions, become impossible.

In many of our families, there is someone who has been judged to be a leper; someone who has been cast out and judged to be incapable of any good, and coldly given up. Jesus would pause in front of these people, look at them with so much faith, and love them with a love that was so disarming, with such simplicity and gentleness, and with so much faith in the goodness in them that He would have brought forth from their callous-covered hearts inexpressible bursts of gratitude, wonder, and joy. And they would have been touched and healed.

Christ expected the best from everyone. When we expect only the worst, then how will they ever be healed? Behind the most horrid of masks people wear, behind their most intricate defence mechanisms, their most insufferable arrogance and bluffing and cursing and silence, there is a child who has never been loved enough and who has stopped growing. Behind the most leprous sinners, there is a fixated and arrested child whose developmental process can come to life with a touch of love. Every child stops developing precisely at the point where significant others have ceased believing in that child.

Touching another person with the love of God means giving them a vocation, a call, a summons. It means summoning from within them the most insistent of all calls in life; it means touching them and stirring up within them a little child who stopped wondering at life and who was therefore no longer either intellectually or emotionally curious about life or about others. To love someone is to call them, to invite them, to surround them, and to patiently and respectfully await their response, their change, and their renewal in growth. No social outcast system can ever hope to accomplish this miracle; no ostracism will ever work.

The outcasts, the so-called lepers in our lives, have to feel that they're loved very deeply, very boldly, and very truly, before they dare appear to be humble and gentle and kind and affectionate and vulnerable. Only the strong can afford these virtues. Only the healthy have the where-with-all to transmit those strengths, those virtues. For the call of Christ demands that the strong share their strength with the weak, the healthy share their health with the lepers, and the holy share their holiness with the sinners. This system is the direct opposite of the system of this world, namely the outcast system. For truly, God's ways are not our ways.

The question for you and me today, my brothers and sisters, is this: Dare we take the risk and reach out and touch the lepers in our lives? Do we have enough faith in ourselves to take that risk or enough faith in God to dare to touch His lepers? Salvation for our society and our own personal salvation hangs or falls on the answer to that question.

# THEME 84
# GOD IS ALMIGHTY

*Isaiah 43:18-19, 21-22, 24-25; 2 Corinthians 1:18-22; Mark 2:1-12*

Our Judeo-Christian history begins with the recognition that God is the Sovereign Power who created the sun, the moon, the stars and the universe, a universe into which God gave life, our human life. That history unfolded as recorded in the Old Testament, a history in which we humans rebelled against God because of our prideful self-will. That rebellion brought with it death and destruction; wars and catastrophes. We just heard the prophet Isaiah reminding them of God's loving care: "I formed people for myself so that they might announce my praise. Yet you did not call upon me, O Jacob, for you grew weary of me, O Israel. You burdened me with your sins and wearied me with your crimes." God's patience with sinful humanity has not been overcome. His love endures forever, Isaiah reminds us.

God cannot be thwarted, nor can our sins cancel His plan and purpose. Thus at the end of today's first reading, we hear that God's creative activity is on-going. "It is I," God declares, "I who wipe out, for my own sake, your offences; your sin I remember no more," an idea we hear repeated in today's gospel account.

Israel witnessed God's sovereignty in many ways, never more so than when He acts to free His people from sin and its consequences, namely when Adam and Eve suffered the loss of their dominion over the earth, the animals, and all that God had given them. In their sin, they were stripped naked of God's graces and were now powerless in facing chaos and death.

Our salvation history gives witness to the truth that God is forever making all things new, restoring them to His original plans and purposes. He is always "Yes" and never "No." His acts astonish us in that He does not abolish the past but continually renews. This, of course, is precisely the mission of Christ in whom Jesus' people saw God at work. The really amazing thing for them is that God's forgiveness is given without reason, beyond the boundaries of reasonableness. This is central to St. Paul's preaching, a piece of which we find in today's second reading which Paul wrote to the Christian community in Corinth. "Brothers and sisters," he wrote to them,

> "As God is faithful, our word to you is not "yes" and "no." For the Son of God, Jesus Christ, who was proclaimed to you by us, Silvanus and Timothy and me, was not "yes" and "no," but "yes" has been in him. For however many are the promises of God, their Yes is to him; therefore, the Amen from us also goes through him to God for glory. But the one who gives us security with you in Christ and who anointed us is God; He has also put his seal upon us and given the Spirit in our hearts as a first instalment."

St. Mark's gospel is all about the question: "Who is Jesus Christ?" The answer is found in all of the healing, the authority of Christ's teaching, and His miracles, especially in and around Capernaum, where Jesus began His public ministry. In today's gospel passage, Jesus forgives sin as only God can forgive. The response of those who witnessed it was: "Who does He think He is?" The question moves us beyond the rhetorical. It prompts us to ask that very same question. "Why does this man speak that way?"This came to the minds of those who heard Him forgiving the paralytic's sins. It's a reasonable question, one that we should ask along with them. Only God can forgive sins is something everyone knows. So just who is this Christ?

So, indeed, which is easier to say: "Your sins are forgiven," or to say, "Rise, pick up your mat and walk?" Which is easier to say and then prove that you have the power to back up those words? Of course, we know the answer, the answer Jesus gave when He instantly and on the spot cured the man of his paralysis and the man immediately walked.

Allow me now to introduce another point. Priests are sometimes challenged to explain why people come to them to forgive sins in our Church's Sacrament of Forgiveness. There are those who, claiming that God alone can forgive sins, accuse priests of usurping the prerogatives of God. In answer to their challenges, I like to bring to their attention the gospel passage we have in front of us today. In it, we find access to Jesus blocked by the crowds of people who were jammed into the door of this house and into the room in which Jesus was preaching. Many things block us also. Four men in their mercy opened up the roof and lowered the paralysed man on his pallet to the feet of Jesus.

We need to stop and realise that they were men of faith. They believed that Jesus had within Him the power of God and that He could cure the man of his paralysis. Jews at that time believed that physical maladies were the result of sin. Sin induces not only spiritual paralysis but physical as well. In today's gospel account, we find Jesus linking the power to forgive sins with the power to heal physical maladies. Curing the sick and those possessed by the demonic dominates St. Mark's gospel accounts. The gospel of Mark is loaded with those cures, something we have seen this year, the year of Mark, the year in which so many gospel accounts are taken from St. Mark's presentation of Jesus Christ in answer to the question: Who is this Jesus?

But there is more. We find St. Mark as well as St. Luke and St. Matthew relating accounts where Jesus passed on to His twelve apostles His mission along with His powers, particularly His power to forgive sins. Significant among them, we find the following in St. Matthew's gospel:

Now when Jesus came into the district of Caesarea Philippi, he asked his disciples, "Whom do men say that the Son of man is?" And they said, "Some say John the Baptist, others say Elijah, and others Jeremiah or one of the prophets." He said to them, "But who do you say that I am?" Simon Peter replied, "You are the Christ, the Son of the living God." And Jesus answered him, "Blessed are you, Simon Bar-Jona! For flesh and blood has not revealed this to you, but my Father, who is in heaven. And I tell you, you are Peter, and on this rock, I will build my church, and the powers of death * shall not prevail against it. I will give you the keys of the kingdom of heaven, and whatever you bind on earth shall be bound in heaven, and whatever you loose on earth shall be loosed in heaven." (Matthew 16:13-19)

Then in St. John's gospel, where he reports the very first thing Jesus did when He rose from the dead, we find this:

On the evening of that day, the first day of the week, the doors being shut where the disciples were, for fear of the Jews, Jesus came and stood among them and said to them, "Peace be with you." When He had said this, He showed them His hands and His side. Then the disciples were glad when they saw the Lord. Jesus said to them again, "Peace be with you. As the Father has sent me, even so, I send you." And when He had said this, He breathed on them, and said to them, "Receive the Holy Spirit. If you forgive the sins of any, they are forgiven; if you retain the sins of any, they are retained." (John 20:19-23)

Let me go back now to the beginning of my homily. God cannot be thwarted, however, nor can our sins cancel His plan and purpose. Thus at the end of today's first reading, we hear that God's creative activity is on-going. "It is I," God declares, "I who wipe out, for my own sake, your offences; your sin I remember no more." When our sins are forgiven, we become God's new creation and, like Adam and Eve in the Garden of Paradise, we walk in the glorious freedom of the sons and daughters of God.

# THEME 85
# MANAGING OUR TIME

*Genesis 9:8-15; 1 Peter 3:18-21; Mark 1:12-15*

Time is a problem for us. We live lives filled with multiple options with an array of many things to do and opportunities to engage ourselves in any number of tasks. Sometimes, maybe most of the time, we have so many things to do, we don't know which ones to tackle first. Our attempts to organise our time seem to be continually frustrated, frustrated by the many new things that come to us each and every day.

Clearly, time is a problem for us. I marvel at what is required of mothers and fathers every day. I find myself asking, "How do they do it?" How do they manage their lives with all that seems to be required of them in caring for their children, getting their children to and from so many commitments, neglecting even the time they, as parents need for each other?

This period of Lent brings to our reflection how well we manage our time. Are there any families left in which everyone in the family shares a Sunday dinner? Do husbands and wives have much time, any time, badly needed time, for themselves --- for the health and development of their own relationships with each other? What has happened to intimacy? Does it have much content anymore?

Our Church organises time, not according to calendar and clock, but according to significant events. The Liturgical Year is her gift to us that, despite all that the world hurls at us, we might steal moments in which we consider what we do with the times we have in our lives along with the significant events that occur in these special times.

New Testament Greek uses the word Chronos to denote time measurement as clocks and calendars measure time. But New Testament Greek also uses another carefully selected word, kairos, moments in which we experience events of significance and meaning.

When you ask someone to marry you, it is an event that occurs in kairos time. Graduation time is another such event. Your photograph album takes you out of Chronos time and puts you into kairos time, the times of your life that more fully and truly measure what has happened in your life.

In today's gospel account, we find Jesus in kairos time. After His baptism by John the Baptist in the River Jordan Jesus, instead of immediately embarking on His public ministry, Jesus puts himself in a place where time doesn't matter. He goes out into the desert for forty days and forty nights, there to come to terms with who He is and what His life is to be all about, and what sort of Messiah His Father has called Him to be. This was for Him a time full of great significance.

He needed to enter into that to maintain a steady balance when He began His public ministry following that initial time in the desert. He needed to have within himself a clear understanding of just what He was about when He faced spiritually and physically diseased people, people who would press in on Him all of the time in the subsequent days to come. He knew He faced living with no place to call home, no home to return to when things got tough. He knew He needed to have a clear head when He had to face the religious and political establishment that would seek to hunt him down. Occasionally He would steal some more kairos time from His Chronos time and go back out into deserted places to do some more praying, getting back in touch again with His Father in heaven.

The forty days of Lent, which the Church offers you and me, is much the same. These forty days of Lent are stolen from our Chronos time so that we can get in touch with who we are, what our lives are all about, as well as get more deeply in touch once again with our Heavenly Father. Lent is kairos time, a significant time in which we can suspend Chronos time for a while.

The forty days of Lent are now upon us, or better said, we are in the forty days of Lent. The Church's Liturgical Year is such that we move from Christmas to Ash Wednesday, to the Great Three Days of Easter, to Pentecost, repeatedly every year in Chronos time so that we can enter into kairos time, a time of meaning and purpose, a time of significance and consequence, periods in which eternal time and temporal time briefly intersect.

When we were conceived in our mothers' wombs, we began to live in eternal time. When we are born, we begin to interact with each other in eternal time. When we are baptised, we begin a new life living in a relationship with God in eternal time. And when we die -- time, for us, does not stop, it only changes. It is then that we will see our entire lives in kairos time. It is then that we will realise that we were always living in kairos time.

What are the times of your life? Do you see them only in Chronos time, or do you see them in kairos time, God's kairos time, the time we had in this life filled with eternal meaning and purpose?

I'm glad you and I are here together during this time when we celebrate the gift God has given us, the gift of sitting at God's table, the Eternal Messianic Banquet during which we celebrate the Wedding Feast of the Lamb, that moment when we celebrate our nuptials with God as He marries Himself to us forever in Jesus Christ, His gift of Himself to us in our kairos time and in our time and place right now.

May Lent be meaningful and significant for you and me.

# THEME 86
# LIFE TESTS US

*Genesis 22:1-2, 9, 10-13, 15-18; Romans 8:31-34; Mark 9:2-10*

In the reading from the book of Genesis that we just read, the author (or authors) tells us that God put Abraham to test. To be honest with you, I have a problem with that. My question is, why would God need to test Abraham? Moreover, why would God need to test any one of us? He already knew what was in Abraham's heart, and He already knows what's in our hearts. Maybe these are not really tests at all. I tend to think that these are opportunities that allow us to find out what's deep down within us.

Abraham was found to have faith, a tremendously deep faith in the goodness of God. Because he had such deep faith, he was prepared to act courageously, to act with a courage that could only come from his deeply held faith in the goodness of God. The lesson for us is that courage comes forth from faith.

In today's second reading, St. Paul was calling the Christians in Rome to have that courage. Said he: Brothers and sisters: If God is for us, who can be against us? He who did not spare His own Son but handed Him over for us all, how will He not also give us everything else along with Him? Who will bring a charge against God's chosen ones? It is God who acquits us, who will condemn? Christ Jesus died, or rather, was raised, who is also at the right hand of God, who indeed intercedes for us.

In today's gospel, we find Jesus being transfigured in front of Peter, James, and John. That event occurred just before Jesus was to go to Jerusalem, there to suffer, to be judged, to be tortured and to die on His

Cross. It was a time of testing, a time of particular testing for Peter, James, and John.

In the end, faith carried Jesus through His death on the Cross and into His resurrection from the dead. That happened because of His faith in His Father's love. And likewise, in the end, the faith of Peter, James, and John carried them through their times of testing not only in the death of Jesus but subsequently after His resurrection and Ascension when those disciples and many early Christians along with them suffered testing and martyrdom because of their faith in and loyalty to Jesus Christ.

Deep within us, there is a reality that we only discover when we face a major trial. We go about our daily lives, lives filled with doing this, that, or the other thing, commitments that require our time and attention. There is a busy-ness that oppresses so many of us, draining us, and causing us to wonder who we are, what our lives are all about, and whether or not we mean anything to others. Most of the time we don't pay, we can't pay much attention to our inner selves.

Then along comes a major event, a testing. We suffer a serious blow to our health. It may be that we find we have cancer, it may result from a heart attack, we may find we no longer have a job or some such similar thing that crashes down on us. Perhaps we discover that our wife or our husband suffers from an incurable illness, or perhaps one of our children or one of our parents is struck down. It could be a terrible accident; it could be that some dreadful thing happened to one of our children.

Life tests us. Is it God's doing? Many people easily blame God for whatever has gone wrong. I am not one of them. I don't believe God is pleased either to inflict pain on us or is pleased to see us suffer. I do believe, however, that life tests us and that many times we suffer because of decisions made by others, decisions made through an uncaring lack of concern for us or decisions resulting from their selfishness. There is an evil force that wants to separate us from God.

In such moments we have an opportunity to see what we're made of. In such moments we face self-revelation, and we can find God's good graces and His love abiding deep within us. Such was the case when the inner Jesus came to the surface in His transfiguration before the eyes of Peter, James, and John.

Facing as we do so many daily tasks, we seem not to have the opportunity to go within ourselves, to pay attention to what we're made of. Yet our faith tells us that God made us in His image and likeness. Our faith tells us that who we are is made up of the gifts of God with which He has endowed us.

When we received the Sacrament of Confirmation, the Church reminded us that we have been gifted by the Holy Spirit, gifted with wisdom, understanding, wonder and awe, right judgment, knowledge, courage, and reverence for God and the things of God. In times of our own testing, in times of our own trials, we need to give grateful attention to these gifts from God. They are a part of our inner reality, our inner selves.

So when a trail or misfortune comes your way, when you are faced with a serious challenge, do not lose heart. Call upon your faith in God and His help. Courage will come your way, itself being a gift from God. Remember, you are a child of Abraham, our father in faith. Call upon those who have gone before you. After all, we belong to the Communion of Saints, our family of faith. Draw closer to God. Perhaps like Abraham and so many others who have gone before you, you will discover what's deep within you. You will find out what you're really made of. And along with Jesus, you will pass through your Good Fridays into Easter Sundays, and rise up in glory into a new life.

# THEME 87
# MEETING GOD AS A FAMILY

*Exodus 20:1-17; 1 Corinthians 1:22-25; John 2:13-25*

Why was this church building built? If everyone here answered that question, you might be surprised at some of their answers. Moreover, the answer that is obvious to me might not be so obvious to some of you.

Well, then, why was this building built?

My answer is that it was built to be a temple. It was not built just to be a meeting place, or an auditorium, or a place much like a theatre where we go to experience a drama. A temple is a building that is purpose-built in order to immerse us in the drama of our relationship with God. Notice that I said, "*our* relationship with God," not "*my* relationship with God." While we may come here for private prayer, the main reason we are here is that this is where we as God's family play our roles in the great drama of God coming to us and our going back to God as His family. Isn't Jesus our Brother and didn't He teach us to pray to God as Our Father?

A temple is certainly a building dedicated to God. But it's more than that. It's a dedicated space, a sacred space, a space unlike all others and in which we enter to be with God. A temple is God's house, not a theatre, a lecture hall, an auditorium, or a place where we go to have churchy sorts of assemblies. It is a place where God and I, where you and I and God, can be together with each other. At the same time, it is a place where I can be alone with God when no one else is here.

God is present here. This is God's house, not just our house. That flickering red candle with its eternal flame always burning is a signal telling us that the Eternal One dwells in this space. We, therefore, ought to conduct ourselves reverently in this space. We genuflect to the Real Presence of Christ dwelling here in this tabernacle. Out of respect, men do not wear hats. We respect those who are praying, and we conduct ourselves in ways that are not ordinary. We genuflect to the presence of Jesus Christ in the Blessed Sacrament. This is an extraordinary space in an extraordinary building that is God's house, a temple of the Lord.

All of this helps explain the angry and violent reaction of Jesus when He entered the Temple in Jerusalem and found it treated more like a shopping centre, or a bank building. Any time that which is sacred, that which is God's, is desecrated, it is a slap in God's face. To corrupt that which is holy is a terrible and personal insult to God. The corruption of the temple's sanctity caused Jesus to blaze out in anger.

But the reality of God's temple is more than being simply a church building. In His Resurrection from the dead, Jesus built a new temple in which He can be found, His Mystical Body, a Body that is composed of Temples of the Holy Spirit, you and me.

Each one of us here is a temple that is purpose-made. Each one of us here is a temple of the Holy Spirit. Each one of us here was brought into being and designed by God for a purpose, namely the purpose of making Him present to others, especially when they enter into who we are. Each one of us here is a walking, living temple in which God is made present to others, *available* to others.

What sort of trafficking goes on inside your temple, inside the temple that you are? What sorts of activities are being carried on inside you? Your answer to that fundamental and radical question is the "stuff" of Lent. Lent is given to us each year to examine and perhaps change what is happening inside of us.

God's expression of Himself, God's Eternal Word, is made flesh and blood in each one of us here. We receive the living Body and Blood of Jesus Christ in Holy Communion in order that He might not only dwell within us but also to become actually who we are and what we are as persons. We constitute the living stones of God's temple here on earth.

On the night before He died, during His Last Supper with His disciples, St. Jude asked Jesus if He would reveal Himself to the whole world. Christ's answer to St. Jude is instructive. He said: *If anyone loves me, he will keep my word, and my Father will love him, and we shall come to him and make our home with him.* [John 14:23]

Moments later, when Jesus was praying out loud to His Father, He prayed: *They do not belong to the world any more than I belong to the world. Consecrate them in the truth; your word is truth. As you sent me into the world, I have sent them into the world, and for their sake, I consecrate myself so that they too may be consecrated in truth. I pray not only for these but also for those who believe in me through their words. May they all be one, Father, may they be one in us, as you are in me and I am in you, so that the world may believe it was you who sent me. I have given them the glory you gave to me, that they be one as we are one. With me in them and you in me, may they be so completely one that the world will realise that it was you who sent me.* [John 17:16-23]

There are quite a few passages in the Bible in which we are told that we are --- each one of us --- "temples of the Holy Spirit." If that is so, if that is the mind of God, if that is why you are walking the face of the earth, then what goes on inside the temple that you are is of immense importance, not only to you but to God Himself.

Lent comes to us in the springtime. We plant, fix up and clean up so that our dwelling places can be healthy places in which to live, and inviting places for others to enter.

Shouldn't we do the same at the very least for God? Or do we want who and what we are to be nothing more than materialists that insult

God as we carry on like the moneychangers in God's temple? If we simply don't care, then the fate of those moneychangers there in God's temple may be our fate as well.

# THEME 88
# GOD IS NOT PASSIVE IN THE FACE OF OUR FAILURES AND SINS

*2 Chronicles 36: 14-16, 19-23; Ephesians 2: 4-10; John. 3:14-21*

Today is Laetare Sunday. Joy is its theme, joy because we are halfway through Lent and thus very close to the joy of Easter when our elect will be baptised, confirmed and receive Holy Communion. Our candidates will be received into our Communion of Faith and likewise receive Holy Communion. There is joy, too, because, despite our sins, God in His love has acted to enter our sinful world and redeem our sinful souls. God has not remained passive in the face of our failures and sins. He has taken actions, decisive actions. He has been in motion, perpetual motion, and we are the recipients of His energy, His energetic love.

In today's first reading, we learn that God inspired a non-Jew, Cyrus, King of Persia, to release the Jews from their captivity in Babylon and allow them to return to their native land. Not only that, but Cyrus was also inspired to rebuild God's house in Jerusalem! This was quite amazing, even more so when we learned that the Jews had been unfaithful to God. Today's first reading began with these words:

*In those days, all the princes of Judah, the priests, and the people added infidelity to infidelity, practising all the abominations of the nations and polluting the Lord's temple which He had consecrated in Jerusalem. Early and often did the Lord, the God of their fathers, send His messengers to them, for He had compassion on His people and His dwelling place? But they mocked the messengers of God, despised His warnings, and scoffed at His prophets.*

The Jews had suffered from their infidelities because sin brings with it indifference toward God. Sin makes the soul lazy. Sin stops movement toward God. It causes us to wallow in the darkness of the soul. Sin makes us spiritually flabby.

God's love, however, is a fire that cannot be extinguished and so in our second reading, we hear St. Paul exhorting Christians in Ephesus:

*Brothers and sisters: God, who is rich in mercy, because of the great love He had for us, even when we were dead in our transgressions, brought us to life with Christ --- by grace you have been saved, raised us up with Christ.*

We rejoice because this gift God has given us, given to us even when we have been sinners, has united us to Christ and has given us the right to share in His glorious resurrection and inherit heaven through Him.

All of this brings us now to today's gospel account in which we find Jesus speaking to Nicodemus saying:

"Just as Moses lifted up the serpent in the desert, so must the Son of Man be lifted up, so that everyone who believes in Him may have eternal life. For God so loved the world that He gave His only Son, so that everyone who believes in Him might not perish but might have eternal life. For God did not send His Son into the world to condemn the world, but that the world might be saved through Him."

What has been our response to all that God has done for us? That question is the big question of Lent, the question we must all face and answer. If you are anything at all like me, you feel uncomfortable answering that question. A soul in motion tends to stay in motion, while a soul that is wallowing in indifference tends to continue in simply not caring.

Isn't that what sin does? Does not sin simply not care about God and the things of God? We know that it does. Thus, a sinful attitude continues by using many lies, lies like: "I'm too busy," or "The Church is filled with hypocrites," or "there is no life after death," or "God is going to save me anyway," or other such seductive lies. The greatest lie of all, the lie that is becoming more popular in our culture each day is: "There is no God anyway."

This is Laetare Sunday, "Rejoice Sunday." We have much about which to rejoice. I realise that many voices tell us that the world is in a mess, that dreadful thing are upon us, that our Church has much within it that is wrong, and that the Second Vatican Council was a bad mistake. Many want to take the Church back to its pre-Vatican II state. I disagree with them. I disagree with them because the voice of Pope John XXIII still speaks to my heart and soul.

Allow me, therefore, to quote Good Pope John's words that he spoke in his opening address to that great Council held back in the early 1960s. In his opening talk he declared:

*In the daily exercise of our pastoral office, it sometimes happens that we hear certain opinions which disturb us --- opinions expressed by people who, though fired with a commendable zeal for religion, are lacking in sufficient prudence and judgment in their evaluation of events. They can see nothing but calamity and disaster in the present state of the world. They say over and over that this modern age of ours, in comparison with past ages, is definitely deteriorating. One would think from their attitude that history, that great teacher of life, had taught them nothing. They seem to imagine that in the days of the earlier councils, everything was as it should be so far as doctrine and morality and the Church's rightful liberty were concerned. We feel that we must disagree with these prophets of doom, who are always forecasting worse disasters, as though the end of the world were at hand.*

Good Pope John's vision was a vision of hope, a joyful vision of hope, hope for the world and hope for the Church based on his unshakeable faith in the love of God and his awareness of God's active and powerful hand at work in our world.

Thus, I repeat the words of the antiphon for beginning today's Mass: "Rejoice with Jerusalem, and be glad for her, all you who love her; rejoice with her in joy…" The Church is God's New Jerusalem, loved by Him and renewed over and over again in the power of His unconquerable love.

And so I close using St. Paul's words in his letter to the Philippians:

"Rejoice in the Lord always; again, I will say, Rejoice. Let all men know your forbearance. The Lord is at hand. Have no anxiety about anything, but in everything by prayer and supplication with thanksgiving, let your requests be made known to God. And the peace of God, which passes all understanding, will keep your hearts and your minds in Christ Jesus. Finally, brethren, whatever is true, whatever is honourable, whatever is just, whatever is pure, whatever is lovely, whatever is gracious, if there is any excellence, if there is anything worthy of praise, think about these things." (Philippians 4:4-8)

# THEME 89
# GOD CALLS US TO LOVE

*Ezekiel 37:12-14; Roman 8:8-11; John 11:1-45*

*"There Are None So Blind As Those Who Will Not See"* is a proverb that has been around for ages. When you read the New Testament, you realise that Jesus Christ spent a lot of time and energy combating the darkness found in the human heart and soul and curing those who were spiritually blind. What was true then is true now. Many voices in the world surrounding us are declaring that the Catholic Church's beliefs and teachings are nothing but superstition, that our Church hates gays and women, and that it is medieval and repressive, using fear and power to try and control human beings. Our critics' minds are made up, and they don't want to be confronted with the facts.

What amazes me is the number of non-Catholic who declare what the Catholic Church teaches without knowing what it truly teaches. Some non-Catholics, fortunately just a few, are fond of telling us what we believe and then what we ought to believe. Question: How can someone who does not share our beliefs tell us they know what we believe or ought to believe? They are blind, and they want to lead the blind. It is they who are prejudiced and repressive, not the Church. Their fear, suspicion, and conspiracy theories have captured the minds of many and corrupted the thinking processes of others against our Church.

A popular spiritual writer and columnist of our day, Father Ronald Rolheiser, wonders if we may be living in a post-ecclesial era because so many people seem to prefer a king but not the kingdom, a shepherd with no flock, to believe without belonging, wanting a spiritual family with God as my Father, as long as I'm the only child. They want spirituality without religion, faith without the faithful, and Christ without His Church. So they drift away from her, get mad at the Church, grow lax, join another church, or just give it all up.

I have often encountered all-or-nothing thinking in others, a type of thinking that leads them into false dilemmas, generalisations, mental filters in seeing things, ridiculing positive ideas, making mountains out of molehills, and especially using emotional reasoning. Along with these, I have found many folks filled with "should statements." They insist on how things should be rather than how things really are, imposing rigid rules they believe should always apply in all circumstances.

We all have our human weaknesses of different kinds. Some of us suffer from the cross life has laid upon us as it happened to Job, St Paul, and suffered by martyrs. We all struggle with prejudices we received from our parents, schooling, friends, churches we go to and so forth. We all have to struggle with "conventional wisdom" and against prejudices and modern superstitions perpetrated by newspaper opinion columnists, those who have taken the place of the medieval Popes and bishops! We all live in society and have to struggle with collective ignorance and irrationality. We struggle with prejudices among our families and friends.

Throughout the centuries, the Catholic Church has built and staffed schools, colleges, and universities. The pursuit of truth and the acquisition of knowledge permeates our seminaries, schools, and c olleges. Our Church has nothing to fear from the truth. In fact, it embraces truth, knowledge, and wisdom whenever and wherever it finds them.

Today we have with us adults here who are nearing the completion of their Rite of Christian Initiation of Adults process of education and spiritual formation. We should all get down on our knees and thank God for giving them to us. They are His gifts to us. You and I have known many of them, and we know that they make wonderful Catholics who have offered so much to all of us in multiple circumstances.

How apt, then, is the dialogue of Jesus we just heard when He spoke to Martha and said: "I am the resurrection and the life; he who believes in me, though he dies, yet shall he live, and whoever lives and believes in me shall never die. Do you believe this?" She said to Him, "Yes, Lord; I believe that you are the Christ, the Son of God, He who is coming into the world."

Belief in God is difficult for us because belief in our basic institutions has been shaken and difficult. The modern world has interpreted faith in statistical analysis and probability theories in order to avoid risk. Conspiracy theories are presented to us in our news media, where conflict is reported under the notion that crisis and controversy sell their products. In such an environment, faith is seen to be naive.

God, however, calls us to love. When you tell someone that you love them, you are making an act of faith in them. Because you have faith in them, you can make yourself vulnerable to them out of love for them. Love and faith are two sides of the same reality. Both involve risk. To give yourself to another in love is to take a risk. To have faith in another likewise involves risk.

This is why we are here. God believes in us enough to love us. God has drawn near to us. Moreover, God has given Himself to us in Jesus Christ. God offers Himself to us and then waits for our response. Is that not what receiving Him in Holy Communion is all about?

"Come and see," Jesus tells us. And so may we have eyes to see and ears to hear what the God of love has in store for us.

# Globethics.net Publications

The list below is only a selection of our publications. To view the full collection, please visit our website.

All products are provided free of charge and can be downloaded in PDF form from the Globethics.net library and at www.globethics.net/publications. Bulk print copies can be ordered from *publictions@globethics.net* at special rates for those from the Global South.
Paid products not provided free of charge are indicated[*].
The Editor of the different Series of Globethics.net Publications is Prof. Dr Obiora Ike, Executive Director of Globethics.net in Geneva and Professor of Ethics at the Godfrey Okoye University Enugu/Nigeria.

Contact for manuscripts and suggestions: *publications@globethics.net*

## Co-publications & Other

Kenneth R. Ross, *Mission Rediscovered: Transforming Disciples*, 2020, 138pp. ISBN 978-2-88931-369-3

Obiora Ike, Amélé Adamavi-Aho Ekué, Anja Andriamay, Lucy Howe López (Eds.), *Who Cares About Ethics?* 2020, 352pp. ISBN 978-2-88931-381-5

Obiora Ike, *Faith and Action Rooted in Christ Reflections on Spirituality, Justice, and Ethical Living*, 2021, 389pp, ISBN 978-2-88931-415-7

## Global Series

Christoph Stückelberger / Jesse N.K. Mugambi (eds.), *Responsible Leadership. Global and Contextual Perspectives*, 2007, 376pp. ISBN: 978–2–8254–1516–0

Heidi Hadsell / Christoph Stückelberger (eds.), *Overcoming Fundamentalism. Ethical Responses from Five Continents*, 2009, 212pp.
ISBN: 978–2–940428–00–7

Ariane Hentsch Cisneros / Shanta Premawardhana (eds.), *Sharing Values. A Hermeneutics for Global Ethics*, 2010, 418pp.
ISBN: 978–2–940428–25–0.

## Education Ethics Series

Divya Singh / Christoph Stückelberger (Eds.), *Ethics in Higher Education Values-driven Leaders for the Future*, 2017, 367pp. ISBN: 978–2–88931–165–1

Obiora Ike / Chidiebere Onyia (Eds.) *Ethics in Higher Education, Foundation for Sustainable Development*, 2018, 645pp. IBSN: 978-2-88931-217-7

Obiora Ike / Chidiebere Onyia (Eds.) *Ethics in Higher Education, Religions and Traditions in Nigeria* 2018, 198pp. IBSN: 978-2-88931-219-1

Obiora F. Ike, Justus Mbae, Chidiebere Onyia (Eds.), *Mainstreaming Ethics in Higher Education: Research Ethics in Administration, Finance, Education, Environment and Law Vol. 1*, 2019, 779pp. ISBN 978-2-88931-300-6

Ikechukwu J. Ani/Obiora F. Ike (Eds.), *Higher Education in Crisis Sustaining Quality Assurance and Innovation in Research through Applied Ethics*, 2019, 214pp. ISBN 978-2-88931-323-5

Deivit Montealegre / María Eugenia Barroso (Eds.), *Ethics in Higher Education, a Transversal Dimension: Challenges for Latin America. Ética en educación superior, una dimensión transversal: Desafíos para América Latina*, 2020, 148pp. ISBN 978-2-88931-359-4

Obiora Ike, Justus Mbae, Chidiebere Onyia, Herbert Makinda (Eds.), *Mainstreaming Ethics in Higher Education Vol. 2*, 2021, 420pp. ISBN: 978-2-88931-383-9

Christoph Stückelberger/ Joseph Galgalo/ Samuel Kobia (Eds.), *Leadership with Integrity. Higher Education from Vocation to Funding*, 2021, 288pp. ISBN 978-2-88931-389-1

## Theses Series

Sabina Kavutha Mutisya, *The Experience of Being a Divorced or Separated Single Mother: A Phenomenological Study*, 2019, 168pp. ISBN: 978-2-88931-274-0

Florence Muia, *Sustainable Peacebuilding Strategies. Sustainable Peacebuilding Operations in Nakuru County, Kenya: Contribution to the Catholic Justice and Peace Commission (CJPC)*, 2020, 195pp. ISBN: 978-2-88931-331-0

Mary Rose-Claret Ogbuehi, *The Struggle for Women Empowerment Through Education*, 2020, 410pp. ISBN: 978-2-88931-363-1

Nestor Engone Elloué, *La justice climatique restaurative: Réparer les inégalités Nord/Sud*, 2020, 198pp. ISBN 978-2-88931-379-2

## African Law Series

Ghislain Patrick Lessène, *Code international de la détention en Afrique*, 2013, 620pp. ISBN: 978-2-940428-70-0

9 782889 314164